D1304557

THE ORMÉE
OF BORDEAUX

THE JOHNS HOPKINS UNIVERSITY STUDIES IN HISTORICAL AND POLITICAL SCIENCE

EIGHTY-NINTH SERIES (1971)

SAL ALEXANDER WESTRICH

THE

ORMÉE OF

BORDEAUX

A Revolution during the Fronde

THE JOHNS HOPKINS UNIVERSITY PRESS
BALTIMORE AND LONDON

*To the memory of
my father, mother, and brother Michel,
victims of the Nazi holocaust*

PREFACE

AFTER HAVING BEEN ALL BUT IGNORED for more than half a century, the Ormée is once again the subject of historical interest. Philip A. Knachel calls it "the most radical movement to have emerged from the Fronde."[1] Ernst Kossmann refers to it as "one of the most interesting and puzzling phenomena to have come out of those years of trouble."[2] H. N. Brailsford notes that is was "the only attempt ever made to export the English Revolution."[3] And Boris Porchnev is persuaded that "had French bourgeois historians only studied the Ormée's program they would not have been so quick to conclude that the Fronde 'lacked ideas'."[4]

Undoubtedly the Ormée's rediscovery owes much to recent debates on the character of the Fronde. Thus Porchnev cites the Ormée as evidence of the fact that the Fronde constituted a revolt of the lower classes against the "feudal-absolutist order."[5] And Kossmann, who refuses to see the provincial Frondes as popular uprisings, must then reconcile his views to the fact that such an uprising occurred in Bordeaux.[6]

If the Ormée was a popular movement, was it a class movement as well? Roland Mousnier, who has sought to repudiate Porchnev's thesis[7] (but who has never commented on the Ormée), declares in an essay on social stratification: "French society during the seventeenth century . . . was uncontestably a society of orders and estates." However, he proceeds to observe: "I am inclined to agree that at the level of merchants and free peasants a society of classes was emerging that opposed the society of statuses."[8] Aside from obscuring the meaning of the first statement, the concession invites an obvious query: if one is permitted to speak

---

[1] Philip A. Knachel, *England and the Fronde* (Ithaca, 1967), p. 89.

[2] Ernst H. Kossmann, *La Fronde* (Leiden, 1954), p. 167

[3] H. N. Brailsford, *The Levellers and the English Revolution* (London, 1961), 690.

[4] Boris Porchnev, *Les soulèvements populaires en France de 1623 à 1648* (Paris, 1963), p. 520.

[5] *Ibid.*, pp. 518–520, 538–582.

[6] Kossmann, *La Fronde*, pp. 111, 117, 134, 245–58.

[7] See Roland Mousnier, "Recherches sur les soulèvements populaires en France avant la Fronde," *Revue d'histoire moderne et contemporaine*, V (1958), 81–113; and *Lettres et mémoires adressés au Chancelier Séguier (1633–1645)*, (Paris, 1964), I, 187–192.

[8] Roland Mousnier et al., *Deux cahiers de la noblesse 1649–1651* (Paris, 1965), pp. 25, 36.

of merchant and peasant classes, may one not also speak of a class of artisans and petty functionaries and therefore of an Ormée class (since the party was made up predominantly of such people)?

This study will not overlook this last question. Its objective is twofold: to present a history of the Ormée and to offer an analysis of Bordeaux's society during the period of upheaval. Also included is a survey of developments in the two decades that preceded the Fronde, without which the circumstances leading to the outbreak of violence in 1648 would remain unclear. And in the conclusion, the relation of the Ormée to the other urban Frondes will be considered.

*   *   *

The writing of this book owes much to the guidance and encouragement of numerous teachers, colleagues, and friends. I am especially indebted to Professor Orest Ranum who watched and encouraged its progress and whose probing comments led me to abandon a number of false assumptions. I also wish to acknowledge a great debt to my dear late friend, Dr. Peter Geismar, whose insights into the character of popular upheavals—those of the seventeenth century as well as those of the twentieth—did so much to clarify my own thoughts. I am also very grateful to two remarkable teachers, Dr. Jacques Barzun and Dr. Ransom E. Noble, for their interest, support, and inspiring intellectual guidance.

Research for this study was made possible by a traveling grant from Columbia University and a sabbatical leave from Pratt Institute, and I wish to thank both institutions. I also wish to thank the staffs of the Archives Municipales de Bordeaux and the Archives Départementales de la Gironde and especially M. and Mme. Avisseau, Mlle. Giteau, and M. Cavignac for their generous assistance. My thanks also to Nicholas Fessenden, Abby Kleinbaum, and Bonnie Fox Schwartz for offering valuable suggestions, Linda Vlasak of the Johns Hopkins University Press for her fine editorial work, and Kim Weber for reading and criticizing every sentence of the manuscript and typing it twice. Finally, I wish to thank Joyce Westrich, who spent many an hour searching for traces of lost Ormists.

CONTENTS

Preface ix

ABBREVIATIONS

A.B.   Archives Municipales de Bordeaux
A.G.   Archives Départementales de la Gironde
A.C.   Archives de Chantilly
A.E.   Archives du Ministère des Affaires Etrangères
A.N.   Archives Nationales
B.M.   Bibliothèque Mazarine
B.B.   Bibliothèque Municipale de Bordeaux
B.N.   Bibliothèque Nationale

I

BORDEAUX BEFORE THE ORMÉE:
A SOCIETY IN FERMENT

BORDEAUX IN THE FIRST HALF of the seventeenth century was a city of warring corporate bodies. The governor of Guyenne and his feudal retainers fought with the Church and with the *Parlement*; the *Parlement*, with a rival provincial court (the *Cour des Aides*) and with the municipal government (the *Jurade*); the *Jurade*, in turn, with two inferior courts (the *Présidial* and the *Bourse*) and with the guilds. There were clashes within the corporations themselves: in the Parlement, between the appellate chamber (*Grand' Chambre*) and the chambers of primary adjudication (*Chambres des Enquêtes*); within the Church, between the upper and lower clergy and the various religious houses; and in the guilds, between the syndics (*bayles des corps de métiers*) and the rank-and-file members. Corporate rivalries were certainly not new to the seventeenth century; what was new was their scope and intensity: endless disputes over protocol, feuds that embraced entire families and lasted for generations, contested claims that began as legal battles and ended in violent street encounters.[1]

[1] The social history of Bordeaux in the seventeenth century still requires to be written. Our assessment of corporatism derives from such primary sources as the *Inventaire sommaire des registres de la Jurade, 1520–1783* (Bordeaux, 1896–1947; cited hereafter as *Registres de la Jurade*), I, 151, 237; II, 241; IV, 64, 71; V, 228; VII, 298, 376; and the unpublished records of the *Jurade* contained in *A. B.*, Inventaire de Baurein (cited hereafter as "fonds Baurein") "Patissiers," carton 23; "Processions," carton 25; "Préséances," carton 25; "Tailleurs," carton 28. Also from Pierre Damas, *Histoire de la jurisdiction consulaire de Bordeaux* (Paris, 1947); Jean Paul Charmeil, *Les trésoriers de France à l'époque de la Fronde* (Paris, 1964), pp. 333–35, 350–51,

The conflicts within the corporate system can, in part, be explained by the overlapping of authority so characteristic of the sixteenth and seventeenth centuries. Both the governor of Guyenne and the *Parlement* could rightly claim to represent the King in the affairs of the province; the *Parlement* was empowered to register fiscal decrees, but so was the *Cour des Aides*; the *Jurade* dispensed mercantile justice, but so did the *Présidial* and the *Bourse*. Beset by numerous structural defects, corporatism was further undermined by the increasing ossification of the system itself. Thus, while it had been comparatively easy for merchants to enter the *Parlement* prior to 1600 by either marrying into parlementary families or purchasing the office of *conseiller*, this was no longer the case in subsequent years.[2] A similar situation prevailed in the *Jurade* and in the *Bourse*, which by the beginning of the seventeenth century had become self-perpetuating bodies of rich merchants, zealously guarding their privileges against encroachments from above and penetration from below.[3] Even the guilds, which had always limited the number of new members, seemed to have become more restrictive, with masters often refusing to admit those who had acquired the offices newly created by the Crown.[4] With the exception of a small number of residents who managed to rise into the ranks of the bourgeoisie,[5] mobility in Bordeaux society had virtually

---

433–44. Pierre Goubert, "Les officiers royaux des Présidiaux, Bailliages et Elections dans la société française au XVIIe siècle," *XVIIe siècle*, nos. 42–43 (1959), 54–75; François Loirette and Louis Desgraves, "La réforme catholique et le mouvement religieux," in *Bordeaux 1453–1715*, ed. Robert Boutruche (Bordeaux, 1966), pp. 375–96; and Yves-Marie Bercé, "La bourgeoisie Bordelaise et le fisc sous Louis XIII," *Revue historique de Bordeaux*, XIII n. s. (1964), 41–66.

[2] The roster of *présidents* and *conseillers du Parlement* contains virtually no new names after 1600. Prior to 1600, bourgeois families such as the Pontacs, the Dussaults, the Pichons, and the D'Alesmes had managed to penetrate the *Parlement* after making their fortunes in trade and occupying positions of authority in the *Jurade*. The list of *jurats* may be found in *Archives historiques du département de la Gironde*, 58 vols. (Paris-Bordeaux, 1859–1932; cited hereafter as *Archives historiques de la Gironde*), XXXIV, 212–50; the list of *parlementaires*, in *ibid.*, XXXI, 3–62.

[3] A small number of families controlled the various municipal offices. Thus the Minvielles became *juges* or *consuls* of the *Bourse* nine times, the Lestrilles four times, while the Ciraqs were *jurats* on ten separate occasions, and the Constants on five. *Ibid.*, XXXIV, 212–50; Jean Darnal, *Supplément des chroniques de la noble ville et cité de Bordeaux* (Bordeaux, 1666), pp. 196–98.

[4] Examples of such refusals are given below.

[5] Entrance into the bourgeoisie became progressively more difficult after 1610. In 1611, the *Jurade* decreed that "no one shall become bourgeois or benefit from the rights thereof unless he first takes the oath before the *Jurade* . . . and the required document is signed by *Messieurs les jurats*." In 1618, a deputation of *jurats* examined

2

ceased: merchants could not penetrate the venal establishment (and therefore tended to find positions in the socially inferior fiscal bureaucracy);
artisans and small tradesmen could not gain admission into the *Jurade*
and other mercantile preserves; and most journeymen could not enter
the guilds.

In circumstances such as these, corporate strife was inevitable. However,
that the strife should have led to social and political upheaval and eventually to revolution was largely due to the policies of the royal government
and especially to its fiscal activities. Compelled to find additional sums
to pay for the German wars, the government of Louis XIII had increased
the land tax (*taille*),[6] created new offices while raising the nominal value
of existing ones,[7] and reduced the wages of officeholders by 25 per cent.[8]
The effect of the last measures was predictable: the office of *conseiller
au Parlement*, which had sold for 64,000 *livres* in 1627, went for 55,000
livres in 1640; that of *trésorier de France*, which had brought 50,000
livres in 1627, went for 41,000 *livres* in 1642.[9] Such a depreciation during a
period of rapid inflation—the value of the *livre tournois* declined by nearly
17 per cent between 1593 and 1633 and by 25 per cent between 1633 and
1652—was a serious blow to officeholders, some of whom had placed the

---

all letters of *embourgeoisement* received during the preceding ten years "to see if they
meet the requirements set down in the statute." In 1620, it ordered that all bourgeois
of less than 15 years standing present a receipt for the fees paid to enter the bourgeoisie "or be constrained to make payment of same." In 1640, the *procureur syndic* declared that "letters of bourgeoisie were so important that they could not be accorded
without a thorough inquisition [*sans une grande connaissance de cause*]." *Registres de la
Jurade*, II, 432, 440, 442, 466.

[6] The amount of the *taille* collected in Guyenne rose from 1,318,262 *livres* in 1636
to 3,975,479 *livres* in 1648. Yves-Marie Bercé, "Les soulèvements populaires du
Sud-Ouest pendant la guerre de trente ans" (unpublished thesis, Ecole des Chartes,
1959), p. 85.

[7] In 1638, the government ordered the creation of thirteen additional offices in
the *Parlement* of Bordeaux. *A.G.*, 1B 24, fol. 69. In that same year the evaluation
of all offices was increased by 33 per cent. *B.N.*, MS. fonds français 11109, fol. 2.

[8] *A.G.*, C 4726, fol. 8.

[9] *A.B.*, Fonds Drouyn, XXV, 260; XXVI, 387; *A.G.*, 3E 11.726, fol. 1156; *A.G.*,
C 3822, fol. 87. The decline in the value of offices is confirmed by Mousnier who
notes that the price of offices in the *Parlement* of Rouen rose until 1632, then "de-
creased slightly in 1633 and 1635, which can be attributed to the threatened creation
of new offices," and dropped steeply after 52 new offices had been created in 1641.
Roland Mousnier, *La vénalité des offices sous Henri IV et Louis XIII* (Rouen, 1945),
pp. 335–36.

bulk of their fortunes in their charges.[10] There were other financial set-backs of a fiscal origin. For many officeholders were also large landholders, and although they were exempt from the land tax (the *taille*) by virtue of their noble status, this was not true of their peasants who often found that they could meet the royal levy only by defaulting on their feudal and proprietary obligations.[11]

Deprived of a substantial portion of their wages and rents while witnessing the erosion of their invested capital, *parlementaires* and other officeholders were in a contentious and often combative mood.[12] Before the seventeenth century was one third over, a bitter struggle had broken out within the venal ranks, pitting those who felt most threatened by the government's policies against those who had benefitted from—or at least suffered less because of—these policies. The struggle saw the lesser and more turbulent *Chambre des Enquêtes* confronting the *Parlement*'s venerable *Grand' Chambre* and especially its *premier président*, an official appointed by the Crown; the newly created (1629) *Cour des Aides* challenging the century-old *Bureau de Finance*; and the ancient but recently revived *Présidiaux* claiming rights which had until then belonged only to the *Parlement*.[13]

The battle was also joined with the royal government. The dispatching

---

[10] We may cite the example of Anthoine de Tarneau, *président* of the *Parlement* who left an estate of 103,000 *livres* of which 89,000 *livres* represented the value of his office. B.B., MS. fonds Itié, July 7, 1654. On the decline in the value of the *livre tournois*, see Mousnier, *La vénalité des offices*, p. 340; Natalie de Wailly, *Mémoire sur les variations de la livre tournois* (Paris, 1857), p. 256.

[11] As Mousnier points out: "The landlords . . . incited the peasants not to pay the *tailles* or the numerous new taxes imposed by the government because if the peasants paid these royal taxes, they would be unable to pay their feudal dues or rents." Roland Mousnier, "Trevor Roper's 'General Crisis' Symposium," in *Crisis in Europe, 1560–1660*, ed. Trevor Aston (London, 1965), p. 98.

[12] One may gauge their belligerence from the following comment delivered by the officers of the *Bureau de Finance*: "We are left without wages and it is apparently thought that we will accept this as calmly as we have accepted the reduction in wages." Letter from the *Trésoriers de France* assembled in Paris to their colleagues in Bordeaux, May 23, 1648, *A.G.*, C 3989.

[13] See Simone Quet, "La Cour des Aides de Guyenne, ses rapports avec le Parlement de Bordeaux," *Revue historique de Bordeaux*, XXXII, 97–111; XXXIII, 17–22; also *A.B.*, "Jurats," fonds Baurein, carton 17; and "Extraits des registres secrets du Parlement de Bordeaux," especially for 1648 [cited hereafter as "Registres du Parlement"]. There are three copies of the "Registres": one in the Bibliothèque Nationale, another in the Bibliothèque Municipale de Bordeaux, and a third one in the Archives Municipales de Bordeaux. Unless otherwise indicated, all references are to the copy preserved in the Bibliothèque Nationale (fonds français, 22377).

of intendants to Guyenne met with strenuous opposition from the *Bureau de Finance* and the *Parlement,* the latter declaring as early as 1620: "So that we may be fully apprised of what is taking place and thus be in a position to check all abuses, no commissions will be executed unless previously reviewed by us."[14] The decision to impose an extraordinary levy in 1643—the *subvention générale*—produced a parlementary demand that it be abolished "inasmuch as the *subvention* has been established in circumstances that will surely incite the people to further rebellion." The *Parlement* also sought to obtain the suppression of the *Cour des Aides*, and meeting no success, petitioned that the tax on offices (the *paulette*) be reduced "as much as we had previously benefitted from its (the *Cour des Aides's*) incorporation and that our revenues were then much greater than they are at present."[15] Not unexpectedly, it was the *Chambres des Enquêtes* that took the lead in resisting the royal measures. When, in 1636, the Duke of Epernon asked the *Parlement* to register a royal decree creating a number of additional offices in the *Parlement*, he reported being subjected "to all sorts of travesties . . . and particularly from the younger members."[16] In the end, the *Parlement*'s resistance proved futile: new offices were created, the intendants remained at their posts, and the *subvention générale* continued to be collected. But an *esprit frondeur* had been born, with consequences not fully to be felt until 1648.

Subjected to the encroachments of the emerging absolutist state, the *Parlement* and the other venal bodies also faced a spirited challenge from Bordeaux's mercantile element. Dubernet, *premier président du Parlement*, was probably speaking for the entire court when he wrote to the royal chancellor in 1646:

The public's clamor over the abuses committed by Flemish agents and by import controllers (*courtiers*) and other merchants of this city have constrained us to issue the decree of which I am sending you a copy. Our commissioners have examined the ledgers of many of these merchants in order to accomplish their investigations and to appreciate the full scope of the secret monopolies

---

[14] Quoted by F. Loirette in *Bordeaux, 1453–1715*, ed. R. Boutruche, p. 355. An excellent discussion of the relation of the intendants to the various corporate bodies is contained in François Loirette, "Un intendant de Guyenne avant la Fronde: Jean de Lauson (1641–1648)," *Bulletin philologique et historique du comité des travaux historiques et scientifiques* (1957), p. 433–61.

[15] Letter from the *Parlement* of Bordeaux to Séguier, March 8, 1643, *Archives historiques de la Gironde*, II, 219.

[16] Epernon to Séguier, June 22, 1636, in Hovyn de Tranchère, *Les dessous de l'histoire* (Paris-Bordeaux, 1886), I, 303.

that have been committed—principally the atrocious usury to which many people are subjected who dare not raise their voices. I have learned that a number of merchants now intend to present you with a list of complaints—as if to expose malpractitioners and chronic usurers was to endanger the commerce by which we subsist, but only when it is conducted in good faith by merchants who are honest and diligent. Ours, however, are held in such disrepute that everywhere they are called peasant-eaters [*mange-paysans*] and are said to have divided the parishes among themselves in order to devour the poor and to destroy the province, which will surely happen if our goods cannot be sold except at ruinous prices.[17]

Dubernet based his attack on merchants on the fact that they manipulated prices and engaged in usury. He may, however, have had other reasons. For it was merchants (or the sons of merchants) who were acquiring the tax *fermes*, filling the ranks of the fiscal bureaucracy, and administering the various state monopolies. Furthermore, because they controlled the *Jurade*, merchants also posed a threat to the *Parlement*'s political authority, particularly in light of their close ties to the governor of Guyenne.[18]

Confronting such powerful foes—the governor commanded the provincial troops and the *Jurade* commanded the municipal militia—the *Parlement* felt compelled to find allies of its own and turned to the last remaining quarter from which help might be forthcoming: the artisans, shopkeepers, petty functionaries, and others lower still, who collectively comprised that segment of the population known as the *menu peuple*. Supported by the latter, the *Parlement* would be able to face its municipal enemies while it sought to defeat those in the province. However, without popular support, and certainly in the face of popular opposition, the *Parlement* would have no choice but to make peace with its mercantile and feudal enemies and with the crown as well. Thus, the *Parlement*'s fate, and indeed that of Bordeaux and Guyenne, had come to depend on the actions of Bordeaux's unprivileged and often dispossessed lower classes.

What was the state of Bordeaux's popular masses in the years preceding the Fronde? The answer to this question is largely to be found in the prevailing economic conditions: the rise of taxes and prices, the depressed

[17] Dubernet to Séguier, November 29, 1646, *Archives historiques de la Gironde*, XIX, 164–65.
[18] The alliance between the governor and the *Jurade* was a natural development in light of their common hostility to the *Parlement*. How the alliance worked will be discussed below.

value of guild offices, the debasement of coinage. Bordeaux should not have been affected by the rising burden of fiscality, as its residents were legally exempt from all taxes. However, the royal government chose to ignore Bordeaux's privileged status and subjected the city to a variety of exactions in the form of extraordinary levies. In 1635, it imposed a tax of one *écu* on each barrel of wine sold in taverns. In 1638, it ordered the city to pay for the upkeep of three companies of soldiers.[19] In 1643, it created the *subvention générale*—a tax of 5 per cent on all goods sold in the city.[20] The indirect taxes would have sufficed to create popular unrest, but even more likely to increase the ferment were the methods used to collect the direct ones. Rather than resort to a *capitation*—a tax based on wealth— the *Jurade* preferred a consumer tax. "In order to avoid *capitations* which are too time consuming, and at the same time odious and difficult to collect," read a decree of September 27, 1639, ". . . the *pié-fourché* [the tax on cattle entering the city] will be raised to 100 *sols* per head of cattle and 6 *sols* per head of sheep, which is the double of the said *pié-fourché*, and as a consequence the price of meat will be raised to 6 *livres* the pound— and this to continue until the 10th of January, 1640."[21] The *Jurade* had already disposed of the funds of the *Hôpital St. André*, Bordeaux's principal charitable institution, as we learn from a decree of June 1, 1639: "Inasmuch as the raising of a regiment is pressing and the collection [of a *capitation*] would take too long and be too difficult to carry out, the needed funds will be borrowed [from the Hôpital] for the said purpose."[22] The decision was approved by the *Parlement*, and 8,000 *livres* that had been intended for the relief of Bordeaux's indigent and the victims of the then raging plague went instead to meet the city's fiscal obligations.[23]

When the sums obtained from the *Hôpital* and the *pié-fourché* proved inadequate, the *Jurade* had recourse to still another expedient. In 1648, it notified the king that

. . . the city being unable to provide the 800 uniforms, both because of its debts which absorb the revenues of the *Hôtel de Ville* and because of the epi-

---

[19] Loirette, in *Bordeaux, 1453–1715*, ed. R. Boutruche, pp. 324, 326, 330.

[20] Bercé, "Les soulèvements populaires du Sud-Ouest," p. 152. The tax created so much opposition that it was replaced by a tribute of 123,000 *livres*.

[21] *Registres de la Jurade*, V. 272. The new rates, however, were retained and even made steeper. By 1646, the tax on cattle had risen to 160 *sols* the head, that on sheep to 10 *sols* the head. *A.B.*, "Pié-Fourché," fonds Baurein, carton 24.

[22] *Registres de la Jurade*, V, 270.

[23] *Ibid.*

demic which has continuously afflicted the city for the last four years, the inhabitants having assembled in the *Hôtel de Ville* convened the *Cent et Trente* [a consultative assembly of leading merchants and office holders] . . . which resolved to create an additional office in each of the city's guilds.[24]

It was the second time that such action had been taken, for in 1631 two offices had been created, allegedly to assist "the poor victims of the plague."[25] The reaction of the guilds is worth noting. The controllers of salted fish [*compteurs et visiteurs de poisson salé*] complained that " . . . at the time of their founding, their membership had consisted of only two . . . that in 1604 it had risen to six . . . and that during the previous year it had increased by two more" although the percentage of fish to which they were entitled had remained unchanged.[26] The official measurers [*auneurs jurés*] declared themselves "opposed to the reception" of the new members.[27] The sellers of fish (*poissonniers*) also had to be warned "not to trouble the new members on pain of 1,000 *livres.*"[28] Such had been the response to the measure of 1631; what it was in 1647, when four offices were created (and not just one as initially contemplated), is not known, but it had to have been even more negative, especially in light of the intervening decline in the market value of guild offices.[29]

Faced with an increase in taxes and with the depreciation of their invested capital, artisans also had to contend with a sharp rise in prices. Between 1635 and 1648, the price of wheat rose by 60 per cent, that of beef by 20 per cent, that of mutton by 25 per cent, and that of wine by perhaps 30 per cent.[30] The increases were in part the result of natural calamities. Hail—the principal enemy of the vine—fell annually between

[24] *Ibid.*, I, pp. 391–92.
[25] *Ibid.*, I, p. 549.
[26] *A.B.*, "Poissonniers," fonds Baurein, carton 24, July 17, 1632.
[27] *Registres de la Jurade*, I, p. 550.
[28] *A.B.*, "Poissonniers," fonds Baurein, carton 24, March 3, 1632.
[29] Thus the office of master baker which had sold for 200 *livres* in 1631 was sold for 100 *livres* in 1647; that of saddlemaker brought 55 *livres* in 1631 and 50 *livres* in 1648; and that of hosemaker went for 60 *livres* in 1632 and 35 *livres* in 1647. *Registres de la Jurade*, II, 339–49; III, 245; see also *A.B.*, "Selliers," fonds Baurein, carton 27.
[30] Wheat sold at 3 *livres* 10 *sols* the bushel in 1635 and 5 *livres* 3 *sols* the bushel in 1648; beef at 5 *sols* the pound in 1635 and 6 *sols* the pound in 1648; mutton at 8 *sols* the pound in 1635 and 10 *sols* the pound in 1648 (*A.B.*, "Viandes," fonds Baurein, carton 49; *Registres de la Jurade*, V, 545–621.) The fluctuations in the price of wine are less clear (the *Registres* do not provide any figures) but from a vineyard belonging to the church of St. Michel in Bordeaux we learn that the price had risen from 54 *livres* to 60 *livres* the barrel (*A.G.*, G 2140–2142).

1629 and 1639, while floods occurring during the same period destroyed much of the cereals and vegetables.[31] But an equally significant factor was the increasingly unsound monetary situation. France was being flooded with inferior foreign coins: the copper pieces of Sweden, the *florins* of Holland, the *cuartillos* of Spain. The presence of such coinage, coupled with the practices of coin clipping and demonetization, had so reduced the worth of circulating pieces that the *Conseil d'Etat*, in August of 1643, ordered one of the coins, the *denier double*, devalued by one half. Intended as a monetary reform (and as a way of increasing the government's revenues), the action proved particularly pernicious to the lower elements, for as the *Bureau de Finance* had indicated, "the *doubles* have so filled the province that no other coins are to be found among the common people (*parmi le menu peuple*)."[32] Not only had the latter's debts and other obligations suddenly doubled, but they also found that no one would take the coins. "The wheat merchants," the *Jurade* reported, "are refusing to accept the *deniers*, and this has caused murmuring among the common people who are in possession of this money." The resistance was so considerable that the Parlement finally had to issue a decree ordering "all persons to accept the *doubles* . . . on pain of exemplary punishment."[33]

The years preceding the Fronde were thus difficult ones for Bordeaux's lower classes. Forced to carry the brunt of the royal taxes, their response was to rise in revolt, first against the government's fiscal agents, then against the municipal authorities, and finally against the government itself. Disturbances had broken out throughout the reign of Louis XIII, but it was not until 1635, after the one-*écu* wine tax had been imposed, that they assumed an insurrectionary form. Shortly after the tax had been announced, large crowds "from the lower elements of the population" appeared in the streets. They claimed to be looking for tax collectors (*gabeleurs*)—and indeed two such were caught and promptly massacred— but their anger encompassed more than fiscal agents, for having seized the *Hôtel de Ville*, they proceeded to burn its registries and empty its gaol. The uprising which had begun early in May continued until the end of June. By then the houses of a tax assessor (*élu*), a royal bailiff (*sergent-royal*), and two *jurats* had been pillaged and put to the torch; the church of St. Seurin had been invaded and a priest burnt alive; and

[31] Bercé, "Les soulèvements populaires du Sud-Ouést," p. 52.
[32] *Ibid.*, pp. 55 and 56.
[33] *A.B.*, "Monnaye," fonds Baurein, carton 20.

a number of soldiers had been shot. The insurrection ended, but only after Epernon had entered the city at the head of an army and killed more than a score of the rebels.[34]

The revolt of 1635 was not soon forgotten. In September of 1636, disturbances broke out over the exportation of grain and the *jurats* reported: "The artisans are threatening to take up arms and burn the vessels if they are allowed to set sail laden with grain. . . . It is evident that these artisans have been emboldened by the recent sedition and by the weakness of the magistrates—half of the constabulary having succumbed to the plague."[35]

There was good reason for apprehension, for the *jurats* had just learned from the captains of the militia that "many bourgeois and other inhabitants refused to take up arms when ordered to do so and that it was therefor necessary to petition the *Parlement* to issue a decree enjoining all heads of households, *secrétaires audienciers, avocats, procureurs,* and others, to take up arms when ordered to do so by their magistrates and captains."[36] Thus the militia, whose principal function was to assist the *Jurade* in preserving order in the city, had begun to show an incapacity for such action —the effect, more likely, of the events of 1635 than of the plague, as the *jurats* seemed to believe.

The disorders continued. In 1638, the new governor of Guyenne, the Prince of Condé, was informed that "persons who are badly disposed toward the King and who are desirous of upsetting the public order are spreading the rumor that His Highness has arrived to restore the salt tax (*gabelle*)."[37] A year later the *Jurade* had decided on a course of action:

Should a riot or other disturbance occur, the *procureur-syndic* and the chief clerk of the city will throw themselves in the *Hôtel de Ville* taking with them half of the constabulary, one of the captains, and twenty of the most reliable bourgeois; the gentlemen of the *Jurade* will then retire to their respective precincts and with their captains take all appropriate actions; officials in each *quartier* will also be appointed to inform the *Jurade* of all that is taking place.[38]

However, the *Jurade* could do nothing when, early in 1642, it received word "that numerous vagabonds and others without employment were

[34] Aguesseau to Séguier, May 20, 1635, in Boris Porchnev, *Les soulèvements populaires en France de 1623 à 1648* (Paris, 1963), p. 586; *Registres de la Jurade,* V, 120–24.
[35] *Ibid.,* VI, 552–53.
[36] *Ibid.,* V, 131.
[37] *Ibid.,* V, 134.
[38] *Ibid.,* V, 135–36.

assembling each evening, that they committed all kinds of excesses, and that rumors and pamphlets were circulating in the city tending to incite the people to rebellion."[39]

In March of 1643 there was another uprising. The *subvention générale* had just been established at Blaye, and wheat was selling at twelve *sols* the bushel—triple its ordinary price. Hearing that a ship laden with grain was about to leave the harbor, a mob that had gathered on the pier announced that it would kill the boatswain and burn the ship if it set sail. There was even talk of arming several vessels and sending them to Blaye to attack the royal fleet. The *Jurade*, "fearing a general upheaval," thereupon dispatched one of its members to visit the city's arsenal, "to see to it that it was not lacking in munitions and that the arms were in a ready state." This was to be the municipal government's only successful action, for when it ordered the militia to mobilize, the captains reported that "the bourgeois and merchants refused to obey their orders." Abandoned by its own supporters, the *Jurade* had little choice but to heed the insurgents' demand and allow the vessel to be unloaded.[40]

The events of 1643 mark a turning point in the struggle of the lower classes. Having once again challenged the municipal authorities, they had, for the first time, forced them to submit to the popular will. Such an achievement may point to a growth of political consciousness: popular assemblies were being held, and it is probable that the discussion of inequitities perpetrated by the Crown also contained complaints about the actions of the local authorities.[41] But a factor not to be overlooked was the increasingly friendly attitude of the *Parlement*. Thus when in 1642 the units used to measure bread were found to be lighter than required by law—a fact known to the *Jurade* which dispensed them to the bakers— the *Parlement* ordered the former to increase the weights by two ounces, "for, given the ever-increasing scarcity [of wheat], the damage to the populace (*le peuple*) that has resulted from the error has become insupportable." And when famine threatened, as it did in a number of years including 1643, it was the *Parlement* that came to the relief of the afflicted, dispensing 20,000 *livres* to the poor, creating a bureau to provide free nourishment, and ordering the *Jurade* to see to it that whole-grain bread

---

[39] *Ibid.*, V, 137.
[40] *Ibid.*, V, 140–43, 145; VI, 591, 617.
[41] The *Jurade* had reported in March of 1643: "Illicit assemblies dominated by people ill-disposed to the King are taking place." *Registres de la Jurade*, V, 143.

(*pain bis*) was made available. The lower classes thus had ample reasons to believe that in any conflict with the *Jurade* they would not have to contend with the *Parlement*'s opposition and might even be able to enlist its support.[42] The ground had been laid for the First Fronde, when *Parlement* and *menu peuple* would close ranks to fight their common enemy.

As in Paris and elsewhere, the Fronde in Bordeaux began as a revolt of the *Parlement*. On April 30, 1648, the financially hard-pressed government of Anne of Austria had offered to renew the *paulette* and the right to inherit venal offices, but on condition that all officers (save those of the *Parlement* of Paris) consent to surrender up to four years of their wages. The offer not only had been rejected, but the *Parlement* of Paris had then proceeded to merge with the other sovereign courts of Paris.[43] Stirred by this display of defiance, the *Parlement* of Bordeaux began to repudiate all of the Crown's policies in the province.[44] On July 1, it issued a decree prohibiting the raising of taxes not previously approved by itself and, in another decree, revoked the royal decree of the preceding year that had created additional fiscal offices.[45] On July 18, it announced that the intendants would not be obeyed unless their orders were first approved by the *Parlement*.[46] On August 26, it abolished the *Présidiaux* of Libourne, Marennes, Sarlat, and Tulle, on the ground that "the edicts [establishing them] have not been verified by the Court."[47] Two days later, on August 28, it asked for the suppression of the *courtiers*, a royally chartered guild of import controllers, "inasmuch as they have connived to render themselves master of all commerce . . . to the prejudice of good citizens and other merchants of the province."[48] Finally, the *Parlement* began considering a reduction of the *convoy*, the export tax on wine, which in 1637 had been raised from

[42] *Ibid.*, II, 343, 345; VI, 508; *A.B.*, "Pauvres," fonds Baurein, carton 23. Epernon had noted: "The officers . . . are considered by the commoners [*les peuples*] as persons who work for their relief and for the common good." Epernon to Mazarin, August 13, 1648, *Archives historiques de la Gironde*, IV, 290.

[43] Ernst H. Kossmann, *La Fronde* (Leiden, 1954), pp. 47 ff.

[44] Epernon informed Mazarin: "The news we have received here of what is taking place in the *Parlement* of Paris has greatly stirred the spirit of the officers, making it more difficult for me to deal with them." June 25, 1648, *Archives historiques de la Gironde*, IV, 284.

[45] *A.B.*, Registres du Parlement, 1648, fols. 494–98.

[46] Epernon to Séguier, July 16, 1648, in Tranchère, *Les dessous de l'histoire*, I, 401.

[47] *A.B.*, Registres du Parlement, 1648, fol. 498.

[48] *Arrest de la Cour de Parlement de Bordeaux portant défense aux courretiers de prendre plus grands droits que ceux qui leurs sont attribués par l'édit vérifié audit Parlement* (Bordeaux, 1648).

8 *livres* to 14 *livres* on each barrel.[49] The contemplated action, touching on one of the government's most important sources of revenue, was more than the Crown could bear.[50] Epernon learned that "Their Majesties were determined not to suffer that the *Parlement* pronounce itself on the *convoy*."[51] Informed of this development the *Parlement* resolved that "very humble remonstrances would be made before the King on the revocation of the 6 *livres* [tax]" but that in the meanwhile the *fermier* of the *convoy* would desist from collecting the levy.[52]

The initial phase of the *Parlement*'s revolt had ended successfully. The intendants were gone, as were the royal *courtiers*; the newly created subordinate courts had been suppressed; and both the *taille* and the *convoy* had been sharply reduced.[53] The struggle, however, was not yet over. On August 31, Dubernet wrote to Cardinal Mazarin: "The gentlemen from the *Enquêtes* are intent on continuing the disorders which I thought would cease with the *Parlement*'s [annual] recess. . . . They now intend to assemble after the feast of *Notre Dame* in September to deliberate on the affairs of the King and those that concern the public."[54] Not content with having defeated royal fiscality, the *Parlement*—or at least its most radical wing—was apparently bent on supplanting the Crown as the sovereign authority in Guyenne. This goal would be reached if it could force the withdrawal of the Duke of Epernon, governor and military commander of Guyenne, and with the departure of the intendants, the Crown's last source of effective support in the province. (Dubernet and others in the *Parlement* supporting the government would soon be driven from their posts.) A concerted effort was called for, but such was precluded by the balance of power existing in Guyenne. For Epernon could always count on the support of Bordeaux's *Jurade* and militia, thus forcing the *Parlement* to divide whatever forces it could muster between the provincial and municipal struggles, and so reduce considerably its chances of success.

[49] Memoir of Dubernet, August 16, 1648, *Archives historiques de la Gironde*, IV, 293–94.

[50] There were 2,300,000 *livres* collected in 1648. The total revenues of the government in that year amounted to 85,400,000 *livres*. G. Jules de Cosnac, *Souvenirs du règne de Louis XIV* (Paris, 1866–82), VIII, 286–94.

[51] Epernon to Mazarin, September 5, 1648, *Archives historiques de la Gironde*, IV, 300.

[52] *A.B.*, Registres du Parlement, 1648, fols. 637–38.

[53] The reduction of the *taille* had taken place on July 13, and involved one eighth of the annual levy. Memoir of Dubernet, August 16, 1648, *Archives historiques de la Gironde*, IV, 293.

[54] Dubernet to Mazarin, August 31, 1648, *Archives historiques de la Gironde*, IV, 299.

Realizing that it would have to consolidate its hold on Bordeaux before openly challenging the governor, the *Parlement* decided that the moment had come to bring the lower classes into the conflict. The first popular demonstration took place on August 26, when "a great multitude of common people [*menu peuple*], armed with swords and sticks, assembled at the docks to protest . . . [Epernon's decision to permit] the exportation of wheat to Spain."[55] Epernon had no doubt as to who was behind the disturbances: "The rising of the commoners which we witnessed yesterday was most assuredly instigated by the city's principal inhabitants."[56] Dubernet, as we have seen, was even more explicit, having written: "The gentlemen from the *Enquêtes* are intent on continuing the disorders." If the *Parlement* had not in fact planned the demonstration, it lost no time in openly supporting its aims, for it now revoked the passports that Epernon had issued to the exporters of wheat.[57]

The struggle soon intensified. Early in 1649, Epernon placed in readiness the *Château Trompette*, the royal fortress inside Bordeaux, "so that," he explained to Mazarin, "I can mobilize all my strength in case the present evils lead to sedition and armed revolt."[58] The *Parlement* was also active. In February it cancelled the tax of six *livres* charged on each barrel of wine entering Bordeaux "for the sole purpose," wrote Epernon, "of gaining the support of the upper country."[59] In March it outlawed the *Cour des Aides* and ordered the *Chambre de l'Edit*—the court adjudicating disputes arising out of the Edict of Nantes—to merge with it. An outraged Epernon wrote to Mazarin: "The *Parlement* of Bordeaux has begun to challenge us openly." The Duke ordered his troops, most of which had just returned from Catalonia, to march on Bordeaux. He also began to build a fort at Libourne, a city on the Dordogne.[60] This last action meant that the governor, who with his fortress at Cadillac already controlled the Garonne, would soon be in a position to cut all of Bordeaux's water routes to the hinterland. The *Parlement* reacted promptly and energetically. After obtaining the support of the entire populace in the form of a covenant pledging each head of household "to defend the city," it

[55] *Registres de la Jurade*, V, 147–48.
[56] Epernon to Mazarin, August 27, 1648, *Archives historiques de la Gironde*, IV, 298.
[57] Loirette, in *Bordeaux, 1453–1715*, ed. R. Boutruche, p. 336.
[58] Epernon to Mazarin, February 16, 1649, *Archives historiques de la Gironde*, IV, 310.
[59] Epernon to Mazarin, February 16, 1649, in Tranchère, *Les dessous de l'histoire*, I, 433.
[60] Epernon to Mazarin, March 14, and March 30, 1649, *Archives historiques de la Gironde*, IV, 315 and 317.

created a council of finance to collect funds, a Council of Police to oversee the city's defense, and an army of twenty thousand organized into thirty-six companies, each commanded by an officer of the *Parlement*, to engage the enemy.[61] Both sides were apparently determined to wage war and indeed fighting broke out soon after the completion of the above preparations.

The military events surrounding the First Fronde can be summarized briefly. In the first month of hostilities, a Bordelais attempt to capture Libourne produced a bloody setback with three thousand of the attackers perishing in the engagement. Epernon would have liked nothing better than to crush the rebellious city, but revolts had broken out in other areas of Guyenne and he lacked the forces necessary to mount an attack. And so the war continued in typical seventeenth century fashion, with much devastation of the countryside, more skirmishes than actual battles, and successes that were invariably the prelude to subsequent setbacks. Finally, after six months of inconclusive results, Mazarin, who was about to attack the Condé party, decided to seek an end to the conflict. The terms he offered to Bordeaux were extremely generous: the proclamation of a general amnesty, the suppression of the 6 *livres* tax on wine, and the destruction of the fortifications at Libourne. The *Parlement* which had abandoned all hope of defeating Epernon after the disaster of Libourne, lost no time in accepting the proposed terms and on January 7, 1650, peace returned to the strife-torn province.[62]

The *Parlement* emerged from the First Fronde as the undisputed ruler of Bordeaux. Its ascendancy over the city began with the military reversals. Shortly after the defeat at Libourne, it expelled Dubernet and other *parlementaires* known to support Epernon.[63] Then it turned on the *Jurade* which, thinking that Bordeaux would soon be in royalist hands, had ordered the dissolution of the Council of Police and even dispatched one of its members to the King to demand the removal of all litigation before the *Parlement*. The *Jurade*'s order was rescinded, and it was told to disavow the mission to the King or face the wrath of the populace. The *Jurade* complied, but not before disturbances had broken out. On the 23rd of July it learned that there was great turmoil in the city, "that

[61] Jacques Fonteneil, *Histoire des mouvemens de Bourdeaux* (Bordeaux, 1651), pp. 80–97, 121–22.

[62] *Ibid.*, pp. 344–47 and 409–22.

[63] D'Argenson de Séguier, July 16, 1649, in Tranchère, *Les dessous de l'histoire*, II, 27–28; Augeard to Séguier, August 3, 1649, *ibid.*, 36–37.

the shops were closed, that barricades were going up, that shouts of 'to arms, to arms' could be heard everywhere and especially in the vicinity of the [*Parlement*'s] palace." That same day one of the *jurats* "who had sought to appease the popular anger" was attacked and nearly killed.[64] The *Jurade* and its supporters were thoroughly cowed. "All the outstanding members of that wretched company as well as other bourgeois of similar standing are fleeing the city," reported one of Mazarin's agents.[65] A week later, the *Parlement* secured the election of three new *jurats* loyal to it, and its mastery of the city was complete.[66]

The *Parlement* could enjoy the fruits of victory for but a few months. The arrest of the Condé chieftains—the Princes of Condé and Conty, the Duke of Longueville—in January of 1650 had resulted in a feudal revolt implicating such princely notables as the Dukes of Orleans, Beaufort, La Rochefoucauld, Bouillon, and the wife of Condé. The last three personages made their way to Guyenne, whose government had, twelve years before, belonged to Condé's father. In May they appeared before Bordeaux's gates and requested the city's protection.[67]

For the first time since the Fronde's outbreak, *Parlement* and *menu peuple* stood divided. Having obtained a satisfactory peace from the King, the *Parlement* was disinclined to approve an act that would signal the resumption of warfare. But such could hardly be the attitude of Bordeaux's masses who had carried the brunt of the fighting and yet gained nothing for their effort. Indeed, the latter may have desired another war precisely because it would jeopardize the gains won by the *Parlement*. As one of the *parlementaires* sent to Paris to negotiate with Mazarin had perceptively noted: "I am fearful that the clauses of the treaty affecting the *Parlement* will not satisfy the common people and that their zeal for us will be altered once they realize that we are only thinking of our interests and not of theirs."[68] How much "zeal" had been lost—on the part of the common people but also on that of the *Parlement*—was now to become apparent.

The *Parlement*'s response to the request for asylum was to order the *Jurade* to lock the city's gates. A mob thereupon invaded the legal chambers and announced that, if the gates were not opened, the locks

---

[64] Fonteneil, *Histoire des mouvemens*, pp. 206–7; *Registres de la Jurade*, I, 433–35,V, 150–51.
[65] Argenson to Mazarin, August 3, 1649, *Archives historiques de la Gironde*, IV, 371.
[66] Fonteneil, *Histoire des mouvemens*, pp. 260–66.
[67] Loirette, in *Bordeaux, 1453–1715*, ed. R. Boutruche, p. 339.
[68] De Gourgues to Le Comte, October 6, 1649, *B.B.*, MS. fonds Itié.

would be smashed.[69] The *Parlement* was clearly stunned, for it issued an appeal to the *Jurade* "to preserve as best it could the tranquility of the city." What ensued was decidedly not what the *Parlement* had hoped for. "No sooner had the *Jurade* appeared in the street," a correspondent of Mazarin reported, "than they were forced by the people to shout repeatedly, 'long live the King and the Princes,'" and some of the more heated spirits then proceeded to break the locks.[70] In the face of the aroused populace, the *Parlement* wisely decided to submit and allow the Condé party to enter the city. Another setback followed when the *Parlement* refused a proferred alliance with the Princes. A mob was soon in the street, besieging the *Parlement*'s palace, and shouting that it would kill anyone who did not sign the pact. A parlementary decree forbidding anyone "on pain of death to enter the palace with arms" and the threat to end all parlementary sessions both proved unavailing, and the treaty with the Princes was then duly registered.[71] Events had thus shown that the *Parlement* could no longer count on the lower classes which, indeed, were rapidly becoming its foe.

Two months after the arrival of the Condists, war broke out anew in Guyenne. A royal army of 17,000 men attacked Bordeaux which was defended by 8,000 artisans and peasants, the latter probably recruited by the princes in the countryside. The fighting was fierce. The outlaying quarter of St. Seurin was taken by the royalists at a cost of 2,000 men. The attackers then attempted to capture one of the city's gates—the Porte Dijaux—but this time could not gain their objective. There was a counterattack, and it was the royalists who had to give ground. Other reversals followed, and soon the attacking force numbered no more than 8,000 men[72] "We have come to such a point," wrote a royalist commander, "that our soldiers can no longer believe that they are dealing with mere bourgeois."[73] Mazarin who had joined the army with the King was in the throes of despair. "We are in the last extremities," he wrote to Le Tellier, "and unless you can send me additional funds . . . everything

[69] La Vie to Mazarin, June 2, 1650, *Archives historiques de la Gironde*, IV, 442.
[70] Unidentified letter from Bordeaux, July 14, 1650, *B.M.*, MS. 2241, fol. 7.
[71] "Nouvelles de Bordeaux," July 14, 1650, *B.N.*, MS. fonds français 18752, fol. 237; Loirette, in *Bordeaux, 1453-1715*, ed. R. Boutruche, p. 339.
[72] Pierre Cayrac, "Récit de la Fronde a Bordeaux," *Revue historique de Bordeaux*, VII (1914), 206-9, 261-71. *Le véritable courrier bordelois ou nouvelles très assurées de tout ce qui s'est passé tant à Bourg qu'à Bordeaux* (Paris, 1650). *Relation des dernières nouvelles du siège de la ville de Bordeaux* (Paris, 1650).
[73] Unidentified letter, September 12, 1650, *B.M.*, MS. 2241, fol. 32.

will be lost."[74] The funds never came and the Cardinal, convinced of the futility of further operations, decided to end hostilities and make peace. The terms he offered could hardly be rejected: a general amnesty, the dismissal of Epernon, and permission to the Condé element to retire from the city. The terms were quickly accepted, and on the 5th of October Louis XIV entered Bordeaux "to the acclaim of the populace."[75] The latter had good reason to be jubilant, for as a royalist official observed, "the proud Bordelais appeared to be more the victors than the vanquished."[76]

Brief as it was, the Second Fronde had far-reaching social and political consequences for Bordeaux. Epernon was gone, leaving behind a helpless *Jurade*. The *Parlement* had split into rival factions, the *Petite Fronde* and the *Grande Fronde*—the former (and much larger) supporting the Crown, and the latter (made up principally of members of the *Chambres des Enquêtes*) supporting the Princes.[77] As for the lower classes, they had shifted their loyalty from the *Parlement* to the Condé princes. "M. de Bouillon is the absolute master of the common people [*le menu peuple*]," a royalist source noted, "and the latter is the master of Bordeaux."[78]

If Bordeaux's masses had indeed begun to play a major role in the city's affairs, they had as yet made no attempt to effect any significant political changes such as eliminating the *Parlement* or capturing the *Jurade*, and had not even sought a voice in the peace negotiations. Such disinterested behavior would suggest a want of maturity: the *menu peuple* may have been the master of Bordeaux—but only of its streets, not of its institutions or political orientation. As in the First Fronde, it seemed perfectly content to sacrifice its interests to those of others. However, this would soon change.

The interval between the Second Fronde and the final outbreak of violence witnessed an exacerbation of the social conflict. The wars had left Bordeaux thoroughly exhausted. "The city," the lieutenant-general of Guyenne informed Mazarin on October 24, "is in a state of veritable wretchedness with much discord, quantity of debts, and a population ruined by the last war."[79] To repay its debts, the *Parlement* adopted a variety of measures: it taxed the guilds and other corporate bodies, seized

[74] Quoted in Kossmann, *La Fronde*, p. 175.
[75] *Ibid.*, p. 176. Report from Bordeaux, no date, *B.M..*, MS. 2241, fol. 30.
[76] Quoted in Kossmann, *La Fronde*, p. 176.
[77] *Ibid.*, p. 167.
[78] D'Albret to Buisson, August 19, 1650, *B.M.*, MS. 2241, fols. 17–18.
[79] Saint-Luc to Mazarin, October 24, 1650, *Archives historiques de la Gironde*, VI, 427.

funds under consignment, imposed a 5 per cent tax on meat, and when the 1,000,000 *livres* thus raised proved insufficient, placed a tax of one *écu* on each barrel of wine sold in the city.[80] Thus the *Parlement* had finally resorted to the very measure that had precipitated the violent uprising of 1635. The wrath of the lower classes was fully aroused, as a tract of the period, the *Apologie pour l'Ormée*, makes plain:

After having perpetrated innumerable acts of injustice in the administration of private suits and in the performance of charges which they hold only because of chance and wealth, these ambitious little men [*petits ambitieux*] now wish to exercise absolute power over the conduct of public affairs. Having committed, under the guise of performing official business, a thousand acts of banditry in the province, they desire to do the same in our city. . . . Having, with the public's consent, taken charge of the public funds, they have come to regard that function as a legal right, and are nettled when asked to give an accounting. One can only begin to list all their crimes: . . . their overweening pride, their hunger for profit, the cruelty of their justice, the despoliation of widows, the devastation of the churches and of the entire province . . . .[81]

Not all the accusations contained in the *Apologie* can be verified, but those dealing with financial corruption and judicial malfeasance appear well founded. Thus on April 30, 1652, the *Parlement* opened an inquiry into the conduct of two *conseillers* accused of malversations in the collection of the *taille*. Others may have been implicated, for the commissioners of the *taille*, the commissioners of the marine, and others who had collected taxes—all officers of the *Parlement*—were asked to absent themselves from the proceedings, a practice followed when members of the court had close personal ties or were in some way implicated in the affairs of the accused party.[82] Legal improprieties often accompanied financial ones, as is clear from the experiences of one Jean Bordenave, physician of Bordeaux. In a brief filed with his notary, Bordenave charged that Bertrand Despujols, a merchant of Brassac,

. . . taking advantage of the prevailing disorders and of the support of M. de Sudiuraut, *conseiller et sous-doyen du Parlement*, had refused to allow him to take possession of a certain piece of property; that when he, Bordenave, had served Despujols with a restraining order obtained from the King's Council,

[80] Fonteneil, *Histoire des mouvemens*, pp. 80, 94–95, 169, 267, 292–93.
[81] *L'Apologie pour l'Ormée par un de l'assemblée de messieurs les bourgeois*, (n.p., n.d.), 27–29. Cited hereafter as *Apologie pour l'Ormée*.
[82] Registres du Parlement, 1651–58, fols. 88–89.

the other had declared . . . that he could not care less about the said order, as he could always count on the support of a number of people, including M. de Suduiraut.[83]

How many others had had a similar experience is of course beyond our possible knowledge, but it is worth noting that one of the Ormée's most adamant demands was for a general evocation of all litigation pending before the *Parlement*.

The attacks on the *Parlement* that had continued throughout 1651 became sharper in the early months of 1652. The charge was leveled that its members had conspired to reinstate the "tyrant" Epernon; that its deputies to the royal court had "time and time again" betrayed the interests of the city; and "that it had done its best to prolong the war so as to profit from it."[84] This last accusation was repeated in the *Apologie:* "While others were serving the public weal . . . the *Parlement* sought ways to harm it through endless requisitions . . . . It was only interested in the city's troubles as a means by which to satisfy its greed and ambition."[85] Such words could only be the presage of further strife. Indeed, the most violent episode of the *Fronde* was about to occur.

[83] *A.G.*, 3E 12.319, fol. 250.
[84] *La généreuse résolution des Gascons* (n.p., 1652); *Le Courrier de la Guyenne, apportant le véritable état des affaires* (Paris, 1652);*Histoire véritable d'une colombe qui a paru miraculeusement en un lieu appelé l'Ormoye de Bordeaux.* (Paris, 1652).
[85] *Apologie pour l'Ormée*, p. 27.

II

THE ORMÉE SEIZES POWER

THERE ARE AT LEAST THREE VERSIONS of the Ormée's formative moments. According to Jacques Filhot, the author of a chronicle on the Fronde in Bordeaux, the Ormée emerged early in 1651, after rumors began to circulate that the King intended to reappoint the Duke of Epernon as governor of Guyenne. There were protests and eventually a crowd numbering 3,000 assembled in the vicinity of the *Hôtel de Ville*. Warned that it would be fired upon if it did not disperse, the crowd retired to the *Ormière*—a platform planted with elm trees (*ormeaux*)—and proceeded to demand "the annihilation of all Epernonists and Mazarinists."[1] All this, however, is omitted in the account provided by the *Apologie pour l'Ormée*:

It was customary for the more prosperous bourgeois—those not having to remain in their shops—to gather on an elevated platform in a corner of the city. Their discussions turned to the troubled times: the exactions, the forced contributions, the misappropriations, the fact that one who collected revenues had purchased a piece of land worth 6,000 *livres* per annum, that another

---

[1] Armand Communay, *L'Ormée à Bordeaux d'après le journal inédit de Jacques Filhot* (Bordeaux, 1887), pp. 172–73. Cited hereafter as *Journal de Filhot*. The date of 1651, although not given, can be inferred from the rest of Filhot's comments, for he notes that the meetings at the *Ormière* began shortly before the *Parlement* sent a deputation to the King to ask that the government of Guyenne be given to Condé — a development that took place in May of 1651. *Ibid.*, p. 173. A dispatch from Bordeaux's *Bureau de Finance* dated June 12, 1652, would also place the Ormée's first appearance early in 1651: "Diverse disorders which occur daily in this city are the result of a conflict that began more than a year ago." (*A.G.*, C 3888, fol. 4.)

had used the money to pay back a debt of 40,000 *livres*. . . . The public's curiosity having been aroused, the assemblies became larger and more frequent, with the result that the *Parlement*, whose ire had been provoked, ordered that they be outlawed.[2]

References to economic discontent also appear in a report of the Venetian ambassador to France, but here the stress is on the influence of ideas:

The opportunity enjoyed by the English of going yearly to Bordeaux in order to ship wines has given them ample means not only of establishing many connections there, but, under existing circumstances, of impressing their own opinions on the inhabitants of the city. The people there used to assemble daily at a certain spot, more to hear the news than from any idea of insurrection or of anything else. But meeting there in great numbers, they began to discuss the badness of the times, contrasting it with the peculiar prosperity of England. This seems to have led to speeches in favor of liberty, advocating the expulsion of the parliament [sic] and the forming of a more popular one, and, in short, governing themselves.[3]

Thus Filhot would attribute the Ormée's emergence to an immediate cause (the threat of Epernon's return), while the *Apologie* and the report of the Venetian ambassador both point to general and long-term factors (resentment over financial abuses and the influence of English radicalism). The versions are considerably different and yet, as they do not contradict each other, one cannot rule out the possibility that all have some validity. Certainly there can be little doubt of the populace's aversion for Epernon, or of the great hostility felt for those who were managing Bordeaux's affairs, or of the English influence. However, are all of these factors to be given the same weight? Epernon had definitely abandoned all claims to the governorship of Guyenne by May of 1651, having in that month given the province to Condé in exchange for Burgundy.[4] It is therefore unlikely that the demonstrations of which Filhot speaks were in fact unleashed by fear of the Duke's return—especially as they continued long after his departure. At the same time, the crowds that met at the *Ormière* called for the destruction of "Epernonists and Mazarinists"—terms used to describe such supporters of the governor and the

[2] *Apologie pour l'Ormée*, pp. 11–12.

[3] Morosini to the Doge and Senate, May 28, 1652, *Calendar of State Papers and Manuscripts Existing in the Archives and Collections of Venice 1647–1652* (London, 1927), XXVIII, 238–39.

[4] Ernst Kossmann, *La Fronde* (Leiden, 1954), p. 196.

royal government as the *jurats* and the members of the *Petite Fronde*—and it is probable that the continued presence of this element in Bordeaux was the actual cause of the assembly held near the *Hôtel de Ville*. Such a conclusion is not at variance with the explanation offered by the *Apologie*, except that the latter would take a broader view of the Ormée's target, adding to it all those who had managed to enrich themselves in the course of the earlier struggles. Reference by the *Apologie* to "larger and more numerous" assemblies also suggests a process of growth—a more likely occurrence than the sudden eruption described by Filhot. If the Ormée's rise was indeed gradual, then quite possibly radical ideas did come to influence the assemblies, as the Venetian ambassador maintains, for English merchants as well as political agents representing the new republic were active in Bordeaux, and may have succeeded in "impressing their own opinions on the inhabitants of the city."[5] However, that the example of England was sufficient in itself to radicalize the populace, as the ambassador suggests, seems doubtful. The Puritan Revolution may have provided ideological material, perhaps even the impetus for political change, but the Ormée's social dynamism could only have resulted from the discontent generated by local inequities.

Whatever its actual genesis, the Ormée[6] soon acquired an institutional character, as is apparent from a circular that appeared in the middle of 1651. Addressed to "The illustrious *frondeurs* of the Ormaye," it read: "You are advised that next Thursday, the 14th of June, a mass will be celebrated at the Church of Ste. Eulalie in honor of the peace which God in His infinite wisdom has consented to bestow on us. A dinner is then to be served at the Château du Hâ. You are invited to both functions."[7] The Ormée's appearance was not lost on the new governor of the province, the Prince of Condé. The latter was on his way to Guyenne—he had, in July of 1651, been forced to relinquish Paris to the partisans of Mazarin—when he wrote to the Ormée:

[5] The importance of English commercial activity can be gauged from the fact that England accounted for one-third of Bordeaux's exports. See Théophile Malvezin, *Histoire du commerce de Bordeaux* (Bordeaux, 1892), II, 256–57. On the role of English agents, see Chapter III.

[6] We shall employ the most common spelling of the word. Other spellings: Ormaie, Ormaye, Hormée, Hourmée.

[7] *Les illustres frondeurs de l'Ormaye.* . . . B.N., Inv. Res. F 185, Ordonnances Militaires, Boite 15 (1646–50), fol. 337. Labadie in his *Nouveau supplement à la bibliographie des Mazarinades* (Paris, 1904), no. 119, states that the pamphlet appeared in 1653, but Thursday, June 14, occurred in 1651. Could the celebration have been in honor of Condé's recent appointment?

The letter in which you assure me of your good will could not have touched me more deeply. . . . I am confident that the sentiments you express will persist to the very end, as they accord perfectly with your best interests. For had my enemies succeeded in my capture, the return of Cardinal Mazarin would have surely followed, with consequences that you would have been the first to feel. . . . Be assured that I shall remain steadfast in my resolve not to tolerate the return of the Cardinal or any of his creatures.[8]

Condé must have known that in cultivating the Ormée he was jeopardizing his ties to the *Parlement*. Had the Ormée already become so powerful as to convince the Prince that its support was worth more than that of the *Parlement?*

Condé arrived in Guyenne in September of 1651 and remained until March of 1652. Not much is known of the Ormée's activities during this period of six months. If the Ormée was truly dormant, as one of Mazarin's correspondents avers, this can only be said of its policy-making organs and not of the element that filled its ranks.[9] On January 3, 1652, Pontac, a *président* of the *Parlement*, was attacked by a large mob "led by one who carried a sword at his side," and his papers which included a letter from the King were seized. A few weeks later, the *Parlement* learned that a group of "bourgeois" had appeared at the *Hôtel de Ville* to "protest the want of speed with which the decrees against suspects are being carried out."[10]

The defeat suffered by Condé at Agen in March of 1652 was the signal for a further display of Ormée militancy. As Mazarin learned from one of his supporters: " . . . the Bordelais are in a rage at the *Parlement*'s regiment which left Bordeaux with 1,200 men, but reached *M. le Prince* with only 400. . . . The Ormée's assemblies are resuming. . . . The persecution of suspects begins anew."[11] The re-emergence of these "assemblies" was also noted by the *Parlement*. On April 10, the following entry appeared in the *Registres Secrets*—the *Parlement*'s official record: "In spite of the injunction against them, assemblies prejudicial to the King's service, the *Parlement's*

---

[8] *Lettre de monseigneur le prince de Condé, gouverneur de Guyenne à messieurs les bourgeois de l'Ormée de Bourdeaux* (Bordeaux, 1651).

[9] Unidentified letter to Mazarin, March 16, 1652, *Archives historiques de la Gironde*, VI, 314.

[10] Registres du Parlement, 1651–58, fols. 32, 46. Who the suspects were is not indicated.

[11] Unidentified letter to Mazarin, March 16, 1652, *Archives historiques de la Gironde*, VI, 314.

authority, and the public peace form daily at the Hourmée."[12] A day later, the *Parlement* received word that "great numbers of people armed with swords and pistols had gathered at the Hourmée." Questioned on this occurrence, the *jurats* could only report having learned that the purpose of the assembly was "to rid the city of suspects."[13] The news was not calculated to allay the *Parlement*'s fears, especially as rumors were then circulating that three hundred "of the best families" were about to be expelled from the city.[14] The *Parlement* ordered the *Jurade* to put down the disturbances and threatened to "suspend its deliberations as long as the assemblies continued."[15] Not at all cowed by the *Parlement*'s actions, the Ormée proceeded to release the names of nine *parlementaires*—all members of the *Petite Fronde*—it wished ousted. Either because it saw an opportunity to eliminate from its midst a group of troublesome members, or because it had suddenly come to appreciate the wisdom of a conciliatory policy toward the Ormée, the *Parlement* now agreed "that the decree formerly issued against the suspects be executed without delay and that the members of the company suspected of being followers of Mazarin be tried by the Court in the *Chambre du Conseil*." At the same time the *jurats* were enjoined "not to allow any further assemblies at the Ormée and to permit them only at the *Hôtel de Ville*."[16] The Ormée could not have asked for more: the unwanted *parlementaires* would be made to depart, and the assemblies allowed to continue: if not under the elms, then in the *Hôtel de Ville*.

However, a number of weeks passed and still the *Parlement* had not acted. Finally losing patience, the Ormée resolved to take matters into its own hands. On May 2, a mob of several hundred descended on three of the proscribed officers.[17] Again, the *Parlement* issued a decree prohibiting all "unlawful assemblies," but this time authorizing the *jurats* to use force in the event that their orders were not obeyed.[18] The *Parlement*'s decree was thereupon met by one from the Ormée which read:

[12] Registres du Parlement, 1651–58 fol. 66.

[13] *Ibid.*, fols. 67, 68.

[14] *Gazette [de Renaudot]*, April 11, 1652, cited in Gabriel-Jules de Cosnac, *Souvenirs du règne de Louis XIV* (Paris, 1866-82), III, 168–69.

[15] Registres du Parlement, 1651–58, fol. 68.

[16] *Le neufiesme courrier bourdelois apportant toutes sortes de nouvelles* (Paris, 1652). Cited hereafter as *Courrier bourdelois*, with the appropriate issue number given in brackets.

[17] Unidentified letter, *B.N.*, MS. fonds Dupuy, liasse 775, fol. 162.

[18] Registres du Parlement, 1651–58, 104.

On the knowledge obtained by the company of the Ormée—a body loyal to the King and M. le Prince—of an edict of the *Parlement* as injurious as it is unreasonable and whose sole purpose is to obstruct and thwart the good intentions of this honorable assembly, we hereby serve notice on its authors, supporters, and accomplices that in the event of its promulgation all will be summarily executed. We also forbid the said *Parlement*, again on pain of death, to take similar actions in the future and declare ourselves ready to take up arms to enforce our will. Moreover, we exhort the faithful bourgeois [*les fidèles bourgeois*] to remain steadfastly loyal to our rule or be declared traitors to the fatherland [*traitres à la patrie*] and thereby incur the penalty of perpetual banishment and the confiscation of all their property.[19]

On the day the above decree was issued (May 13, 1652), Ormists appeared at the house of d'Affis, a *président* of the *Parlement*, who was duly informed that "they would know how to stop him, were he so rash as to attempt to carry out the so-called decree." The next day, as sergeants were about to proclaim the Court's orders, they were set upon and the documents were torn from their hands.[20]

The war of words was rapidly becoming one of deeds. On the 15th of May came the first armed clash. The city awoke, the *Courrier bourdelois* reported,

. . . to find placards on numerous street corners and notably in front of the [*Parlement*'s] palace. They were addressed "to the Bourgeois of Bordeaux" and proclaimed, among other things, that two *jurats* and the better part of the *Parlement* were Mazarinists, that the city's security required further Ormée assemblies, and that all the culprits would have to be thrown out.[21]

By seven o'clock, the Ormée, "with more arms than have yet been seen," was in possession of the Place de l'Ombrière, the square in front of the *Parlement*'s palace.[22] The palace was then invaded. What followed is described in a letter to Condé:

They beat up a few of the officers' servants and some clerks who had come to the *Parlement*'s rescue. They then kept everyone prisoner until three o'clock in the afternoon, in order to force them to rescind their decree [against the

---

[19] *Manifeste des bordelois, contenant le récit véritable de ce qui s'est passé dans la ville de Bordeaux, les 13 et 14 du passé* (Paris, 1652). Cited hereafter as *Manifeste des bordelois*. The decree is published in the *Archives historiques de la Gironde*, VIII, 385–86.

[20] Registres du Parlement, 1651–58, fols. 103, 104.

[21] *Courrier bourdelois* [XIIe].

[22] Unidentified letter, *B.N.*, MS. fonds Dupuy, liasse 775, fol. 182.

Ormée]. But the officers refused and instead announced that they would not hold further sessions until all assemblies had ceased and their safety was assured. They finally departed, accompanied by Monseigneur [de Conty] but in such disorder that one almost felt pity for them.[23]

The decree of May 13 had contained a separate warning to the "faithful bourgeois"—that is, the more substantial inhabitants of the city—and these too now came to know the Ormée's wrath. The author of the above letter to Condé also revealed: "The conflict is so great and the *Parlement* so ill-treated that unless something is done to change things the rising fire will end in consuming all of us. . . . In the name of God and the Holy Mother and on the part of the good bourgeois [*les bons bourgeois*] I implore His Lordship not to leave us in so desolate a state."[24] The writer was a person of some standing, for he described himself as "an old bourgeois whose only remaining interest is the heavenly reward and and my little commerce [*qui ne respire plus que le ciel et mon petit commerce*]," and would not disclose his identity (beyond saying that he was a former *jurat*) because, he explained, "I am fearful of being proscribed despite my age and family."[25] His apprehensions were apparently shared by many others. Guiraut, a *jurat*, told the *Parlement* that shortly after the commencement of fighting he had sought "to place the good bourgeois under arms but that no one, not even the captains, had responded and that he even found it difficult to mount a guard on the city's gates."[26]

The *Parlement's* decision to suspend its sessions was received with jubilation by the Ormists. A correspondent of Mazarin noted: "One only hears of the victories of our brave Ormée and the successes that it daily scores over our *Parlement*. Each day there is a triumphant procession to the sound of 50 or more drums."[27] The planting of an oak tree—an annual pageant in honor of Palm Sunday—was the occasion of a climactic celebration, as we learn from the *Courrier bourdelois:* "The planting of an oak before the residence of His Highness M. de Conty produced so much rejoicing that words cannot describe it. The entire city was under arms, each *jurat* marching at the head of the regiment from his sector. Throughout the day one only heard volleys of musket shot and the sound of drums.

---

[23] Unidentified letter to Condé, May 16, 1652, *A.C.*, MS. serie P, XII, fol. 258.
[24] *Ibid.*
[25] *Ibid.*
[26] Registres du Parlement, 1651–58, fol. 105.
[27] Unidentified letter to Mazarin, May 23, 1652. *Archives historiques de la Gironde,* LVIII, 30.

The Ormée's assembly was working marvels."[28] When Conty, Condé's brother and the acting governor of Guyenne, thought the moment ripe to ask the two factions to negotiate their differences, he was told by the Ormée that it would henceforth refuse all conversations with the *Parlement*.[29]

The turn of affairs troubled Condé. "What will the others say," his anonymous correspondent had asked, " . . . when they learn that a *Parlement* which has served you so faithfully is deprived of all authority and is the subject of such unparalled abuses? Is it not to be feared that those members of the *Parlement* of Paris which have hitherto been well-disposed toward Your Highness will be led by the bad example to foment division?"[30] The Prince who was then seeking to obtain the support of the *Parlement* of Paris, must have been troubled by the same thought, for he proceeded to make every effort to save Bordeaux's *Parlement*. To the *Jurade* he now wrote:

I ask that you use your credit to bring to a halt the divisions that have come to Bordeaux over the assemblies of the Ormée, for they serve only to favor the evil designs of our enemies.[31]

To the Ormée:

I learn that *Messieurs du Parlement* as well as my other friends have been made the targets of violence by persons whom I had always considered and still consider loyal to me.[32]

To Lenet, his principal agent in Bordeaux:

Above all, you must not permit the *Petite Fronde*, among whom I number some of my best friends, to succumb to the attacks of the *Grande Fonde* and the Ormée. It is not, however, my intention that the last named be destroyed, but simply that it be prevented from carrying things to the extreme as it is presently inclined to do.[33]

---

[28] *Courrier bourdelois* [XIIIe].

[29] Unidentified letter to Mazarin, May 23, 1652, *Archives historiques de la Gironde*, LVIII, 30

[30] Unidentified letter to Condé, May 16, 1652, *A.C.*, MS. serie P, XII, fol. 258.

[31] *Lettre de monseigneur le prince escrite à messieurs les maires et jurats, gouverneurs de Bordeaux avec la lettre escrite à messieurs les bourgeois* (Bordeaux, 1652).

[32] *Ibid.*

[33] Condé to Lenet, June 3, 1652, "Mémoires inédits de Pierre Lenet," in *Nouvelle collection des mémoires pour servir à l'histoire de France*, ed. J. Michaud and F. Poujoulat, 3e série, vol. II (Paris, 1838), p. 547. Cited hereafter as Lenet, "Mémoires."

And again to Lenet:

Inform all my friends that they will make me very happy if they re-enter the *Parlement* . . . I repeat that the Ormée must not be put down altogether, for it is likely that in their usual transport they will accuse us of being on the side of Mazarin and this is to be feared.[34]

Condé apparently believed that the *Parlement* would be content merely to survive and that the Ormée would dutifully accept any arrangement he proposed. He did not realize that the *Parlement* would sooner make peace with the Crown, even at the price of a return to the *status quo ante* 1649, than tolerate the existence of the detestable Ormée, and that the Ormée, once aware that it had the power to destroy the *Parlement*, would not be content until it had done just that.

The Ormée's campaign against the *Parlement* was resumed after the latter, assured by Conty that all illegal assemblies would cease, had begun once more to meet. On the first of June, "seditious" placards appeared in the vicinity of the *Palais*. That same day the Ormée assembly began deliberating on a second list of undesirable *parlementaires*. It released the name of fourteen whose departure, the Ormée announced, would take place "voluntarily or by force."[35] On the 3rd, Conty appeared before a gathering of 1,500 Ormists to plead the cause of the proscribed, but, as he wrote to Condé, "neither my entreaties nor my threats obtained the desired results."[36] He then sought to have the action delayed until the 8th, to allow time for an emissary from Condé to reach Bordeaux, but the Ormée replied that the fourteen would have until three o'clock to leave. It was then two o'clock.[37]

While all this was occurring at the Ormée, the municipal powers were beginning to falter. *Président* Pichon announced that he would no longer attend the *Parlement*'s sessions, as the Ormée had resolved "to drive him from the city, and in case of resistance, to throw him into the street." Dussault, a *conseiller*, reported that the Ormée "was placing everyone under arms and closing all shops; that he himself had seen this taking

[34] Condé to Lenet, June 9, 1652, in Lenet, "Mémoires," pp. 547–48.

[35] Registres du Parlement, 1651–58, fol. 114; *Journal de tout ce qui s'est passé à Bordeaux depuis le 1ᵉʳ juin jusques à present* (Paris, sur un imprimé a Bordeaux, 1652).

[36] Conty to Condé, June 6, 1652, *A.C.*, MS. serie P, XII, fol. 267.

[37] *Ibid.*; *Journal de tout ce qui s'est passé à Bordeaux depuis le 1ᵉʳ juin.*

place, . . . and that the *jurats* no longer dared to appear in public." Summoned before the *Parlement*, the *jurats* admitted that they were "too weak to control the situation." They disclosed that two of their number had been sent to the Ormée "to propose some sort of accomodation and to warn those present of the evils that might attend their rebellion," but that the Ormée had spurned both the offer and the warning. When reminded that they, the *jurats*, were still "chiefs of the bourgeois, colonels [of the militia], and governors of the city," the insurgents had answered that "they were well known as colonels and governors of Mazarin and therefore as traitors."[38]

The 3:00 P.M. deadline having passed, the Ormée prepared to make good its threat. It began by staging a display of its might. To the sound of drums, two thousand armed Ormists, wearing elm branches in their hats, marched through the Chapeau Rouge, the parlementary district, making a point of passing the houses of the proscribed. Soon thereafter, a detachment of specially selected Ormists led by Christophe Dureteste, the president of the Ormée assembly, visited each of the intended victims.[39] Condé's anonymous correspondent has left the following account of the operation:

This man Dureteste, taking with him fifteen or sixteen fusiliers who had been picked from his troops, descended first on M. de Mons, *conseiller aux Enquêtes*, ordering him, in the same of the Ormée, to leave before six o'clock the next morning or risk the loss of his life. They then went to see *M. le Président* Pichon and all the others, in the same manner, adding to their announcement a deluge of threats so outrageous and scandalous that even those who were with them were horrified.[40]

The *Parlement* was ready to capitulate. Lenet, who feared that once outside the city the proscribed would establish a rival *Parlement*, informed Condé that his attempts to keep them in Bordeaux had failed: "All want to depart and save their families."[41] Pichon, who on June 3rd and 4th was

[38] Registres du Parlement, 1651–58 fols. 114, 115. *Courrier bourdelois [XV*]; Journal de tout ce qui s'est passé à Bordeaux depuis le 1er juin.*

[39] Lenet to Condé, June 3 (?), 1652, B.N., MS. fonds français, 6707, fol. 144; *Journal de tout ce qui s'est passé à Bordeaux depuis le 1er juin.*

[40] Unidentified letter to Condé, June 6, 1652, A.C., MS. serie P, XII, fol. 269.

[41] Lenet to Condé, June 3(?), 1652, B.N., MS. fonds français, 6707, fol. 144. Lenet's correspondence with Condé constitutes one of the richest sources of information available on the Ormée. Arriving in Bordeaux just prior to its emergence and remaining until its fall, Lenet witnessed (and sometimes participated in) all the upheavals that followed the Ormée's rise to power. Although too attached to Condé's cause to appreciate the Ormée's aims, his portrayal of men and events is sound and often illuminating.

visited by Conty, Mme. de Longueville (Conty's sister), the Princess of Condé, and Lenet, told the first two that he had always been loyal to the Condé party "but that since they had declared him suspect, he intended to depart and would do so whether he received a passport or not."[42] He left on the 5th, but only after telling "one of the Ormists who had come to pay his respects that he was a scoundrel, and that upon his return, which would be soon enough, he would have him hanged."[43] The departure of Pichon, one of the *Parlement's* most influential members, was the signal for a general exodus. The number of departures was so great that the Court was forced to cancel its sessions for the 4th, 5th, and 6th of June.[44] By the 10th, only fifteen officers were still in attendance.[45] Filhot felt impelled to observe: "Dureteste, who was in charge of the proscriptions, expelled more officers of the *Parlement* in a week than the King . . . in four years."[46]

Although most of the Ormée's attention was taken up by the *Parlement*, the *bons bourgeois* were not ignored. Merchants and others who had not joined the June 3rd demonstration were attacked.[47] On the 5th, Conty learned that the Ormée was about "to throw out Fontenel and de Nort, both of whom are *jurats*; Truchon, *juge de la Bourse*, and the two *consuls* of that body; and 'numerous *bons bourgeois*'."[48] The same news was reported to Condé by his unidentified correspondent: "They threaten to proscribe our first two *jurats*, our *juge*, and a great many *bons bourgeois* who have refused to follow them, and still more from the *Parlement*. If this continues, we will either have to cut their throats or the city will become deserted. We are so bewildered that we no longer know what to do or what to say."[49]

Condé's emissary, Chavagnac, arrived on June 7. He brought with him letters for the *Parlement*, Lenet, and Villars—next to Dureteste the leading Ormist. Each letter made a plea for civil peace.[50] That to Villars vehemently

---

[42] Unidentified letter to Condé, June 6, 1652. *A.C.*, MS. serie P, XII, fol. 269; Lenet to Condé, June 3(?), 1652, *B.N.*, fonds français, 6707 fols. 144, 146.

[43] *Ibid.*, fol. 146.

[44] Registres du Parlement, 1651–58, fols. 115–16.

[45] Lenet to Condé, June 10, 1652, in Lenet, "Mémoires," p. 550.

[46] Communay, *Journal de Filhot*, p. 175.

[47] Unidentified letter to Condé, June 6, 1652, *A.C.*, MS. series P, XII, fol. 269.

[48] Lenet to Condé, June 3(?), 1652, *B.N.*, MS. fonds français, fol. 146.

[49] Unidentified letter to Condé, June 6, 1652, *A.C.*, MS. series P, XII, fol. 269.

[50] Thus Condé urged the *Parlement* to negotiate a peace settlement between its various factions (Registres du Parlement, 1651–58, fol. 122), and he urged Lenet to seek a "reunification of all the spirits" (Condé to Lenet, June 3, 1652, in Lenet, "Mémoires," p. 547).

condemned "certain people who seek to cause harm to my closest friends," whom he proceeded to identify as the *président* d'Affis and the *conseillers* Taranques, Mirat, and Bordes, all members of the *Petite Fronde*. The Prince admonished Villars and "all the bourgeois of the Ormée . . . that they take heed not to offend the members of so distinguished a body [as the *Parlement*] . . . and not to hold further assemblies without the consent of M. le Prince."[51] The letter was brought to the attention of the Ormée assembly but, instead of yielding the expected compliance, it provoked an outburst of wrath. Instigated by Villars himself, the assembly moved to mobilize its forces, seize the *Hôtel de Ville*, and promulgate a new municipal charter. Conty now sought to rally the beleaguered party. He urged a specially convened conclave containing representatives of the *Grande* and *Petite Frondes*, the *Jurade*, the *Bourse*, as well as "a number of *bons bourgeois*," to occupy the *Hôtel de Ville* and concentrate armed forces in areas which might come under attack, such as the Chapeau Rouge.[52]

The clash was not slow in coming. On the night of June 9th a band of Ormists on patrol through the Chapeau Rouge came upon a detachment of "*bons bourgeois*" commanded by the *conseiller* Thibault and the *jurat* Fontenel. There was an exchange of fire, and seven or eight Ormists fell, among them two leaders of the Ormée: Monleau, *procureur au Parlement*, and Lafitte, a ham merchant. Villars informed Mme. de Longueville that "4,000 men stood ready to avenge the deaths of their brothers-in-arms and to burn the entire city."[53] Those of the Chapeau Rouge replied that they would "cut down all attackers."[54] Mindful of the wishes of his brother, Conty made an attempt at pacification. At five o'clock on the morning of the 10th, he and the Princess of Condé visited the two camps. He persuaded the Chapeau Rouge to put down its arms but, as he wrote to Condé, "our efforts did not succeed at the Ormée."[55]

Thus, although it had suffered an initial setback, the Ormée was as

[51] Condé to Villars, [no date], in G.-J. Cosnac, *Souvenirs*, IV, 306-7.

[52] Lenet to Condé, June 10, 1652, in Lenet, "Mémoires," pp. 549-50. Unidentified letter to Mazarin, June 10, 1652, *Archives historiques de la Gironde*, VIII, 390-91; Conty to Condé, June 10, 1652, in Henri d'Aumale, *Histoire des Princes de Condé pendant le XVIᵉ et XVIIᵉ siècles* (Paris, 1863-96), VI, 627-28. Cited hereafter as *Histoire*.

[53] *Courrier bourdelois* [XVᵉ]; *Courrier bourdelois* [XVIᵉ]; Conty to Condé, June 10, 1652, in d'Aumale, *Histoire*, VI, 627. Lenet to Condé, June 10, 1652, in Lenet, "Mémoires," p. 550.

[54] Unidentified letter to Mazarin, June 10, 1652, *Archives historiques de la Gironde*, VIII, 391.

[55] Conty to Condé, June 10, 1652, in d'Aumale, *Histoire*, VI, 627.

intent as ever on continuing the struggle. As it explained to Chavagnac, a compromise was unthinkable, "for the *Parlement* being our enemy would destroy us if it ever got the upper hand."[56] Even Lenet, who was ever suspecting that some outside party—the *Grande Fronde*, or Conty, or Mme. de Longueville—controlled the insurgents,[57] was impressed by the Ormée's resoluteness. "The Ormée which has begun to meet daily," he reported to Condé, "is appointing its members to all sorts of positions, sending deputies on various missions, and loudly proclaiming its intention of expelling de Nort, Fontenel, ten or twelve members of the *Parlement*, and numerous bourgeois. . . . Encouraged by the Huguenots, it is allegedly seeking to control all public affairs. When its members, who invariably carry things to excess, are told that they must not do anything except by order of Your Highness, they reply that you are surrounded by Mazarinists and that someday you will be pleased with everything they have done."[58] Lenet's letter contained a number of revelations: that the Ormée was beginning to develop an administration for Bordeaux; that the Huguenots had joined the struggle; that the Ormée's ties to the Condé party, if not to Condé himself, had begun to dissolve; and above all, that the insurgents now had a clearly defined political objective, "to control all public affairs."

The Ormée's emergence as a self-directed political force coincided with a significant change in the relation of its venal and mercantile enemies, for in the face of the common peril, *Parlement* and *Jurade* drew together. The rapproachement seems to have begun after the clash of May 15, when at least one ex-*jurat* had urged Condé to save the *Parlement*. The Ormée's foray into the Chapeau Rouge—a *quartier* inhabited by *parlementaires* but also by prosperous merchants—must have finally convinced both bodies to set aside former differences, for shortly thereafter Conty informed his brother: "All the bourgeois are reunited, to the great satisfaction of the *Parlement*."[59] The same development was also noted by Lenet: "With the exception of a handful of disgruntled

---

[56] Lenet to Condé, June 10, 1652, in Lenet, "Mémoires," p. 551.

[57] Thus, as recently as June 3, Lenet had written: "His Highness has just now gone to dissolve the Ormée assembly, in which venture, unless I am very much mistaken, he will succeed eminently." Lenet to Condé, June 3, 1652, *B.N.*, MS. fonds français 6707, fol.158.

[58] Lenet to Condé, June 10, 1652, in Lenet, "Mémoires," p. 549.

[59] Conty to Condé, June 10, 1652, in d'Aumale, *Histoire*, VI, 628. On the character of the Chapeau Rouge, see Louis Desgraves, *Evocation du vieux Bordeaux* (Paris, 1960), pp. 296 ff.

members, the entire *Parlement* is overjoyed [at the Ormée's defeat]. All the people of substance praise and bless the conduct of Your Highness."[60]

The link between wealth and office became evident when the *Parlement* asked the *Cent et Trente*—an organ representing Bordeaux's legal and mercantile elite[61]—to find ways "of restoring calm to the city."[62] The *Cent et Trente* met on the 13th of June and adopted the following resolutions:

(1) To create a "union" of "all bourgeois and other residents of the city to act promptly and in concert and for the interests of our Lords the Princes."

(2) To outlaw all assemblies "other than those which the public authority and the magistrates will permit."

(3) To recall all the proscribed.

(4) To request the *Parlement* to order "those who have handled public funds to give an account of their expenditures before commissioners selected by the *Parlement* from among all of the corporate bodies of the city."

(5) To ask the *Parlement* to overlook all past injuries done to it.

(6) To demand that Conty look after the welfare of Monleau's widow and children.[63]

The terms were far from generous: in return for an inquiry into the city's finances conducted by the very element that was to be investigated, the Ormée was expected to condone the return of the exiled *parlementaires*, suspend its assemblies, and submit to a venal-mercantile "union." It is little wonder that the *Cent et Trente*'s session resulted in renewed disturbances, Conty informing his brother that "seditious elements have tried to get the people to take up arms."[64]

The Ormée was momentarily on the defensive. On the 15th of June, the *Parlement* declared that all exiles would be permitted to return.[65] The same day, Conty re-affirmed the ban on unauthorized assemblies and announced that the carrying of arms would incur "all the penalties provided in His Majesty's ordinances."[66] The Prince was so confident that peace had been

---

[60] Lenet to Condé, June 10, 1652, in Lenet, "Mémoires," p. 550.

[61] The *Cent et Trente* was a consultative assembly made up of officers of the *Parlement*, *avocats*, and merchants who had held municipal office. Its function was to consider all "grave and public issues." *Registres de la Jurade*, I, 406. For the membership of the *Cent et Trente*, see appendix.

[62] Registres du Parlement, 1651–58, fol. 123.

[63] Registres du Parlement, 1651–58, fols. 125–26; *Courrier bourdelois [XVIe]*.

[64] Conty to Condé, June 13, 1652, A.C., MS. serie P, XII, fol. 274.

[65] Registres du Parlement, 1651–58, fol. 126–27.

[66] *Courrier bourdelois [XVIe]*.

restored that two days later he left for the army then camped outside of Périgueux.[67] On the 19th the exiles made their re-entry "to the applause of the good bourgeois who demonstrated so much joy at their arrival that one could only conclude that the ousters had been carried out against their will."[68]

The return of the proscribed was the signal for a resurgence of Ormée militancy. On the 20th, shots were exchanged between Ormists, led by Villars, and elements from the Chapeau Rouge.[69] On the 21st, five hundred Ormists affixed their names to a manifesto which Lenet described to Condé as "truly the most offensive action yet taken against the *Parlement* and even against Your Highness."[70] The 23rd was the eve of the feast of St. Jean—Bordeaux's patron saint. It was traditionally a festive occasion with fireworks, a feast at the *Hôtel de Ville*, and a march of the militia and other armed elements. But this time "it was deemed advisable not to allow the people to carry arms lest there be a clash between the Ormée and the Chapeau Rouge."[71]

On the morning of the 24th, some eighty Ormists met in the Church of Ste. Croix to discuss sending aid to the Château of Cadillac, then under siege of Harcourt's army, and to "honor the memory of Monleau."[72] When the *jurat* Guiraut ordered the assembly to disband, "the people, filled with wine," thus runs the account of a *Mazarinade*, "mockingly replied that they would remain assembled whether he liked it or not."[73] Guiraut withdrew, but not before he had announced that he would be back at the head of 500 men and see them cut to pieces.[74] The order was then given to the militants of the Chapeau Rouge and St. Rémy—the merchant's quarter—to take up arms.[75] Led by Guiraut and Fontenel, a

[67] Conty to Condé, June 17, 1652, *A.C.*, MS. serie P, XII, fol. 280.

[68] *Courrier bourdelois* [XVIe].

[69] Lenet to Condé, June 24, 1652, in G.-J. Cosnac, *Souvenirs*, III, 335.

[70] *Ibid.*, 336–37. The manifesto is mentioned in an unidentified letter sent to Mazarin, but no details are provided. *A.N.* KK 1219, fol. 19. According to the *Parlement* it contained "a list of grievances and actions to be taken outside of the Parlement." Registres du Parlement, 1651–58, fol. 130.

[71] Lenet to Condé, June 24, 1652, in G.-J. Cosnac, *Souvenirs*, III, 334.

[72] *Journal de tout ce qui s'est fait et passé en la ville de Bourdeaux, depuis le 24 juin jusques à présent, entre les bourgeois de la ville et les Ormistes* (Paris, 1652). According to Lenet, all this was but a pretext for convening an illegal assembly. Lenet to Condé, June 24, 1652, in G.-J. Cosnac, *Souvenirs*, VI, 335.

[73] *Journal de tout ce qui s'est fait et passé . . . depuis le 24 Juin.*

[74] Ciraq to Dubosq, June 27, 1652, *B.B.*, MS. fonds Itié, no fol.

[75] *Journal de tout ce qui s'est fait et passé . . . depuis le 24 Juin.*

force of 300 to 400 that included the *présidents* d'Affis and Pichon, a dozen *conseillers*, and numerous "*bons bourgeois*" began to move into St. Michel, the artisan's quarter.[76] In the Rue du Pas St. George, it met the Ormée. The ensuing engagement was short but fierce. As one source reported: "Stirred by the presence of the *jurats*, the bourgeois unleashed such a withering fire that the rebels were obliged to barricade themselves inside the houses and fire from behind the windows."[77] The Ormée defenses, however, did not break, and after three hours of fighting and a dozen deaths, Guiraut's forces were compelled to withdraw.[78]

The Ormée now prepared to take the offensive. Late on the 24th, word reached Conty's headquarters at the Archbishop's residence that the Ormée was concentrating its forces in the vicinity of the *Hôtel de Ville*. Hoping to avert another clash, the two Condé princesses—Madame de Longueville and the wife of Condé—summoned the Ormée leaders to a conference. Lenet thus describes their arrival: "With drums beating, each man carrying a sword, they appeared at the head of 200 men whom they posted around the archbishopric with the order not to allow anyone to enter or leave until the audience had ended."[79] The princesses asked the rebels to disarm, but the request was refused. The Ormée had clearly decided on a final confrontation.

[76] *Ibid.*; also Ciraq to Dubosq, June 27, 1652, *B.B.* MS. fonds Itié, no fol.; unidentified letter to Mazarin, no date, *Archives historiques de la Gironde*, VIII, 428–29; Lenet to Condé, June 20, 1652 in G.-J. Cosnac, *Souvenirs*, VI, 335.

[77] *Journal de tout de qui s'est fait et passé . . . depuis le 24 Juin.*

[78] *Ibid.*; unidentified letter to Mazarin, no date, *Archives historiques de la Gironde*, VIII, 429. Ciraq to Dubosq, June 27, 1652, *BB.*, MS. fonds Itié, no fol.; Lenet to Condé, June 24, 1652, in Lenet, "Mémoires," p. 336. The figure of a dozen deaths is that of Lenet. The other sources provide varying figures. According to Mazarin's correspondent, the Chapeau Rouge lost four men and the Ormée three. Ciraq places the total number of casualties at "5 or 6 killed and a few more wounded." And the *Journal de tout ce qui s'est fait et passé . . . depuis le 24 Juin* cites the figure of 40 Ormists killed, most likely an exaggeration. Victims cannot be readily identified, as all of their names do not appear in any of our sources and as most of the *état civil* registries— a likely place where they might have been found — have disappeared. However, from an *état civil* that has survived — that of the parish of Sainte Colombe — one learns that on the 24th of June, "in a disorder that occurred in the city, there perished a son of the butcher de Croisset . . . and one Feiller, a clerk who lived in the Allée des Herbes, and a nephew of M. Reforce, priest and vicar of Pessac" (*A.B.*, G.G., 164, acte no. 542). It is likely that the two were Ormists, as three other casualties are known to have belonged to the Chapeau Rouge: Laverie, the son of a *procureur*, Ducod *le jeune*, and the son of one Castaing.

[79] Lenet to Condé, June 27, 1652, in G.-J. Cosnac, *Souvenirs*, III, 344–45.

On the morning of the 25th, a band of Ormists seized the *Hôtel de Ville*.[80] The tocsin was sounded, and a mob of 4,000 soon filled the streets. The *procureur-syndic* hurried to the archbishopric to announce that the Ormée had taken possession of the city's arsenal and that the *Jurade* had lost all control of the situation. The response of the princesses was to convene an assembly of all the notables of the city: the *conseillers* and *présidents* of the *Parlement*, the *juge* and *consuls* of the *Bourse*, the officers of the *Bureau de Finance* and the *Présidial*, and all the *avocats* and *procureurs*. Meeting on the hour, the assembly quickly agreed to place itself under the command of the two ladies and to order the *"bons bourgeois"* to take up arms. However, nothing came of the order. As Lenet explained to Condé: "In truth, I saw little evidence of vigor, Their Highnesses being the only ones showing any signs of it." Bordeaux's privileged element had apparently lost its nerve; the assembly had been a sham.

On the afternoon of the same day, the Ormée moved on the *Parlement's* quarter, the Chapeau Rouge. The attacking force numbered 3,000 men, many carrying hatchets and mallets. A cart of tarred faggots was brought along—to set fire to the houses—and three cannon. The Ormée's plan appears to have been to launch a three-pronged attack on the Fossé du Chapeau Rouge and the Fossé du Campaure—the two roads that formed part of a single artery extending from the Porte Dauphine to the banks of the Garonne. One contingent would occupy the eastern-most end of the thoroughfare—that is where the Chapeau Rouge reached the river. Another, moving along the Rue Sainte Catherine, a street that intersected the two *fossés*, would assault the enemy's center. But the brunt of the attack would originate from the other, the more elevated end of the Campaure. There the Ormée was to mass the main body of its forces as well as its artillery, which would then be made to descend the length of the street. As the attackers had secured all the routes of escape, the enemy would be caught in a withering cross-fire.

If such was indeed the Ormée's strategy, its execution was perfect.

---

[80] Our reconstruction of the events that transpired on June 25th relies on the following sources: Lenet's letter to Condé, June 27, 1652, in G.-J. Cosnac, *Souvenirs*, III, 344–61; Ciraq's letter to his uncle Dubosq, a merchant then in Holland (Ciraq to Dubosq, June 27, 1652, *B.B.*, MS. fonds Itié, no folio; a letter from a former *jurat* (unidentified letter to Condé, July 1, 1652 in d'Aumale, *Histoire*, VI, 628–33); an unidentified letter to Mazarin (no date, *Archives historiques de la Gironde*, VIII, 428–29); and two *Mazarinades: Journal de tout ce qui s'est fait et passé ... depuis le 24 juin* and *Courrier bourdelois* [XVII*e*].

With the first two forces in position, the main body began its descent. First to fall was the Château de Puy-Paulin, Epernon's former residence. Then the cannon were turned on the house of *président* Pichon, which was taken, then pillaged and put to the torch. The same fate befell the adjoining residence of Madame de Pontac. On the opposite side of the street was a small house belonging to the *conseiller* de La Roche. When its defenders refused to surrender, the cart of faggots was ignited and placed alongside the house which soon caught on fire. More property was destroyed including the houses of the *conseiller* Mestivier and the merchant du Cornet, the wine-cellars of the wholesalers Dijeau and Gerosse, both of whom had previously been expelled, and the offices of the *Bureau du Convoy*. The house of the *conseiller* de Bordes and of the *jurats* Fontenel and Guiraut would have suffered the same fate had not all resistance ceased. The fighting ended on a dramatic note. The vicar of St. Pierre, followed by the princesses and their entourage, paraded the holy sacrament "through the length of the *fossés*, among the combatants and around the Chapeau Rouge." Then, the procession having ended, "the few remaining defenders of the Chapeau Rouge came out with the most heart-rending protestations and oaths of submission. Suddenly, everyone withdrew."

The Ormée had won the day, but at a heavy price. Lenet places the number of Ormists killed at 52, those wounded at more than 60.[81] The *Courrier bourdelois* mentions "more than 60" killed.[82] Condé's correspondent advances the figure of 100 killed and 50 wounded.[83] As to the casualties suffered by the Parlement's forces, Ciraq estimated their number at 5 or 6 killed and 15 to 20 wounded.[84] What could explain the great disparity in losses? Lenet notes that the defenders were well protected, while the attackers made an easy target as they came down the Chapeau Rouge.[85] But no less significant was the fact that the Ormists had little or no military experience while the *Parlement* could rely on professional soldiers. One source relates that at the first indication of trouble " . . . one hundred musketeers were placed in the house of the *président* Pichon, an equal number in that of the *conseiller* de la Roche, 120 archers in the offices of the *Bureau du Convoy*, 20 in the house of du Cornet, and more in the other houses. A number of guards were also sent to help defend the

---

[81] Lenet to Condé, June 27, 1652, in G.-J. Cosnac, *Souvenirs*, IV, 358.
[82] *Courrier bourdelois* [*XVIIᵉ*].
[83] Unidentified letter to Condé, July 1, 1652, in d'Aumale, *Histoire*, VI, 629.
[84] Ciraq to Dubosq, June 27, 1652, B.B., MS. fonds Itié, no folio.
[85] Lenet to Condé, June 27, 1652, in G.-J. Cosnac, *Souvenirs*, IV, 348-49, 358.

house of *président* Pichon."[86] Defending the Chapeau Rouge was thus the work of experienced mercenaries—musketeers and archers from the *Parlement*'s regiment, guards from the city's constabulary. In the face of such adversaries, it is less surprising that the Ormée took such heavy casualties than that it won at all.

While some fighting took place on the 26th, the outcome of the struggle was no longer in doubt. "All of Bordeaux now belongs to the Ormée;" reported a *Mazarinade*, "we honor its standards. Only *conseillers* and followers of Mazarin who must endure the rule of these people in the full knowledge that they will have no relief from adversity appear deeply distressed."[87] And Lenet informed Condé: "The entire *Parlement* with the exception of the *Grande Fronde*, talk of departing. *Président* d'Affis, who fears that his house will be pillaged, and *président* Pichon, whose house has just been, are in great despair."[88] D'Affis, "afraid to lose his life but above all his furniture," had his possessions sent to "a convent for safe-keeping."[89] Similarly, Condé's anonymous correspondent reported: "The city is becoming deserted. Most members of the *Parlement* have, for lack of funds, sent their plates to the mint. As for myself and other *bons bourgeois*, we continue to remove as much as we can, not knowing what will become of us. Each man must now think of himself."[90]

The Ormée had defeated the *Parlement* and the *Jurade*. Would it prove as resourceful in the use of power as it had been in its conquest? Would it have the capacity—or the will—to impose a new order on Bordeaux? The answer to these questions would depend in large measure on the Ormée's character—its social make-up as well as its ideology—and it is this character we wish next to consider.

[86] *Journal de tout de qui s'est fait et passé . . . depuis le 24 juin.*
[87] *Extrait de tout ce qui s'est fait et passé à Bordeaux depuis le 29 juin, 1652, touchant le parti de messieurs les princes et celui des Mazarins* (Paris, 1652).
[88] Lenet to Condé, June 27, 1652, in G.-J. Cosnac, *Souvenirs*, III, 351.
[89] *Ibid.*, 352.
[90] Unidentified letter to Condé, July 1, 1652, in d'Aumale, *Histoire*, VI, 631.

III

THE ORMÉE:
SOCIAL ORIGINS AND IDEOLOGY

CHARACTERIZATIONS OF THE Ormée have often taken the form of judgements of its ends—or of the means that were employed to achieve those ends. Devienne, writing in the eighteenth century, asserted that the movement "acknowledged no authority other than mindless fury."[1] In the following century, O'Reilly described the Ormée as "a blind and bloodthirsty party . . . whose ultimate aim was to transform Bordeaux into a vast cemetery."[2] Cosnac, also a nineteenth-century writer, saw it "not simply as a fortuitous gathering of agitators . . . but as a highly organized body" whose members sought to promote permanent sedition "as the best means of giving free reign to their evil instincts."[3] More recently, Porchnev has referred to the Ormée as "a revolutionary body" dominated by "radical and democratic ideas,"[4] while Kossmann has called it "a party of *petits bourgeois* and proletarians" whose "moderation . . . is proof of a certain incompleteness, a certain want of maturity."[5]

Reflecting more accurately their authors' ideological temper than the movement in question, the above assessments also suffer from an imperfect utilization of historical sources. O'Reilly based his conclusions on

[1] Devienne, *Histoire de la ville de Bordeaux* (Bordeaux, 1771), p. 447.
[2] Patrice-John O'Reilly, *Histoire complète de Bordeaux* (Bordeaux, 1860), I, 70.
[3] Gabriel-Jules de Cosnac, *Souvenirs du règne de Louis XIV* (Paris, 1866–82), III, 161–62.
[4] Boris Porchnev, *Les soulèvements populaires en France de 1623 à 1648* (Paris, 1963), p. 520.
[5] Ernst H. Kossmann, *La Fronde* (Leiden, 1954), pp. 254–55, 256.

the work of Devienne whose research was largely confined to the *Registres* of the *Parlement* and to the *Mémoires* of Berthod and Filhot. Cosnac restricted himself to Lenet's correspondence. Porchnev ignored all primary sources save Lilburne's *Agreement of the People*. And Kossmann, who alone seems to have realized the importance of the *Mazarinades*, overlooked one of the most significant, the *Apologie pour l'Ormée*.

The failure to consider such archival materials as the notarial records, the unpublished registries of the *Hôtel de Ville* (especially those of the prison), and the transactions of the *Chambre de Direction* may well explain another serious shortcoming of existing Ormée scholarship: the absence of sustained social analysis. Who were the Ormists and what position did they occupy in Bordelais society? Did social differences exist within the movement, and if so, were these so pronounced as to invalidate the notion of a distinct Ormée class? Did social differences enter into the relation between Ormists and non-Ormists, and if so, were these sufficiently great to account for the bitterness of the struggle and perhaps for the struggle itself? Heretofore left unanswered, these questions must receive careful consideration before any attempt is made to assess the Ormée's principles and program. Our first task then will be to examine the Ormée's social background, beginning with the occupational roles of the individual members.

The Ormée was a mass movement with thousands of active members. As we have seen, 3,000 attended its initial assembly, 1,500 were present at a gathering addressed by Conty, 2,000 participated in a march through the Chapeau Rouge, 4,000 took to the streets on June 25, and 3,000 fought the subsequent battle. Using the average figure of 2,700 men and adding the likely number of dependents results in a total of between ten and twelve thousand supporters, or no less than one-quarter of Bordeaux's population (indeed, one source reports that during the celebration of Palm Sunday, an event that followed the *Parlement*'s first serious setback, "the entire city was under arms"). Who the militants were is largely unknown. We have identified 124 Ormists, but these occupied positions of leadership in the movement and cannot therefore be considered typical members. Were the others their social inferiors—journeymen and apprentices working in the numerous *ateliers*, servants and other domestics in the employment of the well-to-do, shop clerks and street-hawkers, sailors waiting for their ships and peasants waiting to return to their land, those momentarily unemployed and those who had always been? This

41

would seem likely, but one cannot be certain: how far the Ormée descended remains a matter of conjecture.

An examination of the known Ormists reveals seven occupational activities, with the following numerical breakdown:[6]

OFFICIALS OF JUSTICE

   1 presiding officer of the *Cour des Aides* (*président de la Cour des Aides*)
   5 lawyers of the *Parlement* (*avocats au Parlement*)
   5 solicitors of the *Parlement* (*procureurs au Parlement* or *soliciteurs de procès*)
   5 solicitors of the *Sénéchal* (*procureurs au Sénéchal*)
   1 provost of the *Sénéchal* (*vice-sénéchal*)
   3 legal clerks (*praticiens*)
   1 bailiff of the *Présidial* (*huissier au siège Présidial*)
   1 bailiff of the *Parlement* (*huissier au Parlement*)
   1 bailiff of the *Sénéchal* (*huissier au Sénéchal*)
   4 notaries (*notaires*)

OFFICIALS OF THE MUNICIPALITY
(the asterisk indicates officials with multiple occupations)

  *9 officers of the militia
  *5 members of the *Cent et Trente*
  *3 police officers (*commissaires de police*)
  *2 hospital bursars (*trésoriers de l'hôpital*)
   3 import controllers (*courtiers*)
   1 bailiff (*huissier de l'Hôtel de Ville*)
   1 solicitor of the municipality (*procureur en la maison commune*)

FISCAL AND MONETARY AGENTS

   1 tax concessioner (*fermier d'impot*)
   1 wage collector of the *Présidiaux* (*receveur des gages des Présidiaux*)
   1 officer of the mint (*officier de la monnaye*)
   1 bailiff of the Bureau of Finance (*huissier au Bureau de Finance*)

MERCHANTS

45 individuals

ARTISANS

   4 master goldsmiths
   4 master glovemakers
   3 master bakers

---

[6] The tabulation and subsequent comments are based on the list of Ormists which appears in the appendix.

2 master pastrymen
2 master painters
1 master hosemaker
1 master cabinetmaker
1 master carpenter
1 master tailor
1 master pewtersmith
1 master brazier
1 master shoemaker
1 master engraver
1 master wigmaker

PRACTITIONERS OF LIBERAL AND RELATED PROFESSIONS

3 clerics
1 teacher at the College of Guyenne
1 physician
2 master surgeons
1 apothecary
2 musicians
1 master scrivener

MEMBERS OF THE LANDED GENTRY

8 nobles (*escuyers*)

The first group (the officials of justice) thus consisted of twenty-seven individuals, making it the second largest contingent of Ormée members. With one exception (the *président* of the *Cour des Aides* d'Hosten), it contained no representative of the legal nobility and only a few who could pass as city notables. Thus, while two *avocats* (Clairac and Robert) were the sons of similarly placed fathers, another *avocat* (Villars) was the son of a notary; a *soliciteur de procès* (*Dureteste*), the son of a *sergent de l'Hôtel deVille;* a *praticien* (Lartigue), the son of pastryman; and a *procureur* (Rocques), the son of a domestic.[7] The others appear to have been even more modestly placed, for none of the *huissiers* and only five of the ten *procureurs* and *praticiens* had been admitted into the bourgeoisie, and most of these only recently, while the *notaires* were mere transcribers of legal briefs, with no official position in the courts.

Slightly less numerous than the officials of justice and characterized

[7] *Journal de Filhot*, p. 61; *Archives historiques de la Gironde*, XXX, 171–73 and XXXII, 83; *Registres de la Jurade*, II, 430.

by the same dearth of stature were the Ormists who held posts in the municipal government. The number included no former *jurats, procureurs syndics* (the highest administrators in the municipal government), or *juges et consuls de la Bourse*. It is true that more than half of the functionaries were officers in the militia or members of the *Cent et Trente*, but it must be noted that all heads of households were legally obligated to serve in the militia and that the *Cent et Trente* was a consultative assembly with little or no political power.[8] The other officials were no more important. The *commissaires de police* simply received complaints and served without compensation.[9] The *trésoriers de l'hôpital* were exempt from all taxation and from service in the militia, but in return had to provide assistance to the poor—which no doubt explains why few sought the post. As to the *courtiers*, these appear to have been members of a faction that had petitioned for a royal charter, an action decried by the *Parlement* which noted that, while the other *courtiers* "had, by dint of effort, become prosperous," those seeking the protection of the Crown "were poor and lacking in employment."[10]

The character of the third group of Ormists (the fiscal and monetary agents) mirrors closely that of the first two. It contained a bailiff from the *Bureau de Finance*, but no actual member of that body; a receiver of wages, but no officials from the *Bureau du Convoy* (the tax-collecting body from which the wages were paid); and an inconsequential tax *fermier*. Only one important official is listed: an *officier de la monnaye* (Barthelemy Minvielle) —and he, as we shall see, had special reasons for joining the Ormée.

If the smallest contingent of Ormée members came from the financial bureaucracy, the largest belonged to the world of commerce. The 45 Ormists calling themselves *marchands* were involved in diverse commercial activities: exporting to foreign markets, receiving goods from the country-side, and retailing to the local populace. Only a handful, however, were large-scale entrepreneurs—Mercier and Truchon, who lent money, sold insurance, and were active in the wine trade;[11] and possibly Augier, Cadroy, Castaignet, and Fevielle, who were important enough to be ad-

---

[8] "Milices Bourgeoises," fonds Baurein, carton 20, December 24, 1638; B. Barckhausen in *Livre des privileges* (Bordeaux, 1878), XXII.

[9] *Registres de la Jurade*, III, 649–54 and VII, 370.

[10] *Arrest de la cour de Parlement de Bordeaux portant défense aux courretiers de prendre plus grands droits que ceux qui leurs sont attribués par l'édit vérifié audit Parlement* (Bordeaux, 1648), A.G., C 3784, 5. On the rebellious *courtiers*, see also *Registres de la Jurade*, IV, 80–81.

[11] A.G., 3E 767, fol. 706; 3E 5142, fol. 954; 3E 4320, fol. 658.

mitted into the *Cent et Trente*. The others were, for the most part, small tradesmen or simple shopkeepers, pursuing such occupations as ham merchant (Lafitte), grease merchant (Gardera), draper (Samaruc), and collar merchant (Gauselan). A number may have been no more than artisans: thus Blarru styled himself *"marchand"* when he was in fact a goldsmith.[12]

Another large segment of Ormists originated in the crafts. Little is known of this group, in part because artisans, unlike merchants and functionaries, rarely drafted notarial briefs, in part because of the inconclusive nature of the available data. Thus, while many artisans were tenants, some were property owners; and while a large number were debtors (as Filhot suggests), many others were creditors.[13] It is worth noting, however, that all twenty-four artisans were self-employed and that twelve had become bourgeois—facts suggesting that however limited their wealth, none could be classed with the dispossessed.

Most of the members of the sixth group (the practitioners of liberal and related professions) came from the same social milieu as the small merchants and petty functionaries. This was certainly true of the surgeons (who, as we shall see, were related to a *praticien*) and of one of the clerics (who was related to a merchant), and probably so of the apothecary and the scrivener. However, another cleric (Jannet) was the brother of an *avocat;* a teacher at the college of Bordeaux (Prades) was a protégé of the Epernon family; and a musician (Landé) was the brother of an important and anti-Ormist merchant.[14] The most educated members of the Ormée, these men would play a dominant role in its affairs.

Still another source of support for the Ormée came from the feudal nobility. Eight Ormists were from this element, including the eventual commander of the Ormée troops guarding the fortress at *la Bastide* (Bernard Sauvage, *Sieur* de La Mothe); the city's eventual *aide-major* (Jean Le Breton, *Sieur* de La Perrière); a future member of the *Chambre de Direction* (Jean de Mouchac); and three who would become captains of the militia and members of the *Conseil de Guerre* (de Bonnest, du Puy, and de Tustal).[15]

---

[12] G.-J. Cosnac, *Souvenirs*, VII, 8; Armand Communay, "Notaires, registres paroissiaux, bourgeois de Bordeaux," (manuscript, Bibliothèque de Bayonne), fol. 929.

[13] Communay, *Journal de Filhot*, p. 159; A.G., 3E 1522, fol. 351; 3E 10.787, fol. 469; 3E 3208, fol. 201; 3E 15.253, fol. 258; 3E 2448, fol. 938.

[14] A.G., 4J 170; B.N., MS. fonds français 6711, fol. 57; Communay, *Journal de Filhot*, p. 176.

[15] Registres du Parlement, 1651–58, fol. 191; Communay, *Journal de Filhot*, p. 109, 141; G.-J. Cosnac, *Souvenirs*, VII, 78; *Archives historiques de la Gironde*, XXX, p. 174.

Were these simple mercenaries (Le Breton was paid 150 *livres* a month, Sauvage 100 *livres*)[16] or had they joined the Ormée because they too wished to overthrow the municipal oligarchy? The question cannot be answered with any certainty, but in at least one case promise of financial gain was reinforced by hostility to the *Parlement*. Sauvage had been involved in litigation with Armand de Pontac, his overlord and a *président du Parlement*, over the payment of 154 *livres* in feudal dues. The matter had been taken first to the *sénéchal* of Bazadois, then by appeal of Pontac (the *sénéchal* had apparently ruled in Sauvage's favor) to the *Parlement* of Bordeaux, which ordered Sauvage to pay the stipulated sum as well as the expenses of the Court.[17]

The Ormée's membership thus reveals a diversity of occupational backgrounds. *Avocat au Parlement*, officer of the militia, ham merchant, cabinet maker, feudal warrior—all had found their way into the rebellious party. Must we then conclude that the Ormée lacked a distinct social character? Certainly the opinion of the day would indicate otherwise. According to Filhot, the *Chambre de l'Ormée* did not contain "a single creditor."[18] Samuel Robert, a royal official, described Ormists as "scraped up people [*gens ramacés*]."[19] One of Mazarin's correspondents did not understand how Condé could have allowed himself to be led "by such little people [*petits gens*] as are found in the Ormée."[20] Daniel de Cosnac, Conty's principal advisor, went further, calling the rebels "lowly riff-raff" [*canaille du peuple*]."[21] Individual examples were given: Jannet was "a man of mean background"; le Breton "a person of bad reputation"; and Villars "one who has long been without employment and whose law degree was bought for 60 *livres*."[22]

Obviously exaggerating the Ormée's social abjectness, the Ormée's critics may have been correct in alluding to the underlying social homogeneity of the movement. Ormists such as Dureteste and Tauzin held

[16] *A.B.*, CC 271, Extraits des registres de la Chambre de Direction, (cited hereafter as "Registres de la Chambre de Direction") February 1, 1650; July 31, 1652; July 3, 1653.

[17] *B.B.*, MS. fonds Itié, March 15, 1651; May 2, 1651; and May 22, 1654.

[18] Communay, *Journal de Filhot*, p. 159.

[19] Samuel Robert, *Lettres* (Saintes, 1907), p. 427.

[20] Unidentified letter to Mazarin, December 5, 1652, *Archives historiques de la Gironde*, VIII, 423–24.

[21] Daniel de Cosnac, *Mémoires* (Paris, 1852), p. 45.

[22] *A.G.*, 4J 170; Communay, *Journal de Filhot*, p. 108; *L'exile de l'inconnu dédié aux exilés de la ville de Bourdeaux* (Paris, 1653), p. 19.

different positions and indeed belonged to different corporate orders—the former to the *Parlement*, the latter to the guild of pewtersmiths—yet the two occupied the same social position as seems evident from the fact that Tauzin had married into Dureteste's family.[23] The same conclusion may be drawn from the fact that of the two Auguiers one was a merchant and the other a priest and that a relation of Pierre Lartigue, *praticien*, was married to a sister of Pierre Philipon, *maître chirurgien*.[24]

If familial ties provide one indication of social cohesion, still another one is provided by the bourgeois rolls. Of eighty Ormists (or their families) known to have entered the bourgeoisie, forty nine (that is, 61 per cent), had done so after 1610. By comparison, of eighty three members of the oligarchical *Cent et Trente* assembly, thirty one (or less than 37 per cent) became bourgeois after the above date. The figures for the period 1635–50 are especially revealing: twenty-five Ormists entering the bourgeoisie, with only six members of the *Cent et Trente* doing so.[25] Thus, if a number of Ormists had achieved a degree of affluence—to be admitted into the bourgeoisie, one had to own a house worth at least 1,500 *livres*[26]—most had done so in the preceding four decades and not, as in the case of most of the *Cent et Trente*, more than half a century earlier. Ormists, or at least their leaders, constituted a rising class within the population—a fact that may explain not only their revolutionary zeal, but also the deep hostility with which they were viewed by those whose position they were challenging.

The Ormée's class character is made no less distinct by the fact that a number of its members—one can mention the nobles, the *président* of the *Cour des Aides* d'Hosten, the *marchand* Truchon, and the *officier* Minvielle—were more highly placed than the average member. For an examination of the circumstances surrounding their entry into the Ormée reveals the exceptional character of the association. Five of the eight nobles joined the Ormée only after it had become a power in Bordeaux.[27] Truchon became an Ormist only after he had been promised the post of *Juge de la Bourse*.[28] D'Hosten belonged to the Ormée from the outset, but was soon

[23] Communay, *Journal de Filhot*, p. 122.
[24] Communay, "Notaires," fol. 955.
[25] These figures derive from the two lists that appear in the Appendix.
[26] "Livre des bourgeois de Bordeaux (XVIIᵉ siècle)," in *Archives historiques de la Gironde*, XXXII, VIII.
[27] The signatures of only three appear on the document of May 13, 1652. See Appendix.
[28] Unidentified letter to Mazarin, March 5, 1653, *A.N.*, KK 1220, fol. 21.

plotting its overthrow—an indication that, as with Truchon, the basis for the connection may have been more personal than ideological.[29] As to Minvielle, he had extended large sums to the princes, and may have joined the Ormée simply to protect his investments.[30]

Recruited from the ranks of the lower bourgeoisie, the Ormée's composition greatly explains the orientation of its ideology. As Kossmann has aptly observed: "It [the Ormée] . . . remained throughout its existence a party of *petits bourgeois* and proletarians extremely hostile to a system of which it was the principal victim."[31] The Ormée's hostility to "the absolute state, the elite bourgeoisie and its cohorts" (Kossmann's description of the "system")[32] is indeed explained by the fact that its members were, in the main, "*petits bourgeois* and proletarian." For it was this element that had carried the brunt of the royal fisc and that had fought the *Parlement*'s and the princes' wars only to be burdened with even higher levies. The lessons of 1649 and 1650 had been well learned: "Princes and magistrates," the *Manifeste des bordelois* declared, "are the accomplices of tyranny. If the people expect deliverance from leaders who do not come from their midst, they will only prolong and worsen their miseries."[33]

The *Manifeste* divided society into "the accomplices of tyranny" and "the people." The division was expressed symbolically in the *Histoire véritable d'une colombe*: on one side was a dove, "devoid of bitterness or rancor," and on the other side crows, "birds of prey, vultures who only know how to pillage, plunder, and ruin innocent people."[34] Thus the struggle which the *Manifeste* had interpreted in political terms assumed an added economic dimension in the *Histoire véritable:* if the crows had tyrannized the people, they had also stolen from them. Such was also the conclusion of the *Apologie pour l'Ormée*. The *Parlement* had "perpetrated innumerable acts of injustice in the administration of private suits and in the performance of their charges," had "committed a thousand acts of banditry in the provinces," and had engaged "in the despoliation of widows." The following observations followed:

---

[29] It is worth noting that, shortly before the Ormée's advent, d'Hosten submitted a claim of 600 *livres* to the city "for reason of the expenses incurred as a result of the presence in his house of M. le Marquis d'Aubeterre who had come to defend the city." Registres de la Chambre de Direction, February 4, 1652.

[30] Minvielle had lent the princes 150,000 *livres*. *Ibid*, September 12, 1652.

[31] Kossmann, *La Fronde*, p. 256.

[32] *Ibid*.

[33] *Manifeste des bordelois*, p. 6.

[34] *Histoire véritable d'une colombe*, pp. 5–7.

Wisdom depends neither on wealth nor palaces and can thrive even when men are wholly destitute. It is equality that makes for perfection among individuals . . . [for] it unifies all parts of the republic, fosters peace, and produces concord among the citizenry. . . . The actual cause of sedition and political strife is the excessive wealth of the few.[35]

The principle of class struggle could not have been stated more succinctly: on one side were those possessing "neither wealth nor palaces" (an obvious reference to the Ormists); on the other, the "few" with "excessive wealth" (no doubt *parlementaires* and *jurats*). And since such inequities were the cause of all "sedition and political strife," obviously, Bordeaux would not know civil peace until these were eliminated. How this was to be accomplished is not made clear, but there is little doubt that the author of the *Apologie* would have agreed with the Ormée's chaplain when the latter declared:

Our swords and our other weapons must be used . . . if we are not to share the fate of other cities in the province that perished because they were tolerant of the traitors in their midst.[36]

Seeking the removal if not total destruction of its enemies, the Ormée also aimed at the reconstruction of society and especially of the judicial system. A month after the Ormée had seized power, Mazarin learned from one of his correspondents: "The Ormée is intent on abolishing their [the *Parlement*'s] offices, suppressing venality, and placing the right to dispense justice in the hands of individuals whose probity is well known to all."[37] The *Manifeste des bordelois* provided more details of the proposed judicial reforms: "Judges are to be appointed who will render equitable justice. All litigation must be adjudicated within twenty-four hours. There are to be no briefs or other manifestations of chicanery. *Avocats* or *procureurs* will absent themselves, for a litigant can plead the merits of his case as well as any one else."[38] Thus the Ormée intended to alter radically both the character and operation of justice. The office of judge would henceforth be appointive, decisions would be reached swiftly, and the plaintiffs would be obliged to argue their own case. That individuals might be untutored in the subtleties of jurisprudence was of no conse-

---

[35] *Apologie pour l'Ormée*, pp. 26–27.
[36] *Histoire véritable d'une colombe*, p. 7.
[37] Unidentified letter to Mazarin, May 23, 1652, in *Archives historiques de la Gironde*, VIII, 406.
[38] *Manifeste des bordelois*, p. 8.

quence, since the mere knowledge of legal procedure could in no way enhance the cause of justice. As the *Apologie* explained: "Because the study of jurisprudence will not, by itself, increase the level of virtue—knowing the good and practicing it being so dissimilar— we regard that science as useless . . . and shall ignore it and make no attempt to be versed in it."[39]

In denying the individual the right of counsel, prohibiting the presentation of briefs—therefore, the citation of earlier rulings—and discouraging the study of law, the Ormée was clearly seeking to establish judicial principles and procedures that would afford protection to the members of the party. The declaration that judges would henceforth "render equitable justice" no doubt meant that they could now be expected to side with Ormée litigants. And since it would have made little sense to appoint new judges while preserving the old laws, the citing of earlier rulings was not to be tolerated and those versed in these laws (*avocats* and *procureurs*) not admitted before the court.

The new legal procedures are described in the Ormée's covenant, the *Union de l'Ormée*: "We solemnly swear to arbitrate all disputes or allow the Company to do so, in which case we agree to abide by its ruling. . . . The accord [once reached] becomes irrevocable."[40] Parties to a dispute thus had two choices: they could either accept arbitration or request a trial. If they selected the first procedure then, as we shall later see, the Ormée court was to appoint two arbitrators who would issue a ruling; if the second, then the ruling was to come from the Ormée court itself. In either case, decisions were beyond appeal, thus assuring Ormists of additional protection.

The desire for protection is a theme that recurs through much of the Ormée's literature. The *Histoire d'une colombe* hailed the appearance of a dove as evidence of "God's divine protection."[41] The *Apologie* asserted that Ormists "do not ravish any man's liberty . . . usurp the property of others . . . [or] seek to inflict injury on any one."[42] And three of the eight articles of the *Union de l'Ormée* declared:

Should anyone of the Company be threatened, whether legally or otherwise, he will be protected in every possible and reasonable way. Should he be burdened with debt, we shall lend him money free of interest for a stated period of time.

[39] *Apologie pour l'Ormée*, p. 33.
[40] *Articles de l'union de l'Ormée et de la ville de Bordeaux* (Paris, 1652).
[41] *Histoire véritable d'une colombe*, p. 5.
[42] *Apologie pour l'Ormée*, p. 33.

As soon as one of the Company falls ill, his neighbors will exhort him to take care of his conscience and to arrange his affairs so that his heirs will not be troubled. And when he dies, his widow and orphans will be protected as if he were still living.

Should a member of the Company become impoverished, he will be provided with work. And if this is not possible, he will be given all the necessities of life, and this without the public's knowledge.[43]

The Ormée's guild-like character becomes apparent. As in the case of guilds, the aim was to safeguard the interests of the members: all were to be provided with work, the indigent given public assistance, widows and orphans made wards of the community. Rather than be left to the mercy of competitive forces, individuals would henceforth receive protection from an omnipotent authority—the Ormée "Company." As even one of the Ormée's enemies acknowledged, the Ormists stood "ever ready" to support these who belonged to their party.[44]

The transformation of Bordeaux's social and economic relationships was not the only change envisioned, for with it was to come a fundamental re-ordering of the city's political life. In place of the discredited bodies—the *Parlement*, the *Jurade*, the *Cent et Trente*—a new sovereign power was to arise: the popular assembly. Thus an Ormée pamphlet, the *Généreuse résolution des gascons*, announced:

When it becomes necessary for individuals to constitute themselves into assemblies, it is the height of temerity to attempt to dissolve them; for a society that is bound by the common good [*le bien commun*] is indissoluble. The sovereign law being the common weal [*la loy souveraine estant le salut du publique*], it is the latter that will decide the fate of all states, lowering and even destroying them in order to assert itself.[45]

Assemblies possessed sovereignty because, once constituted, they could not be dissolved. However, other reasons might be advanced, namely that they represented the essential link between the state of nature and the state of society, and that they were the only source of protection from tyrannical rule. "Assemblies," the *Apologie* observed, "are founded on man's desire for society which is one of the strongest impulses that nature has implanted in us. . . . It is upon this foundation that cities and republics have been built so that men may find in them all the goods they need,

[43] *Articles de l'union de l'Ormée.*
[44] *A.G.*, 3E 2448, fol. 938.
[45] *Généreuse résolution des gascons* (n.p., 1652), p. 3.

whether for survival or pleasure, and for which they have such strong appetite."[46] If these words recall Aristotle, the ones that follow were no doubt inspired by Bordeaux's own experiences. Assemblies were designed to defend "the interests and affairs of the public from tyrants and bad magistrates whose crimes would then be exposed."[47] The reader is not permitted to forget the precise nature of the "crimes":

We have seen persons destined to the practice of law . . . make use of the authority of their office to raise all sorts of sums from our citizens, and pushing injustice to the extreme, render themselves both the collectors and dispensers of the sums, a practice truly in contempt of the customs of a city and a community, as indeed of human society and common humanity.[48]

And again:

The *Parlement* is less desirous of rendering us justice, as they profess, than of depriving us of our possessions; and the policies that they wish to introduce are inspired more by their own interests than by those of the public.[49]

Having justified their existence, the *Apologie* proceeds to describe the origins and character of the popular assemblies: "At the very outset of the monarchy the Gauls held assemblies outside the confines of the city and in the fields. It can therefore be assumed that the assemblies of our fathers—assemblies not yet corrupted by luxury and the love of pleasure— functioned in the very manner of our Ormée."[50] The early assemblies may have been legislating bodies, for the *Apologie* adds: "It is in imitation of our fathers that the Ormée deliberates under the trees."[51] On one point, however, the *Apologie* is explicit: the first assemblies were not forerunners of the *Parlements*. The *Parlements* had been created by the King who had then transferred their power to the popular assemblies: "Having deprived the *Parlement* of the authority he had initially vested in it, His Majesty did not intend that human society return to its initial chaos and to the horrors of the state of nature, but rather that the people be left with the natural right to make justice for itself and to retain its liberties and other privileges."[52] As in Locke, the termination of one social compact set the stage

[46] *Apologie pour l'Ormée.* p, 13.
[47] *Ibid.*, p. 14.
[48] *Ibid.*, pp. 15–16.
[49] *Ibid.*, p. 18.
[50] *Ibid.*, p. 31.
[51] *Ibid.*
[52] *Ibid.*, p. 35.

for the creation of another—although here it was the King who acted as ultimate arbiter and not the intermediate bodies.

While the ideas contained in the *Apologie* and in other Ormée tracts must not be too closely identified with subsequent liberal doctrines, neither are they to be seen as mere echoes of past or even current ideas. The author of the *Vindiciae contra tyrannos*, for example, assigned the right to resist tyrants to the "natural leaders, the inferior magistrates, the notables, the estates, the local and municipal officials," and not to "the many-headed multitude."[53] Hotman, in the *Franco Gallia*, placed the sovereign power in the Estates General—arguing that the Estates had evolved from the assembly that had originally elected the King.[54] And Claude Joly, the great exponent of limited monarchy, declared: "It is very just that they [the kings] acknowledge the preeminence of their officers in what concerns justice and laws and principally in all things that can harm others."[55] Thus, all three agreed that the right to rule was a prerogative of the privileged orders, but it was precisely this notion that the Ormée wished to repudiate. "I maintain," the *Manifeste des bordelois* declared, "that the restoration of France can only be accomplished by the people. The great nobles and magistrates are the accomplices of tyranny."[56] Another tract urged Condé to appoint "men of principles," so that he might retain "the good will of the people upon which are built the most solid forms of government."[57] A third defended the presence of laborers in the Ormée's assemblies with the observation: "In these times, men who are willing to execute orders are much more useful than those who only know how to argue."[58] And the Ormée motto proclaimed: "*Vox populi, vox dei.*"[59]

Are we then to conclude that the Ormée favored the establishment of democratic rule? The *Manifeste des Bordelois* declared emphatically that such had actually taken place: "They [the Ormists] have established a democratic government [*ont donné etablissement au gouvernement démo-*

---

[53] Quoted in George H. Sabine, *A History of Political Theory* (New York, 1950), p. 382.

[54] William F. Church, *Constitutional Thought in 16th Century France* (Cambridge, 1941), p. 87.

[55] Claude Joly, *Recueil de maximes véritables et importantes pour l'institution du roy contre la fausse et pernicieuse politique du Cardinal Mazarin* (Paris, 1663), p. 376.

[56] *Manifeste des bordelois*, p. 6.

[57] *Evangéliste de la Guyenne* (Paris, 1652), p. 11.

[58] *Courrier de la Guyenne*, pp. 4–5.

[59] *Manifeste des bordelois*, p. 5.

cratique]."[60] The *Apologie* seemed to agree: "We know of the deeply rooted hostility with which the aristocratic state views the democratic one, and in which it reproaches the latter for its ignorance and poverty . . . —a charge that the *Parlement* now makes against the Ormée."[61] And the following statement of doctrine is found in the preamble of the *Union*: "We maintain that being bourgeois we have deliberative as well as consultative privileges in all the assemblies of the communal government."[62] The evidence therefore does indeed suggest an attachment to democratic ideals. However, the attachment must not be exaggerated or extended along egalitarian lines: the Ormée's ultimate aim was to reorganize the hierarchical structure of power, not to destroy the principle of hierarchy. The doctrine of equality may have been upheld—the *Apologie*, as we have seen, declared that "equality makes for perfection among individuals" —but the intent was to equalize the relation between artisans, merchants, and *parlementaires*, not to obliterate intra-corporate differences such as these separating masters from journeymen. In rejecting the corporatism of the *Parlement* or of the merchants, the Ormée did not abandon the ideals of corporatism itself: the notion of occupational privileges (except, of course, for the outlawed corporations), the principle of social immobility (except, perhaps, for Ormists), and, as we shall see, a reliance on the traditional virtues.

The fact that the *Apologie* had juxtaposed the democratic to the aristocratic state but not to the monarchical one is significant, for it indicates that the Ormée was only considering its relation to the *Parlement* and not to the King. Loyalty to the King at least in the early stages of the rebellion, was an unquestioned tenet. The *Histoire véritable d'une colombe* assured everyone that the Ormée had no other thoughts than "the glory of God, the service of the King and M. le Prince, our very dear governor, and the well-being of the people."[63] And the *Courrier de la Guyenne* insisted that

> . . . the rumors that they [the Ormists] acknowledge neither King nor Prince . . . are as injurious as they are false. They love the King as much as the most faithful subjects in the kingdom; they render to M. le Prince all the homage due to a governor and are so attached to his interests that last March, seeing

[60] *Ibid.*, p. 7.
[61] *Apologie pour l'Ormée*, p. 21.
[62] *Articles de l'union de l'Ormée.*
[63] *Histoire véritable d'une colombe*, p. 5.

how inferior his forces were to those of the Count d'Harcourt, they offered to provide him with a regiment raised at their expense.[64]

That the *Courrier* and other Ormée tracts could claim loyalty to the King while defending those at war with the royal government suggests that the Ormée, in imitation of the first two Frondes, distinguished between the monarch and those who acted in his name. This is not to say, however, that the three revolts shared the same conception of kingship. *"Vive le Roi et le Parlement"* had been the cry of the First Fronde; *"Vive le Roi et Monsieur le Prince"* that of the second. Rejecting both the aristocratic conceptions of the Parlement and the feudal ideals of the Princes, the Ormée opted for a third arrangement: an alliance between the King and the people. An Ormée tract exclaimed:

If she [the Ormée] could only prevail upon the King to dismiss Mazarin, make peace with the princes, unburden the people, and restore tranquility to the state, would this not be a providential stroke? Would it not inaugurate the reign of liberty?[65]

And another demanded to know:

Will not the Ormée appear agreeable and deserving of His Majesty's kindness and special attention? . . . should not its courageous refusal to permit those who would share in His Majesty's rule and impose on the people an alien authority be rewarded? Have we not exposed our body to their violence as a sacrifice to that image of royalty inscribed in our hearts and which tyranny, however ruthless, has been unable to eradicate?[66]

King and people had been victims of the *Parlement*'s "tyranny"; what could be more proper than that they join forces to overcome it?

While many Ormists would have been content with a popular monarchy, some envisioned a more fundamental political change. Soon after the Ormée's victory over the *Parlement*, Condé received word that "one named Prades, a priest and mathematician of the *Collège de Bordeaux*, has announced that he has seen in the stars that Bordeaux is to become a powerful republic."[67] The same prediction was contained in the *Manifeste des bordelois:* "Now that the Ormée has triumphed over the *Parlement* . . . no one doubts that the Ormée will soon raise the banner of liberty and

[64] *Courrier de la Guyenne*, p. 5.
[65] *Généreuse résolution des gascons*, p. 7.
[66] *Apologie pour l'Ormée*, p. 34.
[67] Lenet to Condé, July 1, 1652, in G.-J. Cosnac, *Souvenirs*, IV, 291.

establish a republic."[68] Some thought that Huguenot and English machinations would bring about the change. As a former *jurat* reported: "We are afraid of the Huguenots and of the English alliance with which the Republic menaces us."[69]

The fear was well founded. The Ormée was familiar with Lilburne's *Agreement of the People*—the leveller document had been brought to Bordeaux by Edward Sexby in 1651[70]—and Ormists may have been influenced by its radical content.[71] The turn to republicanism became manifest, however, only after the military situation had begun to deteriorate, early in 1653.[72] In April, envoys were dispatched to England to request that the "English nation" help the Bordelais regain their "liberties and privileges."[73] In May, amidst numerous reports that it was about to proclaim a republic, the Ormée split into two factions, with one openly calling for the establishment of a free and independent government. This faction gradually gained the upper hand, as may be seen in a last appeal for English help drafted on June 12, 1653, which reads in part: "[The people of Bordeaux] declare jointly and severally in the presence of God that they will not lay down their arms . . . until they have achieved the true aim of a free people, a republic modelled on those which have come nearest to justice and good government."[74] The republic, however, was never proclaimed. This was, in part, due to the march of events—by July of 1653, the military situation had become hopeless—but the lack of ideological resolve also played a role. For the "banner of liberty" could have been raised any time after July, 1652, and if this did not occur, it was because the Ormée did not regard the establishment of an independent city-state as essential to its cause. Wishing simply to supplant the *Parlement* as master of Bordeaux, the Ormée began to consider severing its ties to the monarchy only after it became clear that the latter had allied itself with the arch-enemy, and that the *Parlement*'s restoration

[68] *Manifeste des bordelois*, pp. 4–5.
[69] Unsigned letter to Condé, June 6, 1652, *A.C.*, MS. serie P, XIII, fol. 269.
[70] Philip A. Knachel, *England and the Fronde* (Ithaca, 1967), p. 161.
[71] An adaptation of the document entitled "L'accord du peuple," was submitted to Condé by Lenet. For an analysis of its content, see *ibid.*, 189–200. The "accord" is reproduced in G.-J. Cosnac, *Souvenirs*, V, 256–62.
[72] See Chapter V. News of the Ormée's republican leanings even reached Paris. Jean Loret, *La muze historique ou recueil des lettres en vers*, ed. J. Ravenel (Paris, 1857), I, 249.
[73] Quoted in G.-J. Cosnac, *Souvenirs*, VII, 346–54.
[74] Quoted in Knachel, *England and the Fronde*, p. 208.

would, unavoidably, follow a royal victory. The turn to republicanism was therefore a condition of the social struggle rather than the result of ideological conviction—a fact that may help to explain why it failed to achieve concrete results.

The Ormée has been accused of parochialism. In the words of Kossmann, "the Ormée's vision failed to extend beyond the confines of a single city."[75] If this is true of the Ormée's republican aspirations which seem indeed to have been restricted to Bordeaux itself, the same cannot be said of the movement's more general aims. Thus the *Manifeste des bordelois* observed:

The Bordelais have shown themselves ahead of all Frenchmen in their zeal for the public good. They have struggled mightily to break their chains and restore to the entire kingdom the liberties lost in the course of all these centuries. . . . Bordeaux's actions will soon be approved by all France, for its cause is so just, that its laurels must spread throughout the kingdom.[76]

And the *Généreuse résolution des gascons* stated:

A state which only partially collapses may be saved. However, when everything crumbles and the foundation itself begins to crack, then a new structure must be put in the place of the old. A general breakdown can only be corrected by a total upheaval [*un désordre général ne peut estre restably que par une confusion universelle*]; in a word, in order to restore France, we need men who are courageous and forthright.[77]

The tract went on to raise a question: "Will other Frenchmen dare to follow Bordeaux's example?"[78] This was evidently a central concern of the author of the *Apologie*, who explained that the purpose of his work was "to impress the most distant people."[79]

The Ormée thus saw itself as waging a struggle to restore the "privileges and liberties" lost to the centralized monarchy. Such an undertaking was not in itself revolutionary: the *Parlements*, the municipal oligarchies, and the remnants of feudal society all favored a return to the decentralized rule of an earlier era. The Ormée, however, intended to go further: not only were the provinces and cities to regain their sovereignty, but the

---

[75] Kossmann, *La Fronde*, p. 254.
[76] *Manifeste des bordelois*, pp. 7–8.
[77] *Généreuse résolution des gascons*, p. 7.
[78] *Ibid*.
[79] *Apologie pour l'Ormée*, p. 6.

very organization of power was to be altered. The oligarchies of wealth and office would be discarded, and their places taken by "republics" of "free people." As the *Apologie* had pointed out, the disappearance of the *Parlement* would leave the people with "the natural right to make justice for itself and regain its lost liberties and privileges."[80]

A last element may be found in the Ormée's ideology: the yearning to bring about a moral regeneration of society. One cannot read the Ormée's tracts without noting their keen attachment to the cause of righteous conduct. The *Apologie* extolled the Ormée's "piety," "good faith," and "wealth in things of the spirit."[81] The *Histoire d'une colombe* was impressed by its "perfect charity" and "holiness and courage."[82] The *Courrier de la Guyenne* noted its "boundless loyalty."[83] But nowhere are the Ormée's moral aspirations advanced more forcefully than in the *Union de l'Ormée*. Rising to the defense of the victims of society—the indigent, the debtors, the widows and orphans—the *Union* also demanded a reaffirmation of moral principles. The preamble declared:

We, the bourgeois, peasants, and inhabitants of Bordeaux, cognizant of the high marks of favor and assistance obtained from God during the recent and still continuing troubles, have resolved to express our profound gratitude so that we may continue to enjoy God's benign grace. Accordingly, we shall strive to better love our neighbors and particularly those who are on our side. Toward this end we declare the following articles and invite all Christians to do likewise or more, if God so inspires them.

And two of the articles:

We solemnly swear to love and protect each other as brothers and establish between us the peace and concordat of Jesus Christ. . . .
In the eventuality that an individual is leading a scandalous and incorrigible life which is contrary to God's teachings, he shall be banished as unworthy of our society and shall be proclaimed a traitor to his honor and to the public good.[84]

Sacerdotal references notwithstanding, there is little in the *Union* to suggest the beatific ideal. The doctrine to "better love our neighbors and particularly those who are on our side" can hardly be said to capture the

---

[80] *Ibid.*, p. 37.
[81] *Ibid.*, pp. 20–21, 33.
[82] *Histoire véritable d'une colombe*, pp. 4–5.
[83] *Courrier de la Guyenne*, p. 6.
[84] *Articles de l'union de l'Ormée*.

spirit of Christian piety. And the call to establish "the peace and con-cordat of Jesus Christ" is followed with the comment: "toward this end we promise to arbitrate all disputes that shall arise among us"—again a repudiation of transcendent spirituality.

One must conclude that the Ormée was less interested in the state of the soul than in the affairs of men. If men were expected to serve God, it was because in so doing they would also serve themselves. As the Ormée's chaplain observed: "God's providence and the spirit of the Holy Ghost have manifested themselves to an assembly whose pure and simple aim is the service of the people and the Glory of God—the two being inseparable."[85] The same desire to reconcile social and moral ideals was expressed by the *Apologie*: "The virtuous man keeps his word and his good faith, does not ravish any man's liberty but seeks to preserve his own, does not usurp the property of others but is allowed to retain that which is his, neither inflicts injury nor suffers wrongs."[86] The Ormée may have been inspired by religious voices, but its ultimate vision was the secular commonwealth.

The Ormée was a movement of artisans, shopkeepers, petty officials, and small merchants seeking protection from patrician justice, the un-certainties of mercantile capitalism, and the increasingly heavy burden of the royal fisc. Its solution was to return to the particularism of an earlier era: to corporate control in the social and economic spheres, to municipal sovereignty on the level of national politics. Although differing from the *Parlement* in its desire to free society from oligarchical control, the Ormée was one with its rival in opposing the forces that were gradually coming to dominate the course of French history. Undoubtedly, this was the ulti-mate reason for its failure, as it was for the failure of the *Parlement*. The future would belong to the centralized state and not to the cities, to free trade and not to guild controls, to the liberty of the individual rather than to the liberties of the community.

[85] *Histoire véritable d'une colombe*, p. 7.
[86] *Apologie pour l'Ormée*, p. 33.

IV

THE ORMÉE IN POWER:
INSTITUTIONAL CHANGES

THE ORMÉE EMERGED FROM THE BLOODY ENGAGEMENT of June 25, 1652, as the principal power in Bordeaux. In conquering the Chapeau Rouge, it had dealt the *Parlement* a shattering blow, reduced the *Jurade* to complete impotence, and, above all, shown that it had the capacity to pursue an independent course of action. The Condé party was impressed. Lenet suggested that everyone "from Monseigneur de Conty down to the last of the city join the Ormée" as the surest was of destroying it.[1] Condé agreed: "I remain of the opinion that we join the Ormée as it is the much stronger party and as we have been unable to bring it down through either guile or force."[2] The Prince was not the only one to appreciate the wisdom of a pro-Ormée policy, for a group of officers belonging to the *Grande Fronde* now also declared its support of the Ormée.[3]

The weeks that followed the Ormée's victory witnessed a steady increase in the radical party's hold over Bordeaux. On the 27th of June, the Ormée's assembly created a chamber of thirty (*Chambre de Trente*), to "advise the *jurats* when they have need of advice."[4] Two days later, the same assembly ordered that the fourteen *parlementaires* previously proscribed be promptly ousted from the city, that officers of the militia "who have disobeyed [the Ormée's] orders" be dismissed, and that

[1] Lenet to Condé, July 1, 1652, in Gabriel-Jules de Cosnac, *Souvenirs du règne de Louis XIV* (Paris, 1866–82), IV, 288.

[2] Condé to Lenet, July 15, 1652, in Lenet, "Mémoires," p. 557.

[3] Lenet to Condé, July 1, 1652, in G.-J. Cosnac, *Souvenirs*, IV, 288.

[4] Lenet to Condé, June 27, 1652, in G.-J. Cosnac, *Souvenirs*, III, 359.

victims of the fighting be compensated.[5] A measure of the Ormée's power may be gained from the fact that Conty, who had just returned to Bordeaux, could not have the orders rescinded. Four thousand *livres* were distributed to the wounded and to the dependents of those who had been killed. Passports were issued to the fourteen who, "accompanied by a few others," left the city on the 2nd of July. Twenty-eight captains and lieutenants were cashiered and replaced by Ormists, Conty having been previously informed that the action would be carried out "whether he liked it or not."[6]

Free to decide all political questions, the Ormée next moved to gain possession of the city's principal organs—the *Jurade*, the *Cent et Trente*, the *Chambre de Direction*, the *Conseil de Guerre*, and the *Bourse*—all still in the hands of merchants and *parlementaires*. The five bodies eventually came under Ormée control, although how this was accomplished is not always clear. In the case of the *Bourse*, we only know that early in 1653, Crozillac, a leading Ormist, was elected one of its *consuls*, indicating that Ormists had somehow infiltrated the ranks of the forty merchants who chose the officers of that body.[7] As to the *Conseil de Guerre*—the body charged with the conduct of the war and with internal security—little else is known other than that its complexion began to change soon after the Ormée's victory (when members of the *Grande Fronde* replaced those of the *Petite*) and that it passed completely into the Ormée's hands before the end of 1652.[8]

More can be said of the Ormée's seizure of the *Chambre de Direction*, an organ created by the *Parlement* in 1649 for the purpose of collecting and disbursing the city's funds. On the 20th of August, the *Jurade* informed the Court that the Ormée "insisted that it [the *Chambre de Direction*] meet in some convent in the city" and not in the *Parlement*'s chancellery as had been the custom.[9] The Ormée's real intent was revealed the

[5] Lenet to Condé, July 1, 1652, in G.-J. Cosnac, *Souvenirs*, IV, 287.

[6] Unidentified letter to Condé, July 1, 1652, in Henri d'Aumale, *Histoire des Princes de Condé pendant le XVIe et XVIIe siècles* (Paris, 1863–96) VI, 629–30; Lenet to Condé, June 30, 1652, A.C., MS. serie P, XII, fols. 287–91; Ciraq to Dubosq, July 1, 1652. *B. B.*, MS. fonds Itié no fol. no. One of the new captains was Giraut, a leading Ormist. *Journal de Filhot*, p. 108.

[7] *Ibid.*, p. 10. On the manner of electing officers of the *Bourse*, see Jean Darnal, *Supplément des chroniques de la noble ville et cité de Bordeaux* (Bordeaux, 1666), p. 194.

[8] Unidentified letter to Condé, July 1, 1652, in d'Aumale, *Histoire*, p. 630; Communay, *Journal de Filhot*, p. 108.

[9] Registres du Parlement, 1651–58, fol. 182.

next day when the *Chambre de Direction*, taking up the question of military appropriations, reported:

On the proposal made by M. Dubourdieu, [*jurat*] of the city, that the regiment recently raised by the city for its defense and presently quartered in the fort of *la Bastide* receive the necessary provisions and that funds for this purpose be drawn on the receipts of the *Bureau* [*du Convoy*], M. *l'avocat général* rose to say that while it was proper that the said regiment be adequately provisioned it was also proper that those who had received funds for the regiment be made to render an account of their expenditures and that such precede any further outlays. It has therefore been decreed that those who have obtained funds give an accounting before two representatives of the *Jurade* as well as before the gentlemen de Mouchac, Villars, Crozillac, and Dureteste, who have been commissioned for the purpose.[10]

A direct challenge to the *Parlement* which had been in charge of the regiment, the decree was signed by the *jurats* de Nort and Robert, and by the Ormist leaders de Mouchac and Villars. Succeeding decrees would carry the names of other Ormists, but never again those of *parlementaires* (prior to August 20, two officers of the *Parlement* had signed each of the *Chambre*'s decrees). The change in the membership of the *Chambre de Direction* thus confirms the content of the decree cited: that it was the Ormée and not the *Parlement* that now controlled the city's fiscal affairs.

If the *Jurade* participated in the Ormée's capture of the *Chambre de Direction*, it was because it had become an appendage of the radical party. Here victory was obtained through the electoral process. On the 4th of July Lenet assured Condé that "all parties" had agreed on the selection of electors who were "well qualified, with good reputations [and] . . . loyal to Your Highness." As he further explained to Condé, his plan was to place Conty at the entrance of the voting chamber and as the electors passed have him "whisper in their ears your instructions which will remain secret until that moment."[11] Lenet apparently thought that the Ormée would accept such machinations. Condé, who is rarely credited with political acumen, had a more realistic appreciation of the situation. He replied to Lenet: "In my opinion, the *jurats* should be selected from among those who belong to the Ormée. In this fashion we will acquire their support and still their rebellious fervor, for once in power, the same *jurats* will want to uphold the authority of their office and thus feel

[10] Registres de la Chambre de Direction, August 21, 1652.
[11] Lenet to Condé, July 4, 1652, *B.N.*, MS. fonds français 6708, fols. 23–24.

obliged to work toward the Ormée's destruction."[12] But Lenet continued to favor the selection of "well-qualified" candidates. In his letter of July 18th, he reported that the Ormée had "gotten it into its head" to select such "people of substance" as Neursse, de Trevel, and de Pineau, "three rich and allegedly honest men."[13] Kossmann is quick to make the most of this revelation: here is further proof of the Ormée's political immaturity.[14] But were the three really the Ormée's choices? One need only read the rest of Lenet's letter to discover that they were not. The Ormée, Lenet continues, was

... very embarassed, having no inclination for the [other] three or four hopeful candidates whose names have slipped in. . . . If everything happens the way we wish, it will not be difficult to have the electors [*prud'hommes*] take the appropriate action. If, on the contrary, they [the Ormists] should decide to convene the *Cent et Trente* in order to obtain other electors and we are unable to prevent this coup, then I am of the opinion that we wait and see who it is they wish to elect.[15]

One thus learns of the existence of two slates of candidates: one, consisting of "people of substance" whom Lenet may have favored but not the Ormée (why else would the Ormée have had any reason to seek "other electors?"); and another, listing names that had mysteriously "slipped in" and that were in all likelihood the Ormée's real choice.

The *jurats* were chosen by twenty-four electors, in turn selected by the six *jurats* from among the members of the *Cent et Trente*—with the latter empowered to overrule the final choices.[16] Thus, to win the election, the Ormée would first have to gain control of the electors, a maneuver that was successfully accomplished, as the *Registres du Parlement* reveals:

The electors came for the most part from the Ormée. Their number contained neither noblemen nor officers, and of those holding the rank of *avocat* there was only Brassier, *docteur en manteau court*; Robert, in a similar robe; a certain Villars, *en manteau court*; and one named Mathieu, dressed in calico and carrying a sword at his side. In the ranks of the *bourgeois, marchands, et citoyens*, there were to be found the said Brignon [de Vrignon], Pinel, Minvielle, Gardera, Dureteste, Crozillac, Tuquoy [Turquois] and Rigolleau [Rigoulet],

---

[12] Condé to Lenet, July 15, 1652, in Lenet, "Mémoires," p. 557.
[13] Lenet to Condé, July 18, 1652, in G.-J. Cosnac, *Souvenirs*, IV, 32.
[14] Ernst H. Kossmann, *La Fronde* (Leiden, 1954), p. 250.
[15] Lenet to Condé, July 18, 1652, in G.-J. Cosnac, *Souvenirs*, IV, 320–21.
[16] *A.B.*, "Jurats," fonds Baurein, carton 17.

an apothecary— none of whom we would have recognized had they not been named to us. Not one of them was a prominent citizen [*citoyen notable*] or had held the usual offices.[17]

The *Registres* notes that the electors had been selected by the *jurats* "from among a list of candidates drawn up by themselves,"[18] but this seems highly unlikely in light of the *Jurade's* conservative character. It is much more probable that the Ormée used the alternative method of working through the *Cent et Trente* to obtain the desired candidates. Lenet had foreseen such a move and in fact had reported: "The Ormée is at work obtaining electors from the *Jurade* by means of the *Cent et Trente* in order to win the election."[19] But why should the *Cent et Trente*, a body of rich merchants and lawyers, have sided with the Ormée, when the *Jurade*, also made up of rich merchants and lawyers, remained its vehement foe? A shift in the Ormée's tactics coupled with a change in the composition of the *Cente et Trente* may provide the answer. On the 27th of July—less than a week before the election—word reached the *Parlement* that the *Cent et Trente* was about to assemble, to consider the demand "of a number of the bourgeois" that "all fortresses in the vicinity of the city be demolished."[20] That these "bourgeois" were Ormists is made clear by Lenet. "The Ormée and all of Bordeaux are pressing with unprecedented fury for the razing of Budos, . . . La Brède and a number of other *châteaux*."[21] The call to eliminate such rural strongholds of the *Parlement*—La Brède belonged to the *président* Montesquieu, Budos to the family of the *conseiller* d'Espagnet[22]—must have accorded well with the *Cent et Trente*, many of whose members were vying with the *Parlement* for control of the lands of the bankrupt peasantry, intending to apply to agriculture the same techniques of capitalist production previously employed in their commercial dealings.[23] At the same time, the contemplated action was bound to be rejected by the more highly placed members of the *Jurade* whose principal ambition was to enter the *Parlement*, acquire landed

[17] Registres du Parlement, 1651–58, fol. 164. A *manteau court* signified that the wearer occupied the lowest rank in the legal profession.
[18] *Ibid.*, fol. 162.
[19] Lenet to Condé, July 15, 1652, in G.-J. Cosnac, *Souvenirs*, IV, 309.
[20] Registres du Parlement, 1651–58, fol. 148.
[21] Lenet to Condé, July 29, 1652, in G.-J. Cosnac, *Souvenirs*, IV, 335.
[22] *Gazette [de Renaudot]*, 1652, p. 741.
[23] On the relation between Bordeaux and the countryside, see J. Bernard in R. Boutruche, ed., *Bordeaux, 1453–1715* (Bordeaux, 1966), pp. 169–73.

titles, and in general lead the lives of *grands seigneurs*.[24] This no doubt explains why, in the face of the Ormée's assault, the *jurats* rose to the defense of parlementary fortresses (as they had previously risen to the defense of parlementary offices), while the merchants and lawyers of the *Cent et Trente*, more interested in filling their purses than in playing the game of venality, sided with the Ormée in urging their destruction.

The session of the *Cent et Trente* held to consider the issue of the fortresses testifies not only to the Ormée's new found support, but also to the pre-eminent role played by Ormists in the affairs of that body (although how they came to play that role is unknown). When the *Parlement*'s commissioners arrived—their presence having been requested by the *Jurade* in accordance with the tradition that the *Parlement* be represented at all meetings held in the *Hôtel de Ville*—they were met by the Ormist Tustal, "a self-styled spokesman of the assembly," who first demanded to know "whether they came in their quality of bourgeois or as emissaries of the *Parlement*" and then proceeded to inform them that they would be received "as bourgeois, but not as representatives of the Court." Turning to the *jurats* Dubourdieu and Larcebault for an explanation of Tustal's remarks, the *parlementaires* were assured that the *Cent et Trente* had indeed agreed to their presence with only "a few bourgeois" dissenting. "At this point," the report of the commissioners continues, "the said Tustal and one named Dureteste interrupted to say that a subsequent assembly had reversed the decision of the earlier one."[25] Dureteste further observed that representatives of the *Parlement* had no right to be present, as their commission was "an usurpation, pure and simple."[26] The *jurats* must have thought that the Ormists were not speaking for the *Cent et Trente*, for no sooner had Dureteste spoken and the commissioners departed than they proposed their recall. This produced "a great outcry" of protest. We quote from the *jurats'* report to the *Parlement*: "Tustal announced that he had been ordered by his company [that is, by the Ormée] to oppose the entry of the deputies of the Court. . . . Many voices were raised in agreement."[27] The assembly then voted "unanimously" to tear down the fortifications in question."[28] The next day, Conty appeared

[24] Although most *jurats* were never to enter the *Parlement*, the fact that a few such as Dalon and Ardent did may have given encouragement to the others.

[25] Registres du Parlement, 1651–58, fols. 149–50.

[26] Lenet to Condé, July 29, 1652, in G.-J. Cosnac, *Souvenirs*, IV, 335.

[27] Registres du Parlement, 1651–58 fol. 154.

[28] Lenet to Condé, July 29, 1652, in G.-J. Cosnac, *Souvenirs*, IV, 336.

before the assembly, "to voice his anger over what had transpired the day before between them and the deputies of the *Parlement*." Robert rose to explain that the *Parlement* had usurped the right to participate in the deliberations of the *Jurade* sixty years earlier, during the Huguenot difficulties, to which Conty replied that the King would one day decide the question and that meanwhile the practice would continue.[29] The matter thus rested, but the stage had been set for the Ormée's victory in the forthcoming election of the *Jurade*, for having obtained the support of the *Cent et Trente*, it could count on the selection of its own slate of electors.

Its outcome made certain by the electors just chosen, the election of the *Jurade* began with a repetition of the formalities that had preceded the meeting of the *Cent et Trente*. Once again, the *Jurade* requested the presence of commissioners, cautioning that "terrible consequences would result if the Court did not despatch them." The *Parlement* thereupon asked if its representatives could safely participate in the election, to which the *jurat* spokesmen replied "that their authority was so weakened and their liveries so little honored that they did not dare answer," but that in all likelihood "they would not be able to prevent the Ormists from raising objections." Only after receiving Conty's assurance that he would do everything in his power to protect them did the commissioners make their way to the *Hôtel de Ville*, where they found themselves "surrounded on all sides by soldiers from the garrison guarding the *Hôtel de Ville*." Another surprise awaited them inside, for upon informing the conclave that it was customary prior to the election of new *jurats* "to read a certain decree setting forth the rules that apply to the said elections . . . and that this had not been done," they were told that the decree "had been read before their arrival." About to withdraw, the commissioners were prevailed upon to remain by the *jurats* who warned "that disorders would most certainly follow their departure."[30]

The election then proceeded without further incident. To fill the places of the three outgoing *jurats*—Guiraut, Fontenel, and de Nort—, the electors chose Légé de La Brangelie, de Vrignon, and Robert. Légé, the *Registres Secrets* reports, obtained the vote of "nearly" all the electors; de Vrignon, the new *jurat des marchands* (and as such commander of the militia), that of a "plurality;" and in the election of the *jurat des avocats*,

---

[29] *Ibid.*, 336–37.
[30] Registres du Parlement, 1651–58, fols 157–62.

"some voted for one by the name of Villars, but the majority were for Robert."[31]

The new *jurats* were all men who could be depended upon to advance the Ormée's cause. Légé was a nobleman from Périgord who, although not a resident of the *sénéchaussée* of Bordeaux as the law required, was permitted to stand for office because of his "valor, intelligence, and experience in the matters of war" and because he had the advantage "of being the choice of M. le Prince."[32] De Vrignon was a merchant and a captain in the militia. The fact that he had not been purged from that body as had most of the other captains indicates that he was definitely not a foe of the Ormée and more than likely was one of its supporters.[33] As for Robert, the son of a *jurat* and a ranking Ormist, he was, in the words of de Nort who placed his name in nomination, "full of zeal, well-intentioned, and very vigilant."[34] His candidacy was opposed by the more radical followers of Villars, but it was likewise opposed by the "*bons bourgeois*," as we learn from Lenet: "We have tried to impress on our partisans and friends that they [the Ormists] must be given someone of their choice."[35]

In deciding the outcome of the election, the Ormée had inflicted on the *Parlement* another great defeat. How great this defeat was can be gauged from the fact that never before in its history had the Court been forced to abide by the popular will in the matter of selecting new *jurats*. The fifteen officers still attending its sessions were at their wits' end. Lenet wrote of the session held on July 29: "Everyone was railing and fulminating at the Ormée with the exception of M. de Trancars who was very nearly devoured by his colleagues." When Dussault, the *avocat général*, declared himself prepared to prosecute Tustal and Dureteste "but on civil rather than criminal grounds," he was howled down by everyone, including his son-in-law.[36] The next day, the Court decreed that any assembly in which its commissioners were not present would be in contempt of the law.[37] Lenet was incredulous. "Messrs. Nesmond, d'Espag-

---

[31] *Ibid.*, fol. 164.
[32] *Ibid.*
[33] *B.B.*, "Milices Bourgeoises," fonds Baurein, carton 20.
[34] Registres du Parlement, 1651–58, fol. 164.
[35] Lenet to Condé, July 29, 1652, in G.-J. Cosnac, *Souvenirs*, IV, 340–41.
[36] Lenet to Condé, July 29, 1652, in G.-J. Cosnac, *Souvenirs*, IV, 338.
[37] Registres du Parlement, 1651–58, fol. 155.

net and de Massiot erupted with so much fury against the Ormée that I have never seen anything like it. Small as is their number, they actually believe that they can, at a moment's notice, revive the *Parlement*'s authority and destroy the Ormée."[38]

The Ormée's conduct appears on the surface paradoxical: powerful enough to rule by fiat, it had embarked on an election; strong enough to annihilate the *Parlement*, it had allowed it to survive, even held discussions with its emissaries. In the eyes of the *Apologie pour l'Ormée* such behavior was proof of the Ormée's modest ambitions: "Even in victory, the Ormée accepted the restrictions imposed on private men which is evidence of a generosity unheard of in all other states where the winning party seizes the government and takes power."[39] Another explanation, however, might be advanced to account for the Ormée's limited actions. For had the *Parlement* been eliminated in Bordeaux, it would simply have established itself in another city (as it was eventually to do), thereby depriving the Ormée of a potential hostage. Shrewd political calculation may also be evident in the *Jurade*'s takeover. As Lenet wrote to Condé, "I am confident that they [the Ormists] will do nothing to upset the forms [of the election] and will behave properly, because those who aspire to become *jurats* will want to be admitted in the ordinary manner so that with the return of peace they will retain their offices."[40] In operating within the letter if not the spirit of the law, the Ormée no doubt thought that it was insuring its political survival. The Ormée's strategy becomes perfectly clear: to eliminate the *Parlement* and the *Jurade* without actually abolishing them or, to rephrase the *Apologie*, to "take power" without "seizing the government."

Having deprived the *Parlement* of its authority and reduced the *Jurade*, the *Bourse*, the *Chambre de Direction*, and the *Conseil de Guerre* to Ormée fixtures, the new regime proceeded to create organs of its own. The *Apologie* reveals that "soon after" the *Parlement* had been defeated, the Ormée established "diverse chambers . . . which became the scene of a thousand remarkable actions, the description of which would only stretch my narrative to tedious lengths."[41] This unwillingness of the *Apologie*'s author to be "tedious" can only be regretted, for few details of the Ormée's

---

[38] Lenet to Condé, August 1, 1652, *B.N.*, MS. fonds français 6710, no fol. number.
[39] *Apologie pour l'Ormée* (n.p., n.d.), p. 37.
[40] Lenet to Condé, July 18, 1652, in G.-J. Cosnac, *Souvenirs*, IV, 321.
[41] *Apologie pour l'Ormée*, pp. 12–13.

governmental apparatus have survived. Little is known of the way the chambers functioned (whether, for example, decisions required a majority vote), or of their relation to each other, or even of the method of selecting members. Lenet's letters, the notarial records, and the *Mazarinades* take note of the various bodies and often provide valuable information on their activities, but more questions are left open to conjecture than are resolved.

The most representative of the Ormée's institutions was the five hundred member *Chambre de l'Ormée*.[42] This body had very likely evolved from the general assemblies that met during the early moments of the Ormée's revolt, and if such is the case, its function was to formulate basic policies. For it was the general assemblies that had called for the ouster of the undesirable *parlementaires*, initiated the attack on the Chapeau Rouge, and created a new political organ, the *Chambre de Trente*.[43]

With the emergence of the *Trente*, the *Chambre de l'Ormée* began to decline in importance—or so it would seem from the less frequent references made to it. It still issued general directives, but it was the new *Chambre de Trente* that now governed. This is confirmed by the records of the prison of the *Hôtel de Ville*. Most of the arrests were ordered by *"Messrs. les bourgeois de l'Ormée"* or sometimes by *"Messrs. de l'Ormée"*— references that could apply equally well to the *Chambre de l'Ormée* as to the *Chambre de Trente*[44]—but in one instance the entry distinguished between the two bodies. One Bernard Dumas was ordered released "following the deliberations of the *Chambre de l'Union de l'Ormée*. By order of the *Chambre de Trente*."[45] Thus, if the *Chambre de l'Ormée* deliberated, it was the *Chambre de Trente* that took the decisive actions. When initially established, the *Chambre de Trente*'s membership had been changed every fifteen days by the *Chambre de l'Ormée*, but the practice does not appear to have lasted very long, as there is no mention of a change in the *Trente*'s composition after July of 1652.[46]

If the *Chambre de l'Ormée* survived as a legislative body, the *Chambre de*

[42] Communay, *Journal de Filhot*, p. 159.

[43] *Histoire véritable d'une colombe . . .* (Paris, 1652) unidentified letter to Condé, May 16, 1652, A.C., MS. serie P, XII, fol. 258; Lenet to Condé, June 27, 1652, in G.-J. Cosnac, *Souvenirs*, III, 359.

[44] A. G. Livre de l'escroue de la maison commune de la presente ville commencé le 5 Septembre 1652, fols. 28, 59, 63, 92.

[45] *Ibid.*, fol. 94.

[46] Lenet to Condé, July 15, 1652, in G.-J. Cosnac, *Souvenirs*, IV, 308–9.

Trente—sometimes referred to as the Ormée's senate—came to assume the executive powers. It drafted the Ormée's charter, masterminded the election of the new *jurats*, and prosecuted the enemies of the regime.[47] So great was its power that the *Parlement* warned Conty early in September of 1652 that it would sooner abandon the city than "suffer the presence of a chamber of thirty, which takes upon itself the right to decide everything [*qui décide souverainement de toutes choses*] to the prejudice of the King's service and of sovereign justice."[48] The Parlement had good reason to resent the *Trente*, for it was the latter that decided which *parlementaires* were to be expelled—a role previously played by the general assemblies of the Ormée. When so occupied, the *Trente* was joined by the Ormée's partisans in the *Jurade*, the *Cent et Trente*, and the *Présidial*, and became a Chamber of Expulsion (*Chambre d'Expulsion*). Thus the *Courrier de la Guyenne* reported:

Lest anyone persevere in the thought that the expulsion of suspects results from arbitrary decisions, I wish to declare publicly that the matter is first discussed in the *Chambre d'Expulsion*, which is presided over by M. le Prince who is assisted by officers of the *Parlement*. The zealots or Ormists only denounce [the suspects] and execute the orders of the said *Chambre*.[49]

Conty and some officers of the *Parlement* may have attended the *Chambre*'s meetings, but most of those present came from the Ormée. Filhot, in an account of his trial, writes that the tribunal consisted "of about forty diverse judges of which the most important after the Prince's party were the Ormist captains Dureteste, Pontellier, du Puy, Masson, Tustal, Guiraut [Giraut], Crozillac, followed by herring merchants, wine merchants, and others."[50]

Still another function of the *Chambre de Trente* was to act as a military council. When the priest Ithier was arrested, he was brought before "the senate of the Ormée which had that very day been constituted into a *Conseil de Guerre*."[51] Was it then the *Conseil* rather than Conty that came to formulate military policy? Sources indicate that in the last stages of the fighting—when the Condist armies of Balthazar and Marsin were in full

[47] *Ibid.*, p. 321. On the *Trente*'s role as a tribunal, see Chapters VI and VII.
[48] Registres du Parlement, 1651–58, fol. 197.
[49] *Courrier de la Guyenne* . . . (Paris, 1652), pp. 6–7.
[50] Communay, *Journal de Filhot*, p. 108.
[51] François Berthod, "Mémoires," in *Nouvelle collection des mémoires pour servir à l'histoire de France*, ed. J. Michaud and F. Poujoulat (Paris, 1838), X, 611. Cited hereafter as Berthod, "Mémoires."

retreat—it was the *Chambre de Trente* that pressed for the continuation of the war, built fortifications, raised a fleet, and sought foreign assistance.[52] Conty might again be present at the *Conseil*'s deliberations, but he could do little more than concur in its decisions. The despatching of Ormée envoys to England is a case in point. The decision could not have come from Conty, if only because the Condist party already had an agent in London, yet the document accrediting the envoys was duly signed by the Prince.[53]

Endowed with so many political, military, and judicial prerogatives, the *Chambre de Trente* was unquestionably the most powerful organ in the Ormée's governmental structure. Its sphere of competence, however, was restricted to questions affecting the regime. Those of a purely private nature came under the purview of yet another body, the *Chambre de Douze*. Adjudicating all private suits, the *Chambre de Douze* played a key role in safeguarding the interests of individual Ormists, as will be seen subsequently.[54]

The *Chambre de l'Ormée*, the *Chambre de Trente*, the *Chambre de Douze*— such then were the branches of the Ormée government. But the Ormée did not only govern. Under attack from without, a prey to subversion from within, it came to appreciate the value of direct action. Squads of armed men appeared whose task it was to ferret out all opposition to the regime. According to Filhot, Dureteste—who commanded one of these squads—would inform his victim: "Having learned that you were ill, I am bringing you an order to go take fresh air. And if in twenty-four hours you haven't withdrawn, you will be murdered and your body thrown in the river." Addressing *présidents* and *conseillers*, he would exclaim: "I have you, you rascal, and you will not escape from my hands!"[55] The bands were far from ephemeral gatherings. Filhot writes that Villars had "a company" of eighty guards "who slept at this home . . . and for whom nothing was impossible."[56] And the *Hôtel de Ville*'s prison registry contains such entries as: "Albert, soldier in the company of M. de Villars, released on orders of Pierre Eynard, lieutenant of M. Villars." "Pacque-

[52] See Chapters VI and VIII.
[53] Lenet, "Mémoires," p. 605.
[54] References to the *Chambre de Douze* may be found in the following notarial briefs: *A.G.*, 3E 4332, fol. 766; 3E 8753, fol. 74; 3E 6582, fol. 299; 3E 2448, fols. 983, 945; 3E 5142, fol. 552. The *Chambre* is discussed in Chapter VI.
[55] Communay, *Journal de Filhot*, pp. 175–76.
[56] *Ibid.*, pp. 176–77.

reau, bourgeois, [and] Sincrit, *avocat* . . . detained at the request of Eynard, lieutenant, and La Fonde, *enseigne* of *Sieur* Villars." "Pierre Margne, arrested on orders of M. de Vrignon [*jurat*] at the request of Eynard, lieutenant of Villars."[57] All this would indicate that the eighty—for it was certainly they who carried out the arrests—was a permanently constituted force. What made it especially effective as an instrument of coercion was that it did not shirk from the use of force. As one of its victims declared: "The violence perpetrated by the assembly of the Ormée has created so much fear that individuals do not dare raise their voices."[58]

Thus soon after its victory over the Chapeau Rouge, the Ormée possessed all the instruments of power. The *Parlement* continued to survive, but in such a moribund state that it posed no real threat to the new order. Nothing could now impede the Ormée from ruling Bordeaux, and it is the consequences of that rule that we wish to examine next.

[57] *A.G.*, Livre de l'escroue . . ., April 9, 1653; April 15, 1653; May 2, 1653.
[58] *A.G.*, 3E 2448, fol. 938.

V

THE ORMÉE IN POWER:
THE POLITICAL CONSEQUENCES

THE ORMÉE'S EARLY HISTORY was closely linked to military developments in Guyenne. Two months after having defeated Condé's forces at Agen in March of 1652, the royal army under Harcourt was in control of most of the Garonne, and indeed had reached the outskirts of Bordeaux.[1] Harcourt would have liked nothing better than to capture the city and in a stroke end the war, but he had neither cannon with which to breach its walls nor forces sufficient to mount a prolonged siege.[2] Compelled to find another target, he ordered his army to move on Villeneuve, a much smaller city one hundred kilometers to the east of Bordeaux. The attack and eventual siege of Villeneuve proved not only a total failure but the undoing of the attacking force as well. Inadequately provisioned, poorly led, and plagued by desertions, the royal army had become an assemblage of marauding bands, more capable of terrorizing peasants than of engaging the enemy.[3] In October, when Plessis-Bellière was ordered to lead the army to Catalonia —Harcourt had returned to the Court to pursue some private affairs—he reported to Mazarin: "I find the army of Guyenne in the throes of such license that it will be no small miracle if I can persuade it to make the march."[4]

[1] Guitaut to La Bourlie, May 2, 1652, *Archives historiques de la Gironde*, VIII, 383.
[2] Cononges to Mazarin, April 20, 1652, *Ibid*, p. 376; Pontac to Mazarin, April 29. 1652, *ibid.*, p. 381.
[3] St. Luc to Mazarin, August 10, 1652, *ibid.*, pp. 404–5; Vivens to Mazarin, September 16, 1652, *ibid.*, pp. 411–12.
[4] Plessis-Bellière to Mazarin, October 27, 1652, *ibid.*, p. 417. Of 4,000 men originally in Guyenne, only 1,000 remained. Gabriel-Jules de Cosnac, *Souvenirs du règne de Louis XIV* (Paris, 1866–82), V, 76.

The disintegration of the royal army was followed closely by the destruction of the royal fleet. Early in August the fleet, under the command of the Duke of Vendôme, had defeated a Spanish squadron off the coast of Saintonge.[5] About to enter the Garonne, Vendôme received orders to set sail for Dunkirk, then under siege of the Archduke Leopold. The mission was never accomplished, for in the straits the French fleet encountered the English and was roundly defeated, seven of its eight ships being sunk.[6]

The early months of Ormée rule were thus marked by the disappearance of the royal presence from Guyenne. Secure from outside attack, the Ormée could devote its full attention to the task of consolidating its position in Bordeaux, and indeed the period witnessed the final defeat of the *Parlement*, the conquest of the *Jurade*, and the establishment of such new bodies as the *Chambre de Trente* and the *Chambre de Douze*. Helping to strengthen the Ormée's hand was the arrival of much needed military and economic aid. In August, a contingent of twelve hundred Irish mercenaries—paid by Spain and recruited with Cromwell's permission—garrisoned Bourg[7] and in September six ships carrying wheat arrived from Brittany.[8]

The prospect of an all-powerful Ormée regime was apparently as disconcerting to some of its adherents as it was to those the Ormée had just defeated, for on August 22 a group calling itself "*les bourgeois de l'Ormée*" remonstrated to Condé:

Our best citizens are so frightened and shaken by the threats they receive daily from M. Laisné [Lenet]—in both your name and his—that we can anticipate the total defection of your supporters, all of whom he holds in contempt, treating them as enemies and worse than Mazarinists. . . . [Thus,] he recently had the said Dureteste warn M. Jolly, *secrétaire du Roy*, that unless he paid the sum of 100 *pistoles* he would be visited by a detachment of the militia. . . . We also discovered that he was using our names to oppress our relations and friends, and immediately dispatched the *Sieurs* de Prades, de St. Croy, and others of our body to inform them that Dureteste was a liar and miscreant and that he had acted without our knowledge. . . . He is also responsible for the flight of Courtade, the banker, and of many others, who have been forced to abandon the city in order to escape his violence.[9]

[5] Unidentified letter to Mazarin, August 12, 1652, *Archives historiques de la Gironde*, VIII, 406.

[6] Philip A. Knachel, *England and the Fronde*, (Ithaca, 1967), pp. 174, 175.

[7] Unidentified letter to Mazarin, August 12, 1652, *Archives historiques de la Gironde*, VIII, 406; Lenet to Condé, August 8, 1652, in Lenet, "Mémoires," p. 560.

[8] Vivens to Mazarin, September 16, 1652, *Archives historiques de la Gironde*, VIII, 412.

[9] Letter to Condé, August 22, 1652, in G.-J. Cosnac, *Souvenirs*, V, 9–11.

Condé thought that the real aim of his disgruntled correspondents was to hand Bordeaux over to Mazarin and promptly instructed Lenet: "Have the Ormée expel d'Hosten and Prades or have them arrested on some pretext or other. This must be done before the grape harvest, or everything will be lost."[10] The order was executed, but not before an attempt had been made to rally the Ormée to the side of the dissidents. "The *président* [d'Hosten], Prades, and others of their cabal have been heard saying," Lenet wrote to Condé,

. . . that I, as their foremost enemy, was behind their expulsion, that my intention was to drive all the people of substance [*gens de bien*] from Bordeaux, and that therefore I should be dumped in the river. They proceeded to declare that they had no intention of departing and would know how to defend themselves. They also charged that Your Highness was seeking to establish a tyranny and that they would oppose this even at the cost of their lives. . . . Among those voicing the loudest protest was a nobleman [*gentilhomme*] named Justel [Tustal] whom the plotters had sought to elect *jurat*.[11]

In a subsequent interview with Tustal, Lenet remarked that he could not understand why "those who had expelled so many notable persons opposed the expulsion of a few lowly characters." Tustal was reminded that it was Condé himself who had ordered the ousters, whereupon the nobleman had a change of heart, "promising all possible friendship and confessing that others had been behind his actions." By the time Prades and d'Hosten were brought before the Ormée's assembly, all resistance to the ousters had crumbled, for the decision to expel the two was unanimous.[12]

The fact that a number of Ormists had risen in support of Bordeaux's privileged element becomes less surprising when the social background of those involved is known. Prades was a professor of mathematics at the College of Guyenne and had been a tutor in Epernon's family.[13] D'Hosten was a *président* of the *Cour des Aides*.[14] Tustal, we have seen, was a nobleman, and Cavault, another member of the cabal, a tax *fermier*.[15]

---

[10] Condé to Lenet, September 11, 1652, in Henri d'Aumale, *Histoire des Princes de Condé pendant le XVIe et XVIIe siècles* (Paris, 1863–96), VI, 633.
[11] Lenet to Condé, September 23, 1652, in G.-J. Cosnac, *Souvenirs*, V, 31–32.
[12] *Ibid.*, pp. 32–33.
[13] Prades to Condé, October 11, 1652, *B.N.*, MS. fonds français 6711, fol. 57.
[14] Registres de la Chambre de Direction, February 4, 1653.
[15] Lenet to Condé, September 23, 1652, in G.-J. Cosnac, *Souvenirs*, V, 31, 34.

Themselves "people of substance,"[16] it is reasonable that they should have inclined towards non-Ormists of similar standing, especially in light of the action just taken by the Ormée. For the letter to Condé was drafted on the very day following the elevation of Mouchac, Villars, Dureteste and Crozillac to the *Chambre de Direction*.[17] With the city's finances in the hands of such extremists, would not the interests of all "*gens de bien*"—those within the Ormée as well as those outside—begin to suffer?

But more general reasons may have been behind the anti-Ormist ferment. The ravages committed by the royal army,[18] the reluctance of foreign vessels to venture to Bordeaux (in Rotterdam, the insurance rate for ships sailing to that city soared to 45 per cent of the value of the cargo),[19] and the disappearance of regional trade[20] all had ruinous consequences for Bordeaux's economy, as Lenet's correspondence makes amply clear. "Commerce is so sterile," he wrote on July 29, "that I am still waiting for it to produce 100 *écus*. Furthermore, the Spanish assistance is so slow in arriving that I shall have great difficulty in awaiting it."[21] "The *convoy* has not produced a farthing," he observed on October 24.[22] And on December 10: "No vessels are arriving. I have been here eight months and still am not sure whether or not there is a *convoy*, *idem*, the *taille*."[23] Directly affected by the decline in trade, Bordeaux's merchants were also the principal victims of the decline in the city's revenues, for with the disappearance of the *convoy* and the uncertainties of Spanish aid,[24] it was they who became the chief source of funds for the war. Thus 40,000 *livres*

[16] That they considered themselves as such is evident from a comment of Prades: "M. de Tustal does me the honor of liking me because he considers me a man of circumstance [*homme de bien*]." Prades to Condé, October 11, 1652, B.N., MS. fonds français 6711, fol. 57.

[17] Registres de la Chambre de Direction, August 21, 1652.

[18] Thus one of Mazarin's correspondents reported: "Most of the regiments are obtaining their pay from the communities to which they are assigned. . .[but] they are taking more than they are entitled and are ruining the countryside. . . . The army has eaten all the wheat the length of the Garonne from Agen to Villeneuve." Vivens to Mazarin, June 11, 1652, *Archives historiques de la Gironde*, VIII, 392.

[19] De Haes to Dubosq, October 31, 1652, B.B., MS. fonds Itié, no fol. number.

[20] See below.

[21] Lenet to Condé, July 29, 1652, in G.-J. Cosnac, *Souvenirs*, IV, 333.

[22] Lenet to Condé, October 24, 1652, *ibid.*, V. 178.

[23] Lenet to Condé, December 10, 1652, *ibid.*, V, 353.

[24] By December of 1652, only two months of subsidies (160,000 *patagons*) had been received. Conty to St. Agoulin, December 1652, in Lenet, "Mémoires," p. 589.

was obtained from the grain merchants,[25] 100,000 *livres* from the munitioneers,[26] and another 80,000 *livres* from the banker Courtade.[27] These actions met with considerable resistance, as Lenet again reveals: "The rascal Courtade whom I was able to detach from the Ormée has been corrupting all our other creditors. He tells them that the Princes only pay their debts when they have a mind to."[28] To obtain compliance, Lenet had to resort to various ploys. "In the event," he wrote to Condé, "that the munitioneers refuse to advance additional sums, I shall placate them with small repayments and thus manage things; they will not dare to leave me for fear of losing everything."[29]

Faced with the prospect of financial ruin if the Ormée remained in power, a number of Ormists had rediscovered their mercantile origins and loyalties and turned against the Ormée. No doubt, they had joined the Ormée because they shared the latter's hostility for the *Parlement* and not because they felt any particular affinity for Bordeaux's *menu peuple*. Prades could write from exile:

Being absent from Bordeaux is less painful to me than being suspected of having betrayed the party in whose behalf I had sworn to sacrifice my life and possessions. For I have never had any attachment other than to the general good, and have always maintained that the interests of our lords the Princes are so closely tied to those of the people that the ruin of one must bring in its wake the ruin of the other.[30]

But "the people" Prades had in mind were the "*gens de bien*" he and d'Hosten had defended before being driven from Bordeaux. Prades may have been a republican— he had been one of the first to call for the establishment of a republic[31]—but his model was the oligarchical republic of the Dutch and not the popular republic of Naples under Masaniello. It was because he believed that Bordeaux under the Ormée was veering toward the latter that he broke with the regime and sought its overthrow.

[25] Lenet to Condé, July 18, 1652, in G.-J. Cosnac, *Souvenirs*, IV, 318.

[26] Lenet to Condé, July 29, 1652, *ibid.*, p. 333.

[27] Communay, "Notaires," fol. 970.

[28] Lenet to Condé, August 8, 1652, in Lenet, "Mémoires," p. 560.

[29] Lenet to Condé, July 1, 1652, in G.-J. Cosnac, *Souvenirs*, IV, 294. In Paris rumors were circulating that Lenet intended to send "a brigade of Ormists to pillage the houses of those who would not advance the stipulated sums." Marigny to Lenet, September 12, 1652, in Lenet, "Mémoires," p. 573.

[30] Prades to Lenet, October 11, 1652, B.N., MS. fonds français 6711, fol. 57.

[31] Lenet to Condé, July 1, 1652, in G.-J. Cosnac, *Souvenirs*, IV, 291.

With the elimination of the Ormée's conservative element, all power fell into the hands of the radicals. As Lenet informed Condé: "We have silenced the chatter of those in the Ormée who gave us the greatest trouble and those who remain appear so well disposed that they speak of throwing into the river anyone who would prefer to harvest his vine rather than serve your cause."[32] The campaign of terror which had hitherto been directed against the Ormée's known enemies was now broadened to include anyone who opposed the new regime or who placed his personal interests above those of the party. Thus Yzaac d'Escombe, *bayle des maitres serruriers*, was thrown into prison because he would not sign the Ormée's registry (the *Livre de l'Ormée*) and because he had "spoken ill of M. le Prince and of the Ormée, all of whom he had said ought to be hanged."[33] And when Bernard Fayard placed a lien on some merchandise belonging to M. de Vateville, the Spanish commander of Bourg, he was visited by Giraut, Dureteste, and others of the Ormée "who, acting on their own authority, had the said Fayard detained in the prison of the *Hôtel de Ville*, where, using numerous threats as well as force and violence . . . , they succeeded in making him renounce all his claims and demands, to the great prejudice of himself and of his family."[34]

The sharpening of the social conflict was only one consequence of the Ormée's radicalization. The Ormée had never before pursued a military course separate from that of the Princes, or even sought a role in the planning of military operations, or made any concerted effort to mobilize support for the war. All this was now to change. First, it took charge of the troops guarding the fortress at *la Bastide*—troops paid by the city but under the command of Conty. This and subsequent developments are described by the *jurats* in a report to the *Parlement:*

Being in the *Hôtel de Ville* at 10 o'clock in the morning, they [the *jurats*] heard the sound of drums coming from the moat outside, and upon investigation discovered the said La Mothe Sauvage at the head of the hired troops. . . . Before they could apprise M. le Prince de Conty of what was taking place, a number of Ormists entered the *Hôtel de Ville* and announced that the appearance of the troops warranted no special attention as they were needed to demolish the fortifications of the *Château du Hâ*. Later in the day, two of their number were received by M. le Prince, who was greatly vexed by the news

[32] Lenet to Condé, September 30, 1652, in G.-J. Cosnac, *Souvenirs*, V, 54.
[33] Registres du Parlement, 1651–58, fol. 215.
[34] *A.G.*, 3E 7228, fol. 457.

that a house belonging to the King was about to be demolished and that soldiers had entered the city without his orders. He resolved to convene the chiefs of the Ormée, among them the said Mouchac, La Peyrière, and Dureteste, and proceeded to cashier the said La Mothe Sauvage. . . . The following day as they [the *jurats*] were meeting, a band of 50 Ormists commanded by La Peyrière interrupted the session with the announcement that Monsieur le Prince de Conty had agreed to the demolition of the *Château du Hâ*.[35]

Soon after, Conty informed the *Parlement* that he had reinstated La Mothe Sauvage "at the behest of a number of persons," but also that he had ordered a halt to the destruction of the *Château du Hâ*.[36] Renaudot's *Gazette*, however, reports that the *Château* was in fact destroyed. The *Gazette* further reveals that it was Ormée troops which, in late September, captured the *Château de La Brède*,[37] providing additional proof that the Ormée rather than Conty now held the military reins.

The Ormée's assumption of military command coincided with a heightened interest in the war itself. The Ormée had previously supported Condé's war efforts, but only because it feared that a royal victory would be followed by Epernon's return. Unaware of the relation between the provincial struggle and the struggle inside Bordeaux, its participation in war had been sporadic and uninspired. It was with the assumption of power and the realization that it would not survive a royal victory that the Ormée began to take energetic action in support of the war. Scaffolds were erected and the Ormée assembly declared that anyone talking of peace would be severely punished.[38] Processions were organized, as Condé learned from Lenet:

Carrying no arms other than their swords, a group of five to six hundred Ormists made their way through the city, stopping at every street corner to threaten with drowning and the burning of his house anyone advocating a peace separate from that of Your Highness.[39]

The rumor that the *procureur général* of the *Parlement* had accepted the royal amnesty brought a warning that, "in the event he did so without notifying His Highness, he would not live a quarter hour."[40] A band of

[35] Registres du Parlement, 1651–58, fols. 191–92.
[36] *Ibid.*, fol. 196.
[37] G.-J. Cosnac, *Souvenirs*, V, 20.
[38] *Ibid.*, p. 18.
[39] Lenet to Condé, October 28, 1652, B.N., MS. fonds français 6711, fol. 123.
[40] Lenet to Condé, October 31, 1652, in G.-J. Cosnac, *Souvenirs*, V, 182.

Ormists also appeared at the *Parlement* and announced that anyone who declared himself for peace "would be thrown into the river."[41] The Ormée was quite serious, as one *conseiller* discovered. Dandraut had been threatened with dire consequences if he accepted the amnesty but had the temerity to reply "a little rudely," whereupon he was assaulted with guns and swords and only saved from certain death because Durant, the munitioneer, had come to his rescue.[42]

By October of 1652 the Ormée had reached the zenith of its power. It would continue to dominate the city's affairs, but never as effectively as it has in the four months that followed its victory over the Chapeau Rouge. The turn of events can again be traced to the military situation, for on October 13 the French army capitulated in Catalonia.[43] This was a fateful development, for it meant that the army could now be expected to march on Guyenne.[44] The Ormée seemed aware of the new danger; in a letter written on November 14, Lenet informed Condé that the Ormée had offered to raise a regiment of cavalry and another of infantry and when this was rejected by Conty, had proposed that 25 additional mercenaries be placed under each of the 36 captains of the city.[45]

If the Ormée was determined to persevere in its struggle, the same was now also true of the opposition, which, encouraged by the improved military prospects, had begun to revive. Some time in the latter part of November, at "a secret meeting attended by those loyal to the King"— thus went the report that was sent to Mazarin,—

. . . the decision was reached to convene an assembly at the *Hôtel de Ville* to which those of the Ormée would be invited; that under the pretext of being in agreement with them it would then be announced that the sole remedy for the present calamities was to submit to the King's will, accept the amnesty, and curb the violence of the mutinous riff-raff [*refréner l'insolence de la canaille mutinée*]; and that the gentlemen of the *Parlement* would be kept informed of everything, as a large number had sworn to support the decision of the said secret assembly.[46]

[41] *Ibid.*, p. 183.
[42] *Ibid.*
[43] John H. Elliott, *The Revolt of the Catalans; a Study in the Decline of Spain, 1598–1640,* (Cambridge, 1863), p. 540.
[44] Such a development was anticipated by Lenet, who wrote to Condé: "If Barcelona falls, then it will be necessary to place all our infantry and cavalry in Guyenne." Lenet to Condé, October 24, 1652, in G.-J. Cosnac, *Souvenirs,* V. 177–78.
[45] Lenet to Condé, November 14, 1652, *ibid.*, p. 186.
[46] Unidentified letter to Mazarin, November 24, 1652, *Archives historiques de la Gironde,* VIII, 421.

A subsequent conclave in the palace of the *Parlement* was cut short by an unexpected development. No sooner had the session begun when Conty appeared, "followed by many people—the entire Ormée being both inside and outside the *Palais*. He announced that he had discovered the existence of a plot against his person and family [and] . . . that many of the gentlemen of the *Parlement* were implicated."[47] The conspirators were seized by panic. "Those who knew of the plot took fright and began to shout that there was no longer any safety in the *Palais*, and that they were all prisoners."[48] The *conseiller* Massiot then rose and admitted that he had indeed taken part in a plot against the Ormée whose adherents were to have been "exterminated." His remarks ended with the observation that he found it "intolerable that such lowly people [*petits gens*] as the Ormists should rule to the prejudice of the *Parlement*." Thereupon Landé, an Ormist stalwart, revealed that Massiot had offered him and an other Ormist 10,000 *livres* to assassinate the entire Ormée leadership.[49] The mob was ready to dispatch the exposed *conseiller* when Conty announced that he was placing him under his protection. This action succeeded in saving Massiot's life, although not his freedom. "So great was the mob's fury," Lenet reported, "that Milord lost all control over the situation. He could do nothing to prevent the carriage from being dragged to the *Hôtel de Ville* where they arrested M. de Massiot."[50]

Who had been behind this second challenge to the Ormée's rule and with what end? Lenet provides the following answer:

It was very clear that through the connivance of the *Parlement* a number of rich bourgeois [*gros bourgeois*] had been brought into the Ormée with the aim of destroying it in the same way that the assembly of the nobility of Paris had been destroyed. After seizing the *Hôtel de Ville* and doing away with Dureteste, Villars, Guiraut [Giraut], Crozillac and Arnault, the *Parlement* intended to assume absolute control over the city's affairs. . . . The conspirators were divided into two groups. One consisting of Mazarinists planned to arrest the Princes and then make peace. The other, made up of the *Petite Fronde*, intended to defeat the Ormée, seize power, and make Your Highness subservient to its ends.[51]

---

[47] Unidentified letter to Mazarin, December 5, 1652, *ibid.*, p. 423.
[48] Lenet to Condé, December 5, 1652, in Lenet, "Mémoires," p. 591.
[49] Unidentified letter to Mazarin, December 5, 1652, *Archives historiques de la Gironde*, VIII, 423–24.
[50] Lenet to Condé, December 5, 1652, in Lenet, "Mémoires," p. 592.
[51] *Ibid.*

Thus all the conspirators did not share the same objective: the Mazarinists aimed at the restoration of royal authority, the *Petite Fronde* at the restoration of the *Parlement*. That such a division should have existed may be explained by the presence among the plotters of *"gros bourgeois"*—that is, of individuals who were only slightly less opposed to the *Parlement's* return than they were to the continuation of Ormée rule, who had supported Epernon because he had sided with them in their differences with the *Parlement* and who now supported Mazarin in the hope that he would do the same in their struggle with the Ormée.

Following Massiot's arrest, it was the merchants who took the initiative against the Ormée. An assembly of four hundred of the *"grosse bourgeoisie"* convened at the *Bourse*.[52] Though its only overt action was to accuse the *jurats* of being Ormists, this was enough to convince the Ormée that another plot was afoot. "The Ormée took fright," wrote Lenet, "and began shouting that the *Hôtel de Ville* was about to be seized."[53] There was, however, no uprising. The merchants had apparently decided not to risk an open confrontation, placards attacking the Ormée being the only other evidence of their insurgency.[54] They may have been discouraged by the Ormée's resoluteness. When Conty, who still hoped for a general reconciliation, proposed a union "of all the bodies," the Ormée replied that "while he could do.what he wanted, they would never enter into such a relationship."[55] And when the Prince thought that he could take advantage of the Christmas season to order the release of Massiot, the Ormée had guards placed in front of the *Hôtel de Ville* and instructed them "not to permit the said Massiot to be freed regardless of who issued the order."[56]

The failure of Massiot's conspiracy convinced a number of the Ormée's foes of the futility of such enterprises. Gabriel de Pontac, a *président* of the *Parlement* serving as an *intendant* in the army of Guyenne and who was also Massiot's brother-in-law, wrote to Mazarin:

Until the present moment I have never lost an opportunity to urge my relatives and friends in the *Parlement* of Bordeaux to shake off the yoke of the

[52] Unidentified letter to Mazarin, December 5, 1652, *Archives historiques de la Gironde*, VIII, 425.
[53] Lenet to Condé, December 5, 1652, in Lenet, "Mémoires," p. 592.
[54] G.-J. Cosnac, *Souvenirs*, V, 354–56.
[55] Unidentified letter to Mazarin, December 23, 1652, *Archives historiques de la Gironde*, VIII, 427–28.
[56] Lenet to Condé, December 26, 1652, in G.-J. Cosnac, *Souvenirs*, V, 367.

people's tyranny and return to their duties. . . . I had some hope of succeeding but am now obliged to inform Your Eminence that the *Parlement* has been completely defeated and can no longer be relied upon. To think otherwise would be a delusion.[57]

Pontac favored economic measures:

My belief is that there are two ways in which the disorders of Bordeaux can be accentuated: either by confiscating and redistributing the property of the inhabitants or by putting a halt to the sale of wheat from Brittany, punishing those merchants who participate in this trade.[58]

Another of Mazarin's agents, however, favored military action:

Despite our efforts to encourage what remains of Bordeaux's people of substance, we see that they are in no condition to undertake anything without the approach of the army and above all of the fleet. It is this which prompts me to inquire as to when we can expect the latter's arrival.[59]

There was nothing in the one approach that precluded the adoption of the other, and indeed Mazarin embarked upon a joint strategy of military encirclement and economic strangulation. On January 10, Vendôme, whose refitted fleet lay anchored off La Rochelle, received word that troops had just been dispatched to Blaye, "to be used against Bordeaux and elsewhere as the occasion requires but also to prevent the Dutch from continuing to bring supplies and to compel them to pay the charges they owe us."[60] Preparations were also made for a land attack.

"The enemy," Conty wrote to his brother,

has nine regiments under M. de Vendôme . . . ; in Augoumois, there are the regiments of Navarre, of Picardie, of Rambures and of Candalle; in the Limousin and the Périgord are the troops of Folleville, the entire army of Italy sent by St. André Monbrun, and all of the troops which were in Provence under M. de Merceur; in the Rouergue and the Haute Guyenne the army that was commanded by M. le Comte d'Harcourt and which is now commanded by M. de Candalle, as well as the forces that had been in Catalonia under M. de Marsin.[61]

All told, Candalle, the new commander of the army in Guyenne, had

[57] Pontac to Mazarin, January 1, 1653, *Archives historiques de la Gironde*, VII, 257.
[58] *Ibid.*, p. 258.
[59] Bourgeon to Mazarin, January 1, 1653, *A.E.*, France, vol. 891, fol. 2.
[60] Mazarin to Vendôme, January 10, 1653, *B.N.*, MS. fonds français 4186, fol. 13.
[61] Conty to Condé, February 15, 1652, in Lenet, "Mémoires," p. 597.

14,000 foot soldiers and 7,000 horsemen. By contrast, Conty's forces consisted of 2,000 foot soldiers and 1,000 horsemen.[62]

Bordeaux's military situation had suddenly become critical. By the middle of February, three fourths of Guyenne was again in royalist hands.[63] Foraying parties from Blaye devastated the countryside around Bordeaux; loyal cities such as Bourg were under attack.[64] "All of France," Conty wrote to his brother, "longs for peace, and this is especially true of Guyenne where we retain various places only because of our garrisons, which for want of money are dwindling. Unless the Spanish act promptly, the loss of Bordeaux as well as everything else that we possess in Guyenne is a certainty."[65] Bordeaux's fate and the survival of the Ormée had thus come to depend on the action of Spain—that is, of a country notoriously delinquent in meeting its treaty obligations.[66]

The immediate effect of the military encirclement was that Bordeaux began to suffer from a critical shortage of food. As early as December, 1652, Lenet had warned Condé: "There is very little wheat in Bordeaux and unless help arrives during the next two months, we shall be lost."[67] Some wheat arrived with a Dutch convoy,[68] but the supply was soon exhausted as we learn from a letter from Conty to his brother: "We neither have munitions nor wheat nor the money to buy any."[69] This was in February, 1653. By then nearly all trade with Brittany, Bordeaux's traditional supplier of grain, had ceased. From February 1 to February 19 (when the records of the *Amirauté* become silent), only two ships arrived from Brittany; during a comparable period in 1652, the number had been 28; and in 1651—a time of peace—it had been 116.[70]

There were also setbacks of a financial nature. The Dutch fleet departed without paying the *convoy*—Bordeaux's most lucrative source of revenue—using as an excuse the fact that the bureau had been removed to

[62] *Ibid.*, p. 597.
[63] *Ibid.*
[64] Berthod to Mazarin, February 3, 1653, *A.E.*, France, vol. 891, fol. 68.
[65] Conty to Condé, February 15, 1653, in Lenet, "Mémoires," p. 597.
[66] Of the 2 million *patagons* promised by Spain, 1.6 million still remained to be paid. *Ibid.*, 596.
[67] Lenet to Condé, December 26, 1652, in G.-J. Cosnac, *Souvenirs*, V, 370.
[68] Vivens to Mazarin, January 8, 1653, *Archives historiques de la Gironde*, VII, 259.
[69] Conty to Condé, February 15, 1653, in Lenet, "Mémoires," p. 597.
[70] *A.G.*, 6B 283. Amirauté de Guyenne, Desparts des Navires du Port de Bordeaux, 1651–1653.

Blaye (it was not to pay there either).[71] Regional land trade also declined. "I am full of regrets," wrote a Dutch merchant to his counterpart in Bordeaux, "to learn from you letter that almost nothing can descend from the upper country and that you are obliged to look for prunes elsewhere. . . . In case you should be permitted to ship some down, I advise you to purchase thirty to thirty-five sacks."[72] That the permission was not likely to be granted, the same correspondent already knew from an earlier letter: "You inform me that the Ormée has prohibited the sale of all wines originating in the upper country and that the only wine you are able to purchase is that produced in the Graves region."[73] Understandably, the Ormée was disinclined to see Bordeaux serve as an outlet for goods that came from areas under the enemy's control. But ultimately this policy was as harmful to the rebellious city as it was to the enemy, for much of Bordeaux's carrying trade originated in the upper Garonne and beyond, and any reduction in this traffic was bound to be reflected in the city's total exports.[74] The merchants would no doubt suffer most, but the depressionary effects of a decline in revenues was bound, in the end, to affect the entire population.

The Ormée had never faced greater perils. However, if its enemies thought that it would now begin to waver, they were greatly disappointed. When the *curé* of St. Pierre urged his parishioners to overthrow the Ormée, he was ordered arrested—a fate he escaped only by fleeing the city. A number of similarly minded clerics followed his example, including the *curés* of St. Simon and St. Projet, the prior of the Jacobins, and the guardian of the Capucins.[75] We learn from a dispatch sent to Mazarin that the Ormée "intended henceforth to exclude all 'good bourgeois' from its ranks" and that Conty had served notice "on all those who lived in Bordeaux but who were originally from towns that opposed Bordeaux, to depart within 24 hours or be attacked on sight."[76] Measures also were taken in regard to the military situation. "A siege is expected," wrote the

---

[71] G.-J. Cosnac, *Souvenirs*, VI, Guron to Mazarin, February 13, 1653, *Archives historiques de la Gironde*, VII, 269.

[72] De Haes to Dubosq, January 23, 1653, *B.B.*, MS. fonds Itié, no folio number.

[73] De Haes to Dubosq, January 23, 1653, *B.B.*, MS. fonds Itié, no folio number.

[74] We learn that one-third of the Dutch ships left Bordeaux without any cargo. Unidentified letter to Mazarin, February 10, 1653, *Archives historiques de la Gironde*, VII, 268.

[75] G.-J. Cosnac, *Souvenirs*, VI, 36–37.

[76] Unidentified letter to Mazarin, February 10, 1653, *Archives historiques de la Gironde*, VII, 266, 267–68.

same correspondent, "and this explains the construction of fortifications."[77]

Thus, far from faltering, the Ormée seemed as determined as ever to maintain its rule. The baptism of Condé's son, born on the 18th of February, was the occasion for a reaffirmation of Ormist principles.

The lawyers, judge and consuls [of the *Bourse*], joined by a large number of bourgeois, had gathered at the *Hôtel de Ville* to march with the *jurats* to the cathedral of St. André. Just as they were to depart, the Ormée sent word that they could not permit lawyers and bourgeois to march as one body; that they constituted the only legitimate body in the city inasmuch as their members came from all of the orders; that even if the *Parlement* was there, they would not allow it to march except as private persons indistinct from anyone else; that they were the sole rulers of the city and controlled all matters as in a republic; and that to enforce their will, they had placed a large number of armed men in the vicinity of the *Hôtel de Ville*. The lawyers, judge and consuls and the other bourgeois now turned to the *jurats* telling them that the moment had come for them to reassert their authority as all the companies of the city were under arms and only awaited the order to march and defeat the Ormée.[78]

When the *jurats* refused to give the requested order, the malcontents withdrew from the procession, leaving the Ormée to march alone. "At the ceremony," concludes the account, "the Ormée presented the Prince and Princesses with a branch of elm which each held in his hand."[79] The fact that the opposition had been so audacious as to stage an open display of its hostility to the Ormée can only have meant that it was again ready to rise. Indeed, one of Mazarin's correspondents noted:

It is certain that more than three quarters of the people in the city live only for the King and would like nothing better than to return to their duty. But they only dare to make known their sentiments privately and in a few secret assemblies. What they need is someone of authority to lead them. A revolt is sure to break out if the fleet remains in the river and close to Bordeaux, even though the Prince of Conty retains the loyalty of the *jurats*, the more militant Ormists, all the captains of the city, and the *juge de la Bourse*, whom they won over by promising him both the post of *jurat* and a sinecure for one of his children.[80]

[77] Unidentified letter to Mazarin, February 6, 1653, *ibid.*, p. 266.
[78] Unidentified letter to Mazarin, February 20, 1653, *ibid.*, pp. 273–74.
[79] *Ibid.*, p. 274.
[80] Unidentified letter to Mazarin, March 5, 1653, *A.N.*, KK 1220, fol. 21.

Conty was alarmed. On March 3, he informed his brother: "Conspiracies are resuming. I have never seen so much ill will as there is in this city."[81] And a few days later:

What surprises us is that everyone is clamoring for peace. Our old Ormée which used to show such fear every time its enemies—that is, the officers and the rich bourgeois—raised their heads, now tolerates their shouts for peace and still claims to be the master. We find such contradictory behavior most suspect.[82]

Another conspiracy was indeed afoot, but that Conty should have suspected the Ormée to be party to it is difficult to understand, especially as he had just joined the Ormée in ordering the militia to take to the streets and seize anyone who spoke of peace.[83] Had the Prince begun to look for a scapegoat?

Until then, all plots against the Ormée had originated in Bordeaux itself. This time the impulse came from the royal council, which in October of 1652 had resolved "to bring Bordeaux back to its duty and drive out those responsible for the rebellion." Père Berthod, a *Cordelier* monk, was dispatched to Bordeaux "with full powers to act as he saw fit."[84] Berthod reached his destination in late December, only to find that word of his mission had preceded his arrival. His reception did not augur well. "Upon learning of my arrival," he later wrote to Mazarin, "the Ormée decided that I was to be thrown into the river or into a dungeon."[85] After a number of interviews with Conty and Lenet who threatened him with an Ormée trial if he did not agree to work for the Princes, the priest succeeded in making his way out of Bordeaux.[86] The conspiracy, however, was not yet over. During his short stay in Bordeaux, Berthod had met a number of anti-Ormists including Père Ithier, guardian of the convent of the *Cordeliers* and a former confessor to the Queen Mother.[87] Now, from Blaye where he had fled, Berthod began to correspond with Ithier, and a new plot was hatched. Ithier informed Berthod that he had confided in Mère Angelique, the mother superior of the Carmelites, and that she had

---

[81] Conty to Condé, March 3, 1653, *A.C.*, MS. serie P, XIII, fol. 8.
[82] Conty to Condé, March 6, 1653, *A.C.*, MS. serie P, XIII, fol.9.
[83] *Ibid.*; unidentified letter to Mazarin, March 5, 1653, *A.N.*, KK 1220, fol. 21.
[84] Berthod, "Mémoires," p. 601.
[85] Berthod to Mazarin, December 18, 1653, *A.E.*, France, vol. 891, fol. 373.
[86] *Ibid.*, fol. 375; Berthod, "Mémoires," pp. 601-6.
[87] Pierre Cayrac, "Récit de la Fronde à Bordeaux," *Revue historique de Bordeaux*, XI, (1918) 236.

expressed the belief that Villars could be won over, as he had "spoken to his sister [a Carmelite nun] of his great disgust for the life he was leading." A meeting with Villars was even arranged, in which the Ormist made known his willingness to join the conspiracy but only on condition that he be given the sum of 30,000 *écus*, the post of *syndic* of the city, and a letter of acknowledgement from the King.[88]

This was all that Berthod needed to hear. He promptly returned to the Court "to inform the Queen, His Eminence, M. de Servien and M. Le Tellier of the things that were needed to restore Bordeaux to its loyalty."[89] Apprised of Villars' terms, Mazarin agreed to meet all the latter's demands. A royal letter was drafted which read:

Monsieur Pierre de Villars: learning of your good intentions for my service and knowing that you have rejected and are opposed to the proposition that a number of rebels have dared advance regarding the establishment of a republic in my city of Bordeaux . . . , I have wished to send you this letter as an expression of the debt I owe you.[90]

The rest of the letter was a confirmation of the agreement that Villars had made with Ithier. It closed with the words: "I shall never forget what you have done, Monsieur Pierre de Villars, and shall pray that God preserve you in His holy protection."[91]

Other measures were taken as well. A decree was promulgated that enjoined

. . . the bourgeois and inhabitants of Bordeaux . . . to take up arms, assemble and occupy all the necessary places, and fight all those who would oppose them; then to arrest the chiefs and all others of the rebellious party, convene the municipal governing body, and remove from office all *jurats*, captains, and officers of the city, appointing in their place individuals whose devotion to the King's cause is well known.[92]

In return, the King promised a general amnesty, the restoration of the *Bureau du Convoy* and the *Parlement*, the suppression of the surtax on wine, and permission "to collect from the inhabitants of the said city

[88] Berthod, "Mémoires," pp. 607–8.
[89] *Ibid.*, p. 608.
[90] Berthod, "Mémoires," p. 608.
[91] The King to Villars, no date, *Archives historiques de la Gironde*, XLI, 140.
[92] Order of the King to the inhabitants of Bordeaux, February 21, 1653, *B.N. MS. fonds français* 4186, fol. 74.

the sums that have been borrowed."[93] The last concession was evidently intended to reassure the merchants who had lent money to Condé.

When Berthod returned to Bordeaux on the 7th of March, he found the conspiracy much advanced. Ithier had reached an understanding with two merchants—his cousin Pierre Ithier and one Armentary— who, in return for 300 *écus*, had agreed to arm 400 men. Ithier had also been promised by René Le Roux, *receveur des tailles de l'élection de Condomois et Bazadois*, the sum of 90,000 *livres* to be used to finance the conspiracy. In addition, Villars had purchased enough guns to arm 60 peasants, and was at work winning over six leading Ormists, each of whom was to receive 1,000 *écus*. Only the role to be played by Vendôme's fleet still needed to be worked out. Berthod secretly repaired to Blaye where he was assured that the fleet would be at Lormont (1 km. from Bordeaux) on the 20th of March and that it would carry the forces necessary "to sustain the well-intentioned, in the event that they were repulsed by those loyal to the Princes."[94]

The conspirators drew up their final plans for the coup. After arresting Lenet, Villars was to seize the *Hôtel de Ville* and inform Conty that his safety in Bordeaux could no longer be assured. Monks and priests from the various religious houses would then take to the street with shouts of "peace" and "long live the King." Fires were to be started "to better surprise the inhabitants," and a number of gates secured through which the royal troops would enter. While all this was taking place the *parlementaires* still in Bordeaux were to be summoned to the *Palais* and there Berthod was to proclaim the terms of the King's peace.[95]

The plan was excellent in every way but one: it presupposed Villars' good faith, and Villars had disclosed everything to Conty. The news was promptly relayed to Condé. "We had long suspected Villars," Lenet wrote to the Prince, "now we know that he is with us. . . . Yesterday he and eight others of our friends from the Ormée joined M. de Marchin [Marsin], M. de Conty, Madame de Longueville and myself in taking all the necessary precautions. The affair is to erupt in three days."[96] On the 19th of March, Villars accompanied by the six Ormists ostensibly participating in the coup—Castaing, Taudin, Giraut, Crozillac, Blarru, and the

---

[93] *Ibid.*, fol. 75.
[94] Berthod, "Mémoires," p. 609.
[95] Berthod, "Mémoires," p. 609; Lenet, "Mémoires," p. 601.
[96] Lenet to Condé, March 20, 1653, *A.C.*, MS. serie P, XIII, fol. 19.

captain Le Rousseau—had a final interview with Ithier. They were given a few more details about the plot, and paid sums of 1,500 *livres* each. The next day Ithier was arrested.[97]

The conspiracy was now fully exposed. Much of what Ithier had to say was already well known, but there may have been a few unfamiliar details. Thus the monk reported "having heard of a number of other conspiratorial cabals in the city, the principal one being that led by *Sieur* de La Vie [*procureur général* of the *Parlement*] in which *Sieur* Masson [a bourgeois] is implicated, and another led by *Messieurs* de Gent [de Jean, father and son *conseillers* of the *Parlement*] of which Littery [Literie], son of a *procureur*, is also a ringleader, and that all have the support of M. *le président* d'Affis."[98] Pressed to declare the identity of the "*bons bourgeois*" involved in the plots, Ithier at first denied all knowledge of them, but finally admitted "having heard that the *Sieurs* Delamarre, Paul Lesville, Pissebeuf, and Mercier were among those well disposed."[99]

First interrogated by Conty, Ithier was next brought before the *Conseil de l'Ormée*—the assembly of five hundred. Berthod relates what transpired: "The one who acted as *procureur général* and who was an apothecary was for quartering the priest, then placing his limbs on top of the city's gates. One of the older *conseillers* who was a pastry maker urged that he be roasted alive. . . . A number of artisans, *conseillers* in this inequitous assembly, then proceeded to voice their opinion."[100] Once the deliberations of the *Conseil* were over, it was the turn of the Ormée senate—that is, the *Chambre de Trente*. Again we cite Berthod: "He was conducted before the senate of the Ormée which had that day been constituted into a council of war, where he was meted out a sentence that violated all legal norms— a sentence pronounced by false and incompetent judges, Huguenots, criminals, people with neither names nor character."[101] Before being thrown into a solitary cell where he would remain for the rest of his life, Ithier was to have his head shaved, be defrocked, and paraded through the city with a cord around his neck and holding a placard that read "traitor to the fatherland."[102] Although a harsh sentence, it was not harsh enough to

[97] Lenet, "Mémoires," p. 610; Berthod, "Mémoires," p. 609.
[98] Lenet, "Mémoires," pp. 600–1; Berthod, "Mémoires," p. 609.
[99] Lenet, "Mémoires," pp. 601–2.
[100] Berthod, "Mémoires," p. 611.
[101] *Ibid.*
[102] Daniel Cosnac, *Mémoires* (Paris, 1852), pp. 45–46; Lenet to Condé, March 27, 1653, *A.C.*, MS. serie P, XIII, fol. 30; Cayrac, "Récit de la Fronde à Bordeaux," p. 237.

satisfy the Ormée's rank and file. While the *Trente* was in session a mob was outside "howling that it would tear to pieces anyone who opposed the death penalty for the priest and that it would take up arms and push things to the last extremity."[103] We also learn that when Ithier was taken to the prison of the *Hôtel de Ville* he was followed by more than five hundred Ormists armed with muskets and halberds as well as by a multitude of lower types, all shouting "he must die."[104] Why then was Ithier not put to death?[105] The reason may have been purely self protective, as Lenet suggests: "Some Mazarinists have let it be known that if Père Ithier is put to death, the Court will do the same to all of Your Highness's adherents whom it holds prisoner."[106]

The arrest of Ithier was followed by that of the other conspirators: Pierre Ithier (who was made to endure the question), the *président* d'Affis, the *conseillers* de Jean and de Bordes, and the *curés* of Ste. Croix, St. Rémy, and St. Pierre. Le Roux and Armentary managed to escape, but their property was seized. And when the *Cordelier* friars went into the streets to demonstrate in favor of their imprisoned prior, fifty of their number were expelled from the city.[107]

Thus ended Ithier's conspiracy. The Ormée emerged victorious, but also aware of how close it had come to being destroyed. Perhaps for the first time it had a vision of ultimate defeat. "The Ormée is going to be reformed," Lenet wrote a few days after the undoing of the plot,

and the Mazarinists who have managed to slip in are going to be driven out. Whatever their position or standing, all those who have taken part in past conspiracies and who might decide to take part in future ones will be expelled or imprisoned. Measures will be taken to prevent such things from happening again, even contracting an alliance with the Turk if it will save us from falling into the clutches of these traitors.[108]

[103] Lenet to Condé, March 24, 1653, in G.-J. Cosnac, *Souvenirs*, VI, 186.

[104] Berthod, "Mémoires," p. 611.

[105] Of the sixty Ormists who judged Ithier only three voted to put him to death. Unidentified letter to Mazarin, March 28, 1653, *Archives historiques de la Gironde*, VII, fol. 312.

[106] Lenet to Condé, March 24, 1653, in G.-J. Cosnac, *Souvenirs*, VI, 189.

[107] Unidentified letter to Mazarin, March 24, 1653, *Archives historiques de la Gironde*, VII, 305; Lenet to Condé, March 27, 1653, *A.C.*, MS. serie P, XIII, fol. 30; Lenet to Condé, March 24, 1653, in G.-J. Cosnac, *Souvenirs*, VI, 185–89; Daniel Cosnac, *Mémoires*, p. 46.

[108] Lenet to Condé, March 24, 1653, in G.-J. Cosnac, *Souvenirs*, VI, 187.

And again:

> We are going to expel monks and nuns and one hundred or two hundred families and are going to purge the Ormée. We are also going to send *Messieurs* de Trancars, *conseiller*, and Labadie [a Protestant minister] to England to demand help.[109]

And so out of the Ithier affair had come the decision to appeal for English assistance. As with the *Parlement* which had realized that to defeat its enemies it would have to nationalize the struggle—that is, enlist the support of the Crown—the Ormée now saw that everything depended on its ability to expand the struggle beyond the ineffectual Spanish alliance. What could be more natural than for the Ormée to seek the support of revolutionary England, especially as the latter had already given signs of being well disposed to the regime?

On the 4th of April the Ormée issued the following decree:

> *Messrs.* de Trancars, *conseiller* of the *Parlement* and bourgeois of Bordeaux, de Blarru, and Dezert, both bourgeois of Bordeaux, will make their way to London and seek to obtain from the gentlemen of the Parliament of the Republic of England all assistance in men, ships and money deemed necessary to preserve Bordeaux and the province of Guyenne and to restore the ancient privileges.[110]

The decree was signed by Conty, Marsin, Lenet and the entire Ormée leadership. Four days later, the envoys were presented with a series of "Instructions." In return for their aid, which was to be both economic and military, the English were to be offered a port—Arcachon, Blaye, and Royan were among those mentioned—and given a monopoly in the wine trade. There was also the hint of a forthcoming change in Bordeaux's relation to England. The "Instructions" made known that any decision on the future political status of the city would have to await the arrival of the requested aid,[111] and a letter which the envoys were to present to the Council of State concluded with the words: "[The Bordelais intend] . . . to recover the liberties and privileges previously won by the glorious exploits of the English Nation. . . . The men, vessels, money, wheat, and other things which they presently need will be returned to their saviors with

---

[109] Lenet to Condé, March 24, 1653, in d'Aumale, *Histoire*, VI, 641.
[110] Lenet, "Mémoires," p. 605.
[111] *Ibid.*, p. 604.

all conceivable gratitude."[112] Was the Ormée holding out the possibility of a return to the *status quo ante* 1453, when Bordeaux had belonged to the "English Nation"?

However attractive the Ormée's terms may have been, nothing was to come of them. Even before the mission had reached London, some already doubted its success. On May 17, the Venetian ambassador to England wrote to his counterpart in France:

Four delegates from the four orders of the city of Bordeaux are expected here daily on a solemn mission. Under the pretence of trade it is said that they will aim at establishing a good friendship and correspondence between that city and this commonwealth, being chiefly anxious to get help against the royal forces which now threaten that province. The embassy will certainly have a friendly reception, though it is considered unlikely that they will get any help because of the state of affairs here and with the presence of M. de Bordeaux [the French ambassador to England] here, if anything is done for the insurgents it will be under cover of the wine trade, so necessary to England.[113]

Three weeks later he had not changed his mind:

These delegates had audience of the Council of State, [where] they only got fair words, and although they press for an immediate decision, since their affairs at Bordeaux do not permit them to stay long, this does not make them hurry here, and the general belief is that little or nothing will be done for them, since conditions here do not admit of sending troops or other assistance so soon as it is desired.[114]

The Ormée's emissaries were to have numerous audiences with Cromwell and with the Council of State, but all proved fruitless.[115] The future Lord Protector apparently had no intention of coming to the aid of the beleaguered city: at war with the Dutch, he simply did not want France to ally herself with his enemies, and used the threat of intervention only to prevent this from happening. The maneuver succeeded perfectly, as we learn from a dispatch of the Venetian ambassador to France:

The Cardinal entertains some apprehension that the English may finally yield

[112] Letter to the *Conseil d'Etat*, no date, B.N., MS. fonds français 11633, fol. 9, 157–58.
[113] Paulucci to Sagredo, May 17, 1653, *Calendar of State Papers . . . of Venice*, ed. Allen B. Hinds, XXIX, (1653-1654), 73.
[114] Paulucci to Sagredo, June 6, 1653, *ibid.*, p. 82.
[115] Knachel, *England and the Fronde*, pp. 203–4.

to the persuasions of the deputies of Bordeaux, who are now in London. With respect to the embarkation of 4,000 men in England these last days, it is suspected, from the smallness of the number, that they cannot be intended to go to Holland, and they are appealing to the minister in London to prevent a step which would be most prejudicial to France, both in itself and because of the consequences.[116]

The failure of the mission to England proved to have far-reaching consequences for Bordeaux. Left to its own devices, the city would struggle a few more months and then capitulate. But no less consequential was its effect on the Ormée's ideological development. The Ormée, as we have seen, had begun to move in the direction of republicanism. In January of 1653, Lenet could write: "Everyone favors the establishment of a republic [*tous ont l'esprit de république*] for there is so much fear of what the future will bring that these people will turn to anything."[117] In February, the Duke of St. Simon, governor of Blaye, noted in a report to Mazarin: "The news is that Bordeaux has decided to establish a republic. Montauban and La Rochelle are in on the plot which is supposed to take place toward the end of March, when a powerful English force will arrive. . . . The Huguenots, according to our source, are the principal authors of this conspiracy. . . . A plan is afoot to chase M. le Prince de Conty out of Bordeaux."[118] Three months later St. Simon's position had not changed: "I have it on good authority that the strongest and most skilled faction in Bordeaux favors a republic. It is this group which has sent the embassy to England to obtain assistance and support."[119]

Had the decision to turn to England then been the work of republicans? Guron, the bishop of Tulle and one of Mazarin's most trusted informants, thought so. He wrote to the Cardinal:

Last Monday M. le Prince de Conty convened a great council, in order to satisfy the Bordelais who are presently divided into two factions: one, led by Villars and Dureteste, looks to Spain; the other, consisting of elements of the Ormée and of most of the Huguenots, contends that since nothing is to be expected from the Spaniards who are deceiving them, the city should turn to the English republic which would not fail to give them prompt aid. . . .

[116] Sagredo to the Doge and Senate, July 8, 1653, *Calendar of State Papers . . . of Venice, XXIX (1653–1654)*, 95.

[117] Lenet to Condé, January 13, 1653, in G.-J. Cosnac, *Souvenirs*, VI, 18.

[118] St. Simon to Mazarin, February ?, 1653, *Archives historiques de la Gironde*, VII, 264–65.

[119] St. Simon to Mazarin, May 23, 1653, *A.E.*, France, vol. 891, fol. 136.

The latter faction appears to be the stronger: it speaks more boldly and has even proposed the establishment of a republic. As a result M. le Prince de Conty, who is afraid of this last development, announced to the Council that those who favored demanding help from England would be permitted to do so, provided that they cease talking of a republic. His qualification was accepted, as it is a matter of indifference to them if the establishment of a republic is openly advocated or not, as their envoys will be given secret instructions to that effect.[120]

One is surprised to learn that Villars and Dureteste were opposed to the English connection, as both had signed the decree sending the envoys to England. The rest of the letter, however, conformed to what St. Simon and Lenet had noted: that the majority of the Ormée favored the establishment of a republic, and that it was this faction that had been instrumental in seeking an English alliance. The secret instructions alluded to by Guron may have been the "Instructions" mentioned earlier, which read in part:

They [Cromwell and the English Parliament] will no doubt propose that Bordeaux accept an altogether new form of government, and that the city join with those of the [Protestant] religion in affirming their common liberty, in which case it will be very proper to reply that they [the Bordelais] only await the appearance of an English army in the Garonne to proclaim the liberty of the city and adopt the [political] forms and actions needed to preserve it, even at the risk of their lives and fortunes.[121]

It could not have been stated more plainly: Bordeaux would become a republic if England guaranteed her survival. Again everything depended on Cromwell's decision—a decision which, when it came, reflected an attachment not to ideological or religious principles, but to England's national interest. And so in the end it was *raison d'état* that proved the undoing of Ormée republicanism, as indeed of the Ormée itself.

[120] Guron to Mazarin, May 17, 1653, *Archives historiques de la Gironde*, VIII, 153–54.
[121] Lenet, "Mémoires," p. 604.

VI

THE ORMÉE IN POWER:
THE SOCIAL CONSEQUENCES

AN ANALYSIS OF ORMÉE RULE must, above all, take into account the social developments that attended that rule. For while the Ormée was intent on transforming political forms, it was even more intent on altering the pattern of social relationships. The officers of the *Parlement* were to be deprived of their privileges, the royal agents of their fiscal power, the merchants of their wealth—such had been the call of the *Apologie pour l'Ormée*, of the *Histoire véritable d'une colombe,* and of other Ormée tracts. But more was envisioned: once shorn of their social and economic advantages, the ruling oligarchies of wealth and office would be eliminated from public life and their places taken by the lower classes, Bordeaux's long-suffering *menu peuple*. This, then, was the Ormée's social objective. How well it was realized—whether, indeed, it was realized at all—we must now consider.

Among the Ormée's enemies none came to suffer more than the members of the *Parlement*. Of seventy-four officers sitting in the *Parlement* in 1651,[1] only ten remained in Bordeaux when the city capitulated two years later:[2] most had fled, but eight had been arrested and imprisoned,[3] and

---

[1] Registres du Parlement, 1651–58, fols. 6–8.

[2] Trancars, d'Espagnet, Raymond, Mestiviers, Duduc, Lachèze, Grimard, d'Alesme, Fayard, Massip. Gabriel-Jules de Cosnac, *Souvenirs du règne de Louis XIV* (Paris, 1866–82), V, 318; VII, 105; *Journal de Filhot*, p. 126.

[3] D'Affis, de Jean, Bordes, Phelibert Dussault, Castelnau, Mousnier, de Gourgues, Massiot; *Journal de Filhot*, p. 184. Unidentified letter to Mazarin, March 24, 1653, *Archives historiques de la Gironde*, VII, 305; Lenet to Condé, June 26, 1653, in G.-J. Cosnac, *Souvenirs*, VII, 221–22; Lenet to Condé, March 24, 1653, *ibid.*, VI, 185–86; *ibid.*, p. 161; B.N., MS. fonds français 18752, fols. 474–75.

twenty-six forcefully expelled.[4] Ormée mobs sacked or put to the torch the town houses of such *parlementaires* as La Roche, Mestivier, Dussault (a *conseiller* of the *Présidial* and son of the *avocat-général*), Pichon, and Pontac.[5] The last, a *président* of the *Parlement* as well as *intendant* of finance in the army of Guyenne, complained to Mazarin that because of sums he had advanced to the royal government, and "the loss of my possessions and the income from my charges that have resulted from the rebellion," he was now a ruined man.[6] Pontac was certainly exaggerating —it is difficult to believe that one occupying so lucrative a position in the financial administration could have fallen into such dire straits—but there can be little doubt that he and his colleagues had suffered great losses at the hands of the Ormée. For not only had they been deprived of their possessions—it was the Ormée's policy to sequestrate the property of those who opposed the regime[7]—but having been ousted from the *Chambre de Direction*, they could no longer compensate themselves for services previously rendered.[8]

Financial persecution could take an even more direct form. One thousands *livres* was extorted from Jolly, an officer in the *Parlement*'s chancellery.[9] Massiot, a *conseiller* of the *Parlement*, was visited by a deputation of Ormists and duly warned that, unless he paid a pension to a certain convent, "they would know how to take the money from him by force." On another occasion, Massiot was accosted by a representative of Villars and ordered to hand over five hundred *livres*.[10] *Parlementaires* who chose to flee might escape extortion, but not outright thievery. The *conseiller* Montaigne charged in a notarial brief filed after the Ormée's suppression

[4] De Moneins (father and son), Salomon (father and son), d'Arche, Gaston, Montesquieu, Dubernet, la Roche, Pontac, Primet, Pichon, Pomiers de Sauvac, Pomiers de François, Pichon Muscadet, Duzeste, Sabourin (father and son), Martin, du Bourg, la Croix Maron, Lescure, Mirat, le Blanc, du Mont. Registres du Parlement, 1651–58, fols. 71–72; *Journal de tout ce qui s'est passé à Bordeaux depuis le 1er Juin jusques à present* (Paris, 1652), p. 7. Lenet to Condé, December 5, 1652, in Lenet, "Mémoires," p. 591.
[5] G.-J. Cosnac, *Souvenirs*, VI, 16; VII, 94; Lenet to Condé, July 3, 1653, in G.-J. Cosnac, *Souvenirs*, VII, 266; see Chapter II, above.
[6] Pontac to Mazarin, December, 1652, *Archives historiques de la Gironde*, VIII, 426.
[7] Unidentified letter to Vendôme, June 6, 1653, *Archives historiques de la Gironde*, VIII, 439. The Ormée even considered imposing a tax on all officers who withdrew from the city, but whether this was actually done is not known. Lenet to Condé, April 24, 1653, in G.-J. Cosnac, *Souvenirs*, VI, 407.
[8] See Chapter IV, above.
[9] Letter to Condé, August 22, 1652, in G.-J. Cosnac, *Souvenirs*, V, 10.
[10] Registres du Parlement, 1651–58, fol. 199.

that, "taking advantage of the prevailing disorders," one Anthoine Lababaille, "master baker of the present city and former captain [of the Ormée] had, on his own authority, seized a vineyard belonging to the said Montaigne."[11] And the *président* Lalanne complained to Mazarin "of the disorders that I discovered in my affairs upon my return to Bordeaux . . . notably that some of my servants, taking advantage of the prevailing disturbances and the weakness of my mother . . . had absconded with all her possessions."[12]

A letter written in exile by the *président* Pichon to the wife of *président* d'Affis casts light on the state of mind of the persecuted:

The apprehensions and continual alarms of my wife oblige me to request your consent to her departure from the city, for I would not wish to impose on your kindness by having her remain longer with you during so harsh a time as the present one . . . . As one is not able to write freely, surrounded as one is on all sides with spies, I tremble each time I take up the pen, not for my safety, but for the safety of those to whom I write. Since everything is always interpreted in the worst sense, I am only seeking to prevent accidents from taking place. I trust to God that my wife's departure be prompt and that we shall soon have peace.[13]

Contributing largely to the "apprehensions and continual alarms" of the parlementary party was the fact that it could no longer count on the *Parlement* for legal protection. Thus when the wife of the *conseiller* Suduiraut learned "of a certain appointment obtained against her in the Chamber of the Council of the *Présidial*" (a court now serving at the Ormée's pleasure), she could do nothing more than file a notarial brief "opposing" the action.[14] Similarly, when François Liraudein, *avocat au Parlement*, was assailed by Jehan Laurens, "one of the Ormée's oldest and most assiduous members" and threatened with a trial before the *Chambre de Trente*, he could only protest that the Ormée "had no legitimate jurisdiction, whether civil or criminal, over him or anyone else" and that he did not recognize any legal powers "other than the true and natural ones, established by the King before which he intended, as soon as events began to improve, to press for the punishment of all the crimes and excesses com-

---

[11] *A.G.*, 3E 4320, fol. 949.
[12] Lalanne to Mazarin, April 26, 1654, *B.N.*, MS. fonds français 11633, fol. 241.
[13] Pichon to Madame d'Affis, April 12, 1653, *B.B.*, MS. fonds Itié.
[14] *A.G.*, 3E 10.945, fol. 263.

mitted against his person."[15] And when Pailler, another *avocat*, informed his notary that one Pierre Labat, "in the company of numerous other persons had entered his house with the intention of murdering him" and killed his servant, he could only add that he would take appropriate action "at the time and place of his choosing."[16]

Parlementaires (or their relatives) may have carried the brunt of the Ormée's repressive measures but other segments of the legal oligarchy— the officers of the other sovereign courts as well as lower officials of the *Parlement*—were not overlooked. Early in 1653, the Ormée ordered the officers of the *Cour des Aides* "together with all other suspects . . . to leave the city within twenty-four hours or run the risk of being prosecuted as disturbers of the public peace."[17] The order was obeyed but with great protestations. Wrote one of the intended victims: "I was scandalized by what appeared to be a repetition of the unjust procedures that had been followed against the first Christians who were persecuted not for what they had done but because of who they were, who were put to death not for having been criminals but for having been Christians."[18] In contrast to what befell the *Cour des Aides*, there was no mass exile of the lower officials of the judiciary. A number of them, however, was arrested including Raymond Literie, *procureur en la cour du Parlement et auditeur des comptes*, for having participated in Ithier's conspiracy;[19] Guillaume David, another *procureur of the Parlement*, for plotting against the Ormée;[20] and Jean de Raymond, *greffier de l'audience de la Cour des Aides* who, in the waning days of the Ormée's rule, attempted to turn the *Hôtel de Ville* over to the *"bons bourgeois."*[21] A higher price was paid by Chevalier, an *avocat* and son of a *procureur*, who was found carrying papers for Candalle and summarily executed.[22] The four had thus been guilty of counter-Ormist activities. Unlike the treatment accorded the officers of the *Cour des Aides*, the Ormée had turned against these lower functionaries not because of

[15] *A.G.*, 3E 10.787, fol. 469.
[16] *A.G.*, 3E 24.802, fol. 951.
[17] *L'exile de l'inconnu, dédié aux exilés de la ville de Bordeaux* (Paris, 1653), p. 13.
[18] *Ibid.*
[19] Unidentified letter to Mazarin, March 24, 1653, *Archives historiques de la Gironde*, VII, 305; *A.G.*, Livre de l'escroue de la maison commune de la présente ville, March 22, 1653, fol. 111.
[20] *Journal de Filhot*, pp. 108, 111; Lenet to Condé, June 26, 1653, *B.N.*, MS. fonds français 6715, fol. 228.
[21] *Journal de Filhot*, p. 146; G.-J. Cosnac, *Souvenirs*, VII, 191–92.
[22] *Journal de Filhot*, pp. 180–81; G.-J. Cosnac, *Souvenirs*, VII, 192.

"who they were" (many ardently supported the Ormée and were in turn supported by the latter), but because of "what they had done."

The assault on the legal oligarchy in itself constituted a revolutionary action. But the Ormée extended the scope of this endeavor by attacking the agents of the royal fisc. Among its targets was the *Bureau de Finance*, the body which collected all direct taxes in Guyenne. Filhot has left the following account of its treatment: "Numerous treasurers of France who had always shown much zeal in the service of the King suffered injuries both to their persons and possessions, among them *Monsieur* de Richon [*trésorier général des finances*] who was arrested and held for ransom."[23] The *Bureau* eventually moved to Agen, but even this did not mark the end of its misfortunes, as the following, written by one of its officers, indicates: "Our willingness to obey the orders of the King has so incited the Ormée against us that not a day passes that we do not learn of some new act of violence directed against our possessions and families."[24]

Numerous other fiscal officials were arrested or banished from the city, including Latouche, *visiteur du Convoy*, for having written an incriminating letter[25] (the *Bureau du Convoy*, it will be recalled, had been sacked during the June days); Gelon, *receveur de la connétablie*, who, Lenet noted, "has been active in every conspiracy against us";[26] and Jean Roux, *conseiller du roy et receveur des tailles de Guyenne*, René Le Roux, *receveur des tailles de l'élection de Condomois et Bazadois*, and Jacques Filhot, *trésorier général de Montauban*, all for having participated in various plots against the Ormée.[27]

Still another group to feel the effects of the Ormée's wrath was Bordeaux's mercantile element. It will be recalled that during the uprising of June, 1652, the merchant's quarter had been invaded, individual merchants had been assaulted, and business establishments had been sacked.[28] In the face of these attacks, merchants had begun to leave the city. "The city grows desolate," a former *jurat* observed shortly after the Ormée's victory, "many '*bons bourgeois*,' uncertain of what will befall them, have sent their plates to the mint and are fleeing."[29] Flight was not always possible,

[23] *Journal de Filhot*, p.184.

[24] Letter to the officers of the *Bureau de Finance*, no date, B.N., MS. fonds français 11633, fol. 154.

[25] *Journal de Filhot*, p. 181.

[26] Lenet to Condé, January 13, 1653, in G.-J. Cosnac, *Souvenirs*, VI, 20.

[27] *Journal de Filhot*, pp. 111, 179; Livre de l'escroue, June 25, 1653, fol. 218; Lenet to Condé, June 26, 1653, B.N., MS. fonds français 6715, fol. 228.

[28] See Chapter II, above.

[29] Unidentified letter to Condé, July 1, 1652, d'Aumale, *Histoire des Princes de Condé pendant le XVIe et XVIIe siècles* (Paris, 1863–96), VI, 631.

however. In a manifesto issued in July of 1652, the Ormée called for the arrest of Guiraut and Fontenel, both *jurats*, and of du Cornet, Roquette and Tillet, officers of the militia and leading bourgeois.[30] Later, other arrests were ordered including those of Le Blanc Mauvesin, *procureur syndic*;[31] Pierre Armentary, "one of the richest merchants of St. Michel";[32] and Pierre Ithier, merchant and relative of Père Ithier.[33]

As with the *parlementaires*, merchants not arrested or forced to flee were subjected to economic harassment. In October of 1652, the Ormée moved to dissolve the guild of *courtiers* and to assume its functions.[34] Grain merchants feared an even harsher fate: Mazarin received word in August of 1652, that the Ormée was about "to consider the price of wheat, which has begun to rise sharply. They intend to fix its price, and throw into the river any merchant who does not abide by their decision."[35] These moves were only the prelude to a concerted attack on all commercial activity. Lenet wrote in November: "The most bizarre schemes are aired daily in the Ormée, whose outcome we hope to avoid as long as possible. They wish to restrict all trade."[36] What form these restrictions took is revealed in a letter written by a merchant of Rotterdam to his agent in Bordeaux: "I am truly distressed to hear of the disorders that are taking place. You inform me that the Ormée has placed a ban on the shipment of wines from the upper country, and that only wine from the Graves region may be exported."[37] The letter had been written in January of 1653; six months later, it was no longer possible to export any wine at all. A merchant from Brest disclosed in a notarial brief that he had "purchased a certain quantity of wine in the city thinking he would be allowed to load it aboard his vessel in accordance with the permission granted him by His Highness the Prince of Conty on June twenty-seven last [1653]. But because of the opposition of the people and of the bourgeois of the Ormée, he has been forced to relinquish this undertaking."[38]

The Ormée did not only act to curb mercantile activity. Possessing the requisite legal and political machinery, it could also proceed against

---

[30] *Extrait de tout ce qui s'est fait et passé à Bordeaux depuis le 29 juin 1652* (Paris, 1652).
[31] Lenet to Condé, December 5, 1652, 1652, Lenet, "Mémoires," p. 592.
[32] *Journal de Filhot*, p. 179.
[33] *A.G.*, Livre de l'escroue, fols, 65, 192.
[34] Lenet to Condé, October 31, 1652, in G.-J. Cosnac, *Souvenirs*, V, 184.
[35] Unidentified letter to Mazarin, August 12, 1652, *Archives historiques de la Gironde*, VIII, 406.
[36] Lenet to Condé, November 14, 1652, in G.-J. Cosnac, *Souvenirs*, V, 186.
[37] De Haes to Dubosq, January 23, 1653, *B.B.*, MS. fonds Itié, no folio no.
[38] *A.G.*, 3E 4369, fol. 115.

individual merchants as the notarial records again demonstrate. Thus Jean du Laurans, merchant and former *consul* of the *Bourse* testified

. . . that from the 8th of the present month and year [June, 1653] he had been repeatedly persecuted and tormented by Pierre Cayrac and [Guillaume] . . . Tauzin . . . both captains of the present city, with the end of obtaining his signature to certain pretended resolutions and deputations which they had drafted and were about to dispatch to England with M. Trancars, *conseiller du roy en la cour*, the said Blarru, Dezert, and one other. Upon adamantly refusing to commit an act so contrary to his will and conscience, the said Cayrac and Tauzin had warned du Laurans that he and his entire family would be thrown into prison if he did not sign the documents, and that he was jeopardizing everything including his life. . . . [On another visit] Cayrac and Tauzin had employed great force and violence against him, even pointing a pistol at his throat, and thus constrained the said du Laurans to sign the two pretended acts in question.[39]

The attack upon du Laurans had been politically motivated; in the case of other merchants, the attacks had a more personal basis. Pierre Manpetit, one of Bordeaux's wealthiest merchants, described how Gabriel Chartran, *juge* of the county of Ornon (a dependency of Bordeaux) had had him summoned before the Ormée

. . . presumably to have their case adjudicated or to have the sentence that the said Manpetit had obtained from the *Parlement* revoked. But when he appeared before the so-called Union of the Ormée, he was asked whether or not he had signed the covenant and general evocation, and replying in the negative, was presented with the two registries and told that he would not be heard until he had affixed his name to both. This he had at first refused to do, but being threatened with immediate expulsion from the city, he had finally signed the documents in question. He now declared his signature as well as the prejudicial sentence given against him by Rocque and Bastide [the two Ormée arbitrators] null and void.[40]

Claude Godière, merchant, had a similar experience. He declared before his notary that

. . . because he had always preserved in his heart and demonstrated through his actions the loyalty that is owed to the King's cause—as indeed have numerous other good bourgeois of this city—he had incurred the wrath of the

[39] *A.G.*, 3E 12,354, fol. 881.
[40] *A.G.*, 3E 10.945, fol. 107.

Ormée party; that, when his enemies had seen him held in such aversion by the party, they had taken advantage of the occasion to obtain through force what they should have obtained only through justice; that among his enemies was Martin d'Arnault du Pierron, one the principal leaders of the party who often assumed the role of president and chief administrator, who had ordered the said Godière's grape harvesters not to abide by a decree of the *Parlement* of Bordeaux that enjoined the said d'Arnault not to trouble the other in the enjoyment of his possessions; that thereupon, the assembly of the Ormée had decreed that armed assistance be given the said d'Arnault to enable him to carry off the fruits in question, which loss the said Godière had been constrained to suffer in the absence of free justice or officers able to receive his plaint.[41]

Godière was engaged in a dispute with still another Ormist, as the rest of the deposition indicates:

He has this very day been persecuted in the same assembly by Jean Loignon, a captain of the Ormée, who compelled him to accept as arbitrators and adjudicators of their dispute the *Sieurs* Dureteste and Crozillac, two of the principal leaders of the Ormée who stand ever ready to support the members of their party [*qui n'oublient rien pour ceux qui sont dans leur Union*] . . . . He agreed to the ruling of the said assembly and accepted the arbitration of the said Dureteste and Crozillac, but only out of fear for his person and possessions, as he has already received a number of visits from diverse individuals they call commissioners . . . whose threats and other actions strike terror even into the hardiest souls.[42]

Godière must have procrastinated, for a few days later he was visited by Loignon. This incident and the subsequent events are described in another brief:

This morning Jean Loignon, captain of the Ormée, taking advantage of his position and of the prevailing disorders, entered his house at the head of 12 or 15 guards allegedly of Villars's company, all armed with swords and pistols, with the intention of obtaining money from him. After subjecting him to untold outrages and violences, including the seizure of various objects, they forcibly took him to the Chamber they call The Twelve of their Union, where he found himself in the presence of diverse personages unknown to him, who with the said Loignon and others of his band obliged him to sign an agreement stipulating that their differences would be resolved through arbitration

---

[41] *A.G.*, 3E 2448, fol. 938.
[42] *Ibid.*

and that he would turn over to Loignon the sum of ten *livres*. . . . All of this he was constrained to do, but he reserved the right to challenge an agreement extracted from him by force of arms . . . at such time as authentic justice, for the moment suppressed, shall have been restored.[43]

Other examples of Ormée justice may be cited: Alphonse Romerd, *bourgeois et marchand* residing in the parish of St. Eloy (next to St. Pierre the wealthiest parish in Bordeaux) testified that

. . . in consequence of the sentence handed down by the *Présidial* court of Guyenne, reported by M. Dusau [Dussault], *conseiller* of the same, on the 4th of January last [1653] and of the supporting ordinance of the Chamber of Twelve of the Ormée issued on the 26th of the present month and signed by Texier, clerk, terminating his dispute with Jean Prélat, bourgeois of Bordeaux, he had paid to the said Prélat the seventy-four *livres* of rent in question in order to avoid the confiscation of his goods and his imprisonment.[44]

The wife of Pierre du Bosq, a merchant accused of having left Bordeaux to plot with the enemy, registered her opposition

. . . to an appointment given by the lieutenant general of Guyenne [no doubt with the concurrence of the Ormée], dated the 6th of the present month, stipulating among other things that the said du Bosq, her husband, would be required to assume the duties of guardian of the children of the late Jacques Berthet . . . [and this although] the said du Bosq has long been absent from the city as the entire neighborhood will vouch, the present troubles and other difficulties having forced him to depart.[45]

Similarly, Pierre Lauretan, *bourgeois et marchand*, declared his opposition

. . . to a certain appointment obtained against him by Silvestre Ciraq, merchant of Bordeaux, empowering the last named to seize two dozen of his cask hoops valued at 3 *sols* the hoop. He had appealed this action of *Messieurs les juges et consuls de la Bourse* [to the *Parlement?*], but the said Ciraq insisted on receiving the full complement of hoops by reason of the said appointment and of an ordinance of *Messieurs de l'Ormière*.[46]

Thus with the exception of Ciraq — who, it should be noted, had been an early supporter of the Ormée[47]—not a single merchant had managed to

[43] *A.G.*, 3E 2448, fol. 945.
[44] *A.G.*, 3E, 4320, fol. 766.
[45] *A.G.*, 3E 4320, fol. 832.
[46] *A.G.*, 3E 767, fol. 831.
[47] Ciraq to Dubosq, June 27, 1652, *B.B.*, MS. fonds Itié.

obtain the Ormée's protection. It is not difficult to understand why individuals such as Godière should have longed for the restoration of "authentic justice."

Having considered the Ormée's relation to Bordeaux's notables, we wish next to consider its attitude to the rest of society, and especially to the lower classes. Itself belonging to the lower classes, the Ormée's conduct vis-à-vis this element should provide further insight into the movement's underlying aims while illuminating the social aspects of the struggle being waged. For if the Ormèe's hostility, rather than being indiscriminate, was in fact restricted to a single segment of society, then its actions cease to be idiosyncratic (as Kossmann maintains)[48] and become the manifestation of class insurgency. The question of the Ormée's treatment of the lower classes—that is, of the minor clergy, the petty functionaries, the shopkeepers, the artisans, and those of even more modest standing—must therefore receive the closest scrutiny.

Clerics who opposed the Ormée suffered the same fate as the other enemies of the regime. The Ormée arrested or expelled the *curés* of St. Rémy, Ste. Croix, St. Pierre, St. Simon, and St. Projet; the prior of the *Jacobins*; the guardian of the *Capucins*; the provincial overseer of the *Feuillants;* and fifty *Cordelier* friars.[49] However, not all clerics opposed the Ormée, and those who didn't or who actually supported the rebellion —one can mention the Protestant pastors,[50] the Jesuits, the *Minimes*, the *Pères de la Merci*, as well as a number of parish priests—were left in peace and in some instances liberally rewarded.[51] Thus Gay, a priest who had been one of the first to join the insurrection, was granted the title of Ormée chaplain, *Aumonier de l'Ormée*.[52] Du Fresne, a Jesuit, described by one of Mazarin's agents as a "fanatic rebel," received the parish of St. Pierre. Two *Cordeliers* "cut out of the same cloth" (the reference is to

[48] Ernst Kossmann, *La Fronde* (Leiden, 1954), pp. 245–55.

[49] Lenet to Condé, December 5, 1652, in Lenet, "Mémoires," p. 592; Lenet to Condé, January 30, 1653, in G.-J. Cosnac, *Souvenirs*, VI, 37; Lenet to Condé, March 24, 1653, *ibid.*, p. 189; Lenet to Condé, March 27, 1653, *A.C.*, serie P, XIII, fol. 30; *A.G.*, Livre de l'escroue, fol. 111. *Journal de Filhot*, p. 113.

[50] The relation between the Ormée and Bordeaux's Huguenots is not very clear, but there can be little doubt that the latter supported the rebellion, if only tacitly, and that the Ormée was well disposed toward them. Kossmann, *La Fronde*, pp. 247–48.

[51] Unidentified letter to Mazarin, March 24, 1653, *Archives historiques de la Gironde*, VII, 305; Lenet "*Mémoires*," p. 601.

[52] Ernest Labadie, *Nouveau supplément à la bibliographie des Mazarinades* (Paris, 1904), no. 126.

du Fresne) advanced to the pulpits of St. Rémy and St. Projet, whose regular priests had been expelled from the city.[53] Père Romain, *Correcteur des Minimes*, and Frère Jean Gilles Joly, a member of the same order, were reported to have "intrigued themselves in the affairs of Milord the Prince of Conty . . . and to have done everything in their power to preserve the people in a state of rebellion," although what they gained from this action is not made clear.[54]

Why had some clerics rallied to the Ormée, while so many others remained its implacable foes? Political loyalties provide part of the answer. The *Cordeliers* were staunch advocates of the royal cause, while the Jesuits were enemies of Mazarin and, with their Spanish connection, of the Bourbon dynasty as well.[55] The Jesuits had still another reason for siding with the Ormée, for the *Oratoriens*, a rival teaching order, supported Mazarin.[56]

Political ties and religious rivalries do not suffice to explain the clerical divisions, inasmuch as a number of orders were themselves torn by division. Thus Mazarin was urged to have the *Cordeliers* expelled from Bordeaux and have their places taken by friars "not badly disposed toward us"[57]—an indication that the order was not without its recalcitrant members. Indeed, while fifty *Cordeliers* were ousted from the city by the Ormée, two were held in sufficiently high esteem, as we have seen, to be given parishes. Had these and other clerics then thrown their support to the Ormée in the hope of gaining some desired preferments? Père Galtery, a *Cordelier* with close ties to Conty and possibly to the Ormée, was accused by the superior of his order of

. . . having forgotten his profession and having committed acts of unheard of violence within as well as outside his monastery, all prompted by considerations of ambition and shameful avarice, namely that he aspired to become guardian of the Bordeaux monastery and provincial father of the Order without regard for the wishes of our assembly and in direct contravention of the constitution and the laws of the Church.[58]

[53] Bourgeon to Mazarin January 5, 1653, *A.E.*, France, volume 891, fol. 8.
[54] *A.G.*, 3E 12.253 fol. 497.
[55] Unidentified letter to Mazarin, March 28, 1653, *Archives historiques de la Gironde*, VII, 312. That the Jesuits supported the Ormée is revealed in a letter from Lenet to Condé, March 17, 1653, in G.-J. Cosnac, *Souvenirs*, VI, 164.
[56] G.-J. Cosnac, *Souvenirs*, VI, 57.
[57] Vendôme to Mazarin, July 9, 1653, *Archives historiques de la Gironde*, IV, 336.
[58] *B.N.*, MS. fonds français 11633, fol. 565.

Priests whose actions invited expulsion from the Church—the archbishop of Bordeaux had excommunicated all adherents of the Ormée—must have been strongly motivated. And since questions of religious doctrine do not appear to have entered the dispure, one can only surmise that the decision to support the Ormée had been guided by "considerations of ambition," perhaps even by "shameful avarice."[59] Seen in this light, the challenges of Galtery, du Fresne, Romain, and Joly appear as the clerical counterpart to the struggle for power then being waged in the other corporate bodies.

As in the case of other members of the lower bourgeoisie, some priests saw in the Ormée's ascendancy an opportunity for legal redress. Alexandre Maurian, the *curé* of Ste. Eulalye, described how Simon Bourousse, another priest, had withdrawn some litigation pending before the *Parlement*,

. . . in the belief that there would soon be an evocation by virtue of the inter-dict placed on the *Parlement* of Bordeaux. However, seeing that nothing had come of this, Bourousse had obtained a decree from the *Chambre* of the Ormée [the *Chambre de Douze?*] which stipulated that the sentence given by the *Sénéchal* of Guyenne against the said Maurian be carried out, even though the latter had had the sentence reversed by the *Parlement* prior to its interdiction.[60]

The social standing of the litigants may well account for the Ormée's action (as indeed that of the *Parlement*). Bourousse was a minor cleric: in the brief he is referred to simply as "a priest." Maurian on the other hand was a personage of distinction, for he headed an important parish and had close ties with the mercantile bourgeoisie, as can be gathered from the fact that a number of merchants, including Etienne Hucgla, former *jurat* and one of Bordeaux's most prosperous citizens, had declared themselves ready to testify on his behalf.[61] The Ormée had been made to choose between two unevenly placed clerics and had taken the side of the one more lowly placed.

The Ormée's treatment of the clergy thus differed markedly from that accorded to the groups discussed earlier. Not only was there no attempt made to destroy the church, but priests indifferent to the regime were tolerated and those loyal to it rewarded with sinecures and preferential justice. If some officers of the *Parlement* and merchants had been spared

[59] François de Montglat, "Mémoires," *Nouvelle collection des mémoires pour servir à l'histoire de France*, ed. J. Michaud and F. Poujoulat (Paris, 1854), XXIX, 283.
[60] *A.G.*, 3E 181, fol. 502.
[61] *Ibid.*

it was because they had actively supported the Ormée. Unlike the priests who could escape persecution by remaining passive, the others had to demonstrate their loyalty to the regime to obtain the same consideration.

The favorable attitude shown by the Ormée toward the lesser clergy characterized its relation to the entire "*menu peuple.*" This was particularly evident in the area of justice, which prior to the Ormée's advent had been in the hands of the patrician courts: the *Parlement* which dispensed venal justice, the *Jurade* and the *Bourse* which could always be expected to side with the mercantile litigants. How deeply this state of affairs had been resented can be gauged from the fact that one of the Ormée's first acts was to demand an evocation that would have transferred all litigation pending before the *Parlement* to the *Conseil du Roi.*[62] The evocation, it is true, had not been carried out, but what was done proved even more drastic, for the *Parlement* was altogether eliminated and all litigation transferred to the *Présidial* and the chambers of the Ormée. With the judicial power firmly in its hands, the rebellious party proceeded to redress earlier wrongs. The Dirouard case is illustrative. Charged by the public prosecutor with "*excès et crime de rébellion*"—the only part of the indictment that has survived—Dirouard and three others had, in August of 1651, come before the Court of the *Jurade.*[63] From the records of the *Parlement* one learns that the accused had been sent to prison, freed, and then in September of 1652 re-imprisoned by order of the *Parlement.*[64] Why the *Parlement* should have chosen to reopen the case can only be left to conjecture. Perhaps in arresting a rebel it hoped to show that it had lost none of its power. Whatever its reasons, the *Parlement* must have been disheartened by what followed. "The Court has received word," reported the *Registres secrets*, "that a so-called *Chambre de Trente* of the Ormée, having been unable to persuade the *jurats* to release the prisoner, had him removed by force."[65]

Many others came to benefit from Ormée justice. As shown earlier, the Ormée sided with Gabriel Chartan, a county judge, in his dispute with Pierre Manpetit, merchant; with Jean Prélat, rather than with Alphonse Romerd, merchant; with Silvestre Ciraq, merchant but supporter of the Ormée, and not with Pierre Lauretan, merchant; and with Jehan Laurens, glove maker, in his differences with François Lirandein, *avocat* of the

[62] Unidentified letter to Mazarin, June 24, 1652, *A.N.*, KK 1219, fol. 391.
[63] Sentences de l'Hôtel de Ville, 1649–1667, *A.G.*, 12 B7.
[64] Registres du Parlement, 1651–58, fol. 190.
[65] *Ibid.*

Parlement. Additional examples of Ormée justice include the case of Thomas Castaing, a tax *fermier* who had a suit pending in the *Parlement* against a number of individuals, including one—Rolland—who was an Ormist. He already had received a favorable hearing from the *Parlement* and was about to have the case adjudicated when the other litigants "had the said Castaing summoned before the officers of the *Chambre de Douze*, which concluded that all the parties would have to submit briefs before *Sieur* Croizet, a member of the said *Chambre*."[66] One may also mention the case of Helies La Croix, master button maker, who with his son-in-law Pierre Bonin, also button maker, had rented a shop from Jean Bourard, *procureur* of the *Parlement*. The latter had sought to cancel the lease and obtained from the *Présidial* a decree ordering the two to vacate the shop. Bonin then launched an appeal to the *Chambre de Douze* which ruled that Bourard would have to abide by the original agreement.[67] Another official fared even worse. Pierre Augeau, *procureur en la prévosté royale de Blaye*, charged that, although he had never had any dealings with Laurens Rolland (the same Rolland as above) the latter, "taking advantage of the prevailing disorders and of the fact that he was held in high esteem by the Ormée, had, with the help of five or six other Ormists, seized and thrown him in the prison of the *Hôtel de Ville* where he had languished for sixteen days and from which he was released only after he had paid his captors twenty-five *louis*."[68] Then there was the dispute between Bernard Damazac, *notaire* and a former captain of the militia, and Gabriel Aubry, an Ormist captain. The former had been asked by Aubry "to present himself before the *Chambre de Douze*, in order to terminate all their differences and litigation," but had refused, pleading that he "could not present himself as soon as the said Aubry desired because of an illness." Another summons produced the desired results. The *Douze* must have ruled against Damazac, for the latter challenged Aubry "to declare whether or not he intended to abide by the terms of the evocation which calls for the removal of all litigation pending before the *Parlement* to a court outside of the city."[69]

Officers of the *Parlement* and rich merchants had been the victims of Ormée justice, while artisans and small merchants had been its beneficiaries. The conclusion that Ormée justice had a distinct class character

[66] *A.G.*, 3E 6582, fol. 299.
[67] *A.G.*, 3E 12.354, fol. 307.
[68] *A.G.*, 3E 12.219, fol. 69.
[69] *A.G.*, 3E 12.354, fol. 732; 3E 5142, fol. 552.

thus seems wholly justified. It is true that not every dispute brought before the Ormée tribunals involved patrician and lower bourgeois litigants, but when such happened, the Ormée invariably sided with the latter. The merchant Godière had charged that Ormists never failed to "support those of their party." He might have said the same of the Ormée's treatment of the lower classes in general.

Control of the machinery of justice had yielded highly beneficial results. By equal advantages also accrued from the Ormée's control of such political and financial organs as the *Chambre de Trente*, the *Chambre de Direction*, and the *Jurade*. The *Chambre de Direction* rewarded the faithful by providing them with work,[70] purchasing supplies from them,[71] and reimbursing them for losses incurred as a result of the war.[72] The *Jurade* may have lost much of its power, but it retained the authority to admit individuals into the ranks of the bourgeoisie, which it now used on behalf of those previously excluded.[73] As to the *Chambre de Trente*, it was active in a number of ways: using funds obtained from the defeated party to feed the poor and compensate widows and orphans of fallen Ormists;[74] prohibiting the export of wine and the hoarding of grain;[75] requisitioning goods from known enemies of the Ormée;[76] and, perhaps most important, reducing all rents by one quarter.

As the clearest evidence of the Ormée's support for the lower classes, the action concerning rent merits special consideration. The decree ordering the rebate had been issued in January of 1653 in the name of Conty and read:

Because of representation made to us by the artisans, tenants, and other inhabitants of this city to the effect that since the commencement of the present disturbances they have suffered the loss of trade and income due as much to

---

[70] Countless numbers worked on Bordeaux's fortifications. Registres de la Chambre de Direction, April 12, 1653, and May 1, 1653.

[71] Vampulle received 2,160 *livres* for 30 cases of gunpowder. His loyalty to the regime is attested by his declaration that "he did not want to profit from the said sale but wanted only to serve the city." *Ibid.*, January 27, 1653.

[72] Thus Henry du Puy, an Ormist, received 100 *livres* "in compensation for losses incurred in the public service." *Ibid.*, September 8, 1652.

[73] Such may be inferred from a decree of the *Conseil d'Etat*, promulgated on March 30, 1655, which declared "null and void all letters of bourgeoisie expedited from August 1, 1652 to the same month in 1653." *Registres de la Jurade*, II, 476.

[74] See Chapter II.

[75] See Chapter VII.

[76] Thus in May, 1653, the Ormée seized a vessel that belonged to du Laurans, an enemy of the regime. *A.G.*, 3E 5142, fol. 727.

the difficulty of obtaining the necessary merchandise as to the expenses of mounting a guard and defraying other public costs; that in spite of this loss they have paid the full amount of their rents which they can no longer do; and that therefore they respectfully request to be discharged of one half of the said rents, we have resolved that, although we cannot comply with the above request, all tenants, including artisans, and other bourgeois and merchants of the said city who rent houses, shops, rooms, and other quarters shall be discharged of one quarter of their rent. We further forbid all propietors to compel their tenants to pay more than the required sum, and prohibit all guards, sergeants, and bailiffs from pursuing anyone for reason of the said quarter, on pain of losing their charges.[77]

This was not the first time that a rebate had been granted, for in April of 1650, an assembly of artisans and small merchants had forced the *Parlement* to declare a similar reduction in rents.[78] The action, however, had been nullified by the stipulation that the rebate should "not prejudice the rights of proprietors who, on the basis of previously granted leases, seek to obtain redress from the Court."[79] Opposition to the rebate was understandable in light of the extensive property held by individual *parlementaires*: thus Bernard de Pichon, *président* of the *Parlement*, owned eighteen houses[80]; Ogiers de Gourgues, *trésorier de France* and member of an important parliamentary family, seven;[81] Michel Millanges, *avocat*, three; [82] Anthoine de Tarnau, *conseiller*, two in Bordeaux and one in Talence, a village adjoining the city.[83] As these houses constituted an important source of income—Pichon, for example, earned 5,979 *livres* in rent annually[84]—the loss of the quarter of rent was more than the *parlementaires*, already suffering from a sharp decline in venal income, could bear.

The decree of 1653 produced a wave of resistance. Demoiselle de Taranque, widow of an *avocat*, explained (after the Ormée had been suppressed) that she had ignored it,

---

[77] *A.G.*, C4700, Decree of the Prince of Conty, January 15, 1653.
[78] *Arrest de la Cour de Parlement de Bordeaux portant que tous les manans et habitants demeureront quittes et dechargéz du payement des loyers d'un quartier des dites locations* (Bordeaux, 1650).
[79] *Ibid.*
[80] F. Giteau, in *Bordeaux, 1453–1815,* ed. Robert Boutruche (Bordeaux, 1966), p. 490.
[81] *A.B.*, fonds Drouyn, vol. 13, fol. 549.
[82] *A.G.*, 3E 12.354 fol. 841.
[83] *B.B.*, MS. fonds Itié, July 7, 1654.
[84] Giteau, *op. cit.* (Note 80, above), p. 490.

. . . as it would have been a sheer mockery to avail oneself of a pretended ordinance favoring the tenants given by Milord the Prince of Conty at the behest of certain people who during the recent disturbances comprised a chamber of sedition of which the said Castaignet [her tenant] was one of the leaders and therefore an interested party.[85]

When Arnault Maurian, *procureur*, was about to leave the city "following
the permission received by M. le Prince de Conty" and sought to return
his house keys, he found that the proprietor—an *avocat*—would not accept them "under the pretext that the said Maurian still owed a quarter
of the rent."[86] And when Pierre Branda, secretary of Conty, informed his
landlord, Michel de Bruhl, *procureur en Guyenne*, that he intended to avail
himself of the rebate, he was not only refused but promptly evicted.[87]

Dame de Massiot, widow of a former *président*, complied with the decree,
but only because her tenants would not pay their rents unless they were
first granted the rebate. She duly declared that she would take "appropriate
measures to obtain restitution of the said quarter by the voice of right
and reasonable justice at the time and place of her choosing."[88] Jeanne de
Sallignac, also widow of a *parlementaire*, found that two of her tenants
had refused to pay the quarter of rent, "using as a pretext an imaginary
rebate." She had threatened to take punitive action, but to no avail.
"However," her plaint continued, "now that the said lady knows that the
rebate will not be granted [it was September, 1653, and the Ormée had
just fallen] she demands to be paid in full."[89] Similarly, Gerault de Robil-
lard, *escuyer avocat*, declared that

. . . because of the high esteem in which he holds M. le Prince de Conty and
his ordinances, he intends to reduce his tenants' rent by one quarter, but re-
serves for himself the right to collect the sum at the appropriate time.[90]

In a few instances, the rebate was granted without any altercation.
Yzabeau de Gaxies, widow of a *procureur*, agreed to give her tenant the
quarter "because of the ordinance of M. le Prince de Conty."[91] And Guillaume Ferandert, a master baker whose shop belonged to Jean Lentillac,

[85] *A.G.*, 3E 15.253, fol. 258.
[86] *A.G.*, 3E 15.253, fol. 204.
[87] *A.G.*, 3E 1522, fol. 284.
[88] *A.G.*, 3E 9752, fol. 22.
[89] *A.G.*, 3E 14.850, fol. 52.
[90] *A.G.*, 3E 10.945, fol. 124.
[91] *A.G.*, 3E 4047, no fol. (May 5, 1653).

avocat of the *Parlement*, obtained the reduction after he informed the latter that he was "without means . . . and lacked the wheat and flour with which to bake bread."[92]

The cases cited above all involved members of the legal order. But the Ormée's action did not affect this group alone. Claude Godière, merchant, was the owner of eight houses;[93] Pierre Manpetit, merchant, of eleven;[94] Gratien Pissebeuf, former *juge de la Bourse*, of more than a score.[95] Thus Bordeaux's merchants felt the burden of the rebate as keenly as did the *parlementaires*—and proved just as contentious. Bernard Latreille, simple inhabitant of Bordeaux, complained that he had not been given the rebate, as did Arnault Bastide, linen maker, Jean Eynard, barrel maker, Arnaud Texier, roofer, François Carrier, tailor, Bernard Lacheize, bailiff of the *Bourse*, François Dupeyrat and Julien Machade, small merchants, and François Terrier, occupation unknown. The response of their landlords, most of whom were important merchants, is worth noting. In two instances, the tenants were ordered evicted. In one, an appeal was made to the *Parlement* (which began to meet in Agen in April of 1653). In another, the rebate was granted, but with the understanding that "it will never be repeated, even for reasons of war, plague, or anything else." In still another, the landlord claimed that he could do nothing, since he did not own the house but leased it from two merchants "who had refused to grant the said rebate." And finally, we have the response of the wife of the merchant du Bosq, who announced that "being unalterably opposed to the ordinance and the pretended rebate, she reserved the right to require payment of the said quarter at her pleasure."[96]

The struggle between the landlords and tenants again points to the class, and not just corporate, character of the upheaval. Some proprietors were indeed members of the privileged estate, but all were investors of capital; tenants may have figured in an inferior corporate order, but they also belonged to the class of the economically dependent. Any attempt to explain

[92] *A.G.*, 3E 8753, fol. 159.
[93] These houses were worth 50,000 *livres* and brought Godière an annual rent of 2,500 *livres*. *Archives historiques de la Gironde*, XXV, 194–205.
[94] *A.G.*, 3E 120.318, fol. 356.
[95] The precise number of houses cannot be given, as Pissebeuf groups all his possessions together. In all, he owned 58 pieces of property, including vineyards, woodlands and storage places. *A.G.*, 2E 2309, Pissebeuf.
[96] *A.G.*, 3E 12.354, fol. 922; 3E 767, fol. 873; 3E 5212, fol. 163; 3E 4320, fol. 650; 3E 12.354, fol. 259; 3E 5142, fols. 718, 754; 3E 24.802, fols. 265–67; 3E 15.253, fol. 190.

the rebate and its consequences in purely corporate terms—as a struggle over privilege and prerogative—must therefore be rejected. If the Ormée's action was intended as a challenge to patrician status—and none of the sources suggest such a motive—it was more directly intended as a challenge to patrician property. This would explain why merchants and judicial officers—traditional enemies—had consented to join forces: in the face of the common economic challenge, corporate rivalries could be set aside.

The rebate and other Ormée measures had clearly enhanced the well-being of Bordeaux's lower classes. But even greater gains could be realized by simply joining the Ormée, for the latter rewarded its most loyal adherents with offices formerly held by *parlementaires* and their clients, as well as with positions in the newly created Ormée organs. Gardera, an Ormist stalwart, rose to become *receveur du Bureau de Libourne*.[97] Cayrac, Ormist captain, advanced to the position of *controleur général du Convoy*.[98] Truchon became *controleur du Bureau des Bourgeois* (that is, of the *Chambre de Direction*);[99] de Vrignon, Ormist *jurat*, was named *intendant de la Marine*;[100] and Deboigues, another Ormist, became secretary of the *Chambre de Direction*, a post eventually filled by Dureteste himself.[101] The Ormée chieftains assumed a variety of posts: Villars was both commander of the Ormée guards and a leading figure in the *Chambre de Trente*;[102] Crozillac, a *consul* of the *Bourse*, was also a member of the *Chambre de Trente*;[103] Dureteste combined the function of secretary of the *Chambre de Direction*, member of the *Chambre de Trente* and of the *Chambre de Douze*, and *président* of the *Chambre de l'Ormée*.[104] The offices could be highly remunerative. Gardera received 800 *livres* per annum,[105] Truchon 500 *livres*,[106] Deboigues 720

---

[97] *A.B.*, CC271, Registres de la Chambre de Direction, December 12, 1652.

[98] Pierre Cayrac, "Récit de la Fronde à Bordeaux," *Revue historique de Bordeaux*, VII (1914), 8.

[99] Registres de la Chambre de Direction, December 12, 1652.

[100] *A.G.*, 3E 5142, fol. 727.

[101] *Archives historiques de la Gironde*, XXX, 172. Deboigues had occupied the post since 1651. Whether he had been given the post to placate the Ormée or for some other reason is not known.

[102] G.-J. Cosnac, *Souvenirs*, VII, 5; *Journal de Filhot*, pp. 176–77.

[103] G.-J. Cosnac, *Souvenirs*, VII, 6.

[104] *Ibid.*; *A.G.*, 3E 2448, fol. 938; *B.N.*, MS. folds français 6707, fol. 144.

[105] Dureteste became secretary of the *Chambre de Direction* in December of 1652. The subsequent entries are in his handwriting; *A.B.*, CC 271, Registres de la Chambre de Direction, December 22, 1652. This was the sum received by *controleurs de Libourne, ibid.*, June 12 1652.

[106] *Ibid.*, December 12, 1652.

livres—wages that exceed those paid to the *conseillers* of the *Parlement*.[107] Dureteste, Villars, Crozillac and de Vrignon fared even better, for in addition to whatever compensation they received as officers of the Ormée, they were paid a monthly stipend by Lenet.[108] Villars and a number of his cohorts are also reported to have made "substantial sums" from the issuance of permits that allowed the entry of prohibited goods into Bordeaux.[109] Membership in the Ormée could indeed be highly profitable.

Enemy of the patrician party, defender of the interests of the lower bourgeoisie, what was the Ormée's attitude to Bordeaux's proletariat— the journeymen who would never become masters, the apprentices and domestics whose very survival depended on the benevolence of others, the peasants who had sought refuge in the city only to join the beggars and vagabonds as "*gens sans métiers*"? The Ormée did seek to alleviate the lot of the poor. As we have noted, funds were distributed to the needy and restrictions placed on the exportation of wine and on the hoarding of grain (in part to keep their prices down); and one of the charges leveled against the conspirator Filhot was that he had wanted to see "the poor people starve to death." [110] Did the Ormée then support the journeymen in their struggle with the masters? Not enough decisions of the Ormée courts have survived to permit a conclusive answer, but with so many masters belonging to the Ormée, this is not likely to have been the case. Class interest, not social altruism, guided the Ormée's actions. If it supported the poor, it was because it wished to enlist their support, not because it sympathized with their plight. The Ormée's treatment of Bordeaux's itinerant peasants makes this clear. In the early months of the Ormée's rule, peasants had gained entrance to the city without difficulty— indeed had been well-received.[111] But in May of 1653, the *Chambre de Direction* declared:

Upon the testimony presented to the *Chambre* that the city contains numerous useless persons including many whom the enemy has driven out and who have sought refuge therein and that they consume a great deal of bread of which the city may find itself in short supply, it is hereby decreed that all beggars save those of the city and its environs will be placed outside the said city

[107] *Ibid.*, September 15, 1651.
[108] In May of 1653 Dureteste received from Lenet 700 *livres*, Villars 500 *livres*, de Vrignon 600 *livres*, B.N., MS. fonds français 6715, fol. 250.
[109] Lenet to Condé, February 4, 1653, B.N., MS. fonds français 6713, fol. 153.
[110] *Journal de Filhot*, p. 123.
[111] Cayrac, "Récit de la Fronde à Bordeaux," pp. 14, 16.

by *Messieurs les jurats* and their subordinates, that an eyebrow of each will be cut so that they be recognized, and that each is to be given 4 *sols* worth of bread.[112]

The decree was harsh, but it must be remembered that even before it was issued, the Ormée had already begun to persecute some of its own adherents: bakers were being searched, butchers were being arrested.[113] In the face of the rapidly deteriorating military situation, the Ormée may have felt compelled to eliminate the "useless" elements—those who placed their own welfare above that of the regime, as well as those whose presence in Bordeaux had become more of a burden than anything else.

The Ormée's domination of Bordeaux had far-reaching social consequences. The oligarchies of wealth and office were overthrown and their places taken by a new power: the *"menu peuple."* Long suppressed, the latter now sought to recover the security that had been lost in the course of a century of monarchical and mercantile expansion. Its source of support should have been the *Parlement*—and indeed prior to 1651, the two had been allies—but the *Parlement* had come to see that it had more to fear from the mob than from the Crown, and had made peace with the latter. And so the Ormée found itself fighting the entire ruling establishment: the Crown, the *Parlement*, and the merchants. The outcome of such a struggle could not long remain in doubt.

[112] Registres de la Chambre de Direction, May 15, 1653.
[113] See Chapter VII.

VII

THE DEFEAT OF THE ORMÉE

PERHAPS THE MOST REMARKABLE ASPECT of the Ormée's dominance over Bordeaux is that it lasted as long as it did. Under royalist attack from the very beginning of its existence, the Ormée did not succumb until August of 1653. By then its armies had been shattered, Bordeaux was encircled and on the brink of starvation, Conty had deserted, and the *"bons bourgeois"* were in full revolt. Defeat was unavoidable: as with La Rochelle twenty-five years earlier, Bordeaux could not withstand the armed might of the monarchy. However, because the defeat resulted from military weakness rather than political exhaustion, it did not mark the end of civil strife. The Ormée was indeed destroyed, but not the spirit that had sustained it through two years of warfare and revolution. The Ormée's end would be both violent and prolonged, its final disappearance taking place only after the *Parlement* had been restored in November of 1654.

The royal advance continued throughout the early part of 1653. On April 17, Conty wrote to his brother: "Bazas has capitulated. Only Bordeaux, Libourne, Bourg, Bergerac, Ste. Foix, Tartas and Périgueux are still loyal to us. In the last few days we have lost all our posts on the Garonne."[1] Much of the countryside around Bordeaux was in enemy hands. "The loyal cities can no longer be provisioned," Lenet informed Condé on April 23, "the enemy is at Lormont and at a number of other places in Entre-deux-mers and we cannot get anything out of Bordeaux."[2]

[1] Conty to Condé, April 17, 1653, in Lenet, "Mémoires," p. 606.
[2] Lenet to Condé, May (no day), 1653, *A.C.*, MS. serie P, XIII, fol. 129.

Lormont fell on the 26th of May, placing the royal army at less than one kilometer from Bordeaux.[3]

Faced with a critical military situation, an empty treasury,[4] and a serious shortage of grain,[5] the Ormée was now confronted with a number of new attempts against its rule. On April 18, a conspiracy was uncovered involving one Mme. de Lure, a friend of the Duke of Epernon, and *Père* Landé, a *Cordelier* friar. The latter had urged his brother—the same Landé whom we have already encountered—to place himself at the head of the bourgeoisie, gain control of the city's gates, and with the connivance of Marsin (Condé's chief military representative in Guyenne) introduce a detachment of cavalry into Bordeaux. No sooner was the conspiracy exposed than the Ormée had the ringleaders arrested, tried by the *Conseil de Guerre*, and sentenced to imprisonment for life.[6] The Ormée reacted with equal resoluteness when, a few days later, it received word that Chambon, an emissary from Candalle, had entered the city with a message for Conty. "The Ormée having assembled," Lenet reported, "a number of its leading members announced that the traitor from Saintes had just arrived and that he was to be thrown into the river or hanged as an example to others."[7] Arrested, Chambon was being led to the *Hôtel de Ville* to stand trial when his carriage was stopped by a mob "which fell upon him, struck him with a thousand blows, and began to drag him to the gallows that stand before the *Hôtel de Ville*." There was no hanging, but only because the mob, at the last moment, was prevailed upon by Conty's guards to allow the prisoner to stand trial.[8]

The Ormée was apparently determined to continue the struggle until the very end, as is evident from still another incident. On May 4, a royal letter arrived in Bordeaux addressed to the *sénéchaux* of the chapters of St. André and St. Seurin, the *juge et consuls* of the *Bourse*, and the captains of the militia which offered the city the choice of a general amnesty or

---

[3] Guron to Mazarin, May 27, 1653, *Archives historiques de la Gironde*, VIII, 171.

[4] Lenet owed more than 360,000 *livres* and wrote to Condé: "Unless money arrives from Spain, the future will be ominous. Our credit here is not going to last forever." Lenet to Condé, May (no day), 1653, *A.C.*, MS. serie P, XIII, fol. 129.

[5] As early as March, Lenet had written: "We no longer have any wheat." Lenet to Condé, March 31, 1653, *A.C.*, MS. serie P, XIII, fol. 35.

[6] Lenet to Condé, April 22, 1653, *B.N.*, MS. fonds français 6713, fol. 279; *A.G.*, Livre de l'escroue, April 18, 1653.

[7] Lenet to Condé, April 24, 1653, Gabriel-Jules de Cosnac, *Souvenirs du règne de Louis XIV* (Paris, 1866–82), VI, 406.

[8] *Ibid.*, pp.406–7.

defeat "by force of arms."[9] The letter was read to the Ormée assembly, where, in the words of Lenet, it evoked "unheard of derision." "There then arose," Condé was further informed, "cries of 'Long live the King and *Monsieur le Prince!*' and an oath was then taken to live and to die for your cause, with more than a thousand Ormists participating."[10]

The above had taken place shortly before the fall of Lormont; the weeks that followed were marked by other displays of intransigence. Marsin was severely reprimanded by Dureteste for not having gone to the relief of Lormont—the two coming to blows over the issue.[11] On the 29th of May, the Ormée assembly resolved to expel anyone who spoke in favor of peace and to send deputies to Cromwell "with new proposals."[12] The next day it arrested the *avocat* Chevalier, as he was about to leave for Candalle's camp. He was found carrying letters from the *conseiller* Mousnier, which contained the news that "nearly everyone in the city has had his fill of the tyrannical rule of Villars, Dureteste, Guiraud [Giraut] and Crozillac," and that a number of individuals, including the *conseiller* de Bordes and the *jurat* Thodias, were about to make another attempt against the Ormée. Villars's guards were immediately dispatched to seize Mousnier, but in the ensuing skirmish in which one man was killed, the latter made good his escape. The next day, the *Conseil de Guerre* sentenced Chevalier to death and he was executed within two hours.[13]

Steps were also taken to meet the military threat. Earthworks were put up at Bacalan, a village on the outskirts of Bordeaux, and the city's garrison was strengthened.[14] On May 30, the Ormée seized all the vessels still in the harbor and these were sent to the aid of La Bastide, the fort facing Bordeaux on the Garonne.[15] If such actions could not avert the

---

[9] Royal letter to Bordeaux, April 26, 1653, *ibid.*, VII, 95–97.

[10] Lenet to Condé, May 8, 1653, *ibid.*, pp. 99–100.

[11] Unidentified letter to Berthod, May 29, 1653, *Archives historiques de la Gironde*, VIII, 175.

[12] Lenet to Condé, no date, B.N., MS. fonds français 6715, fol. 157; Gissard to Mazarin, no date, *Archives historiques de la Gironde*, VIII, 177–78.

[13] Lenet to Condé, no date, B.N., MS. fonds français 6715, fol. 157; unidentified letter to Vendôme, June 6, 1653, *Archives historiques de la Gironde*, VIII, 439. Guron's reaction to Chevalier's death is worth noting: "The people of Bordeaux should not be spared since they hang the King's subjects with so much ease." Guron to Mazarin, June 7, 1653, *ibid.*, p. 443.

[14] Guron to Mazarin, June 3, 1653, *ibid.*, pp. 179–80.

[15] *A.G.*, 3E 5142, fol. 727; unidentified letter to Vendôme, June 6, 1653, *Archives historiques de la Gironde*, VIII, 439.

city's capture, they might at least delay it until help arrived. For some still clung to the hope that the city would soon be relieved. Marsin had written: "We are awaiting the armed fleet which is supposed to arrive in less than three weeks. We are doing everything that we can [to survive until then]."[16] And a correspondent of the Cardinal: "A man very devoted to our cause has just reported hearing from a very reliable source that the Spanish fleet will soon be here. Everyone is in great suspense over this."[17]

And so the one-sided struggle continued. Before the end of June, Candalle's forces had reached Bordeaux's walls, Bourg was under attack, and Libourne's Irish garrison had defected.[18] Even the Protestant city of Montauban which had remained steadfastly loyal to Bordeaux now decided to make peace with the royal government.[19] On the first of July, Lenet made a last plea for Spanish aid. "If Bordeaux is to be saved from starvation," he wrote to Vateville, then in Spain, "you must despatch the fleet and engage the forces of Mazarin in the river. . . . But come, come or everything is lost. Your actions until now have been insufferable; with the result that we are about to lose our most powerful and able ally in France."[20]

Bordeaux was at the end of its tether. Not only had most of the province been lost, but there were signs that the city itself was beginning to falter. Entire areas were deserted. The chapter of St. Seurin could not decide "whether or not to continue to hold services in the said church inasmuch as the quarter has been completely abandoned and the soldiers that fill it are ravaging everything."[21] There was an acute shortage of food—the price of meat had soared to 20 *sols* the pound[22] and grain was virtually unobtainable. One observer reported: "The bakers have only enough flour for 15 days."[23] And another: "The people are howling for bread and peace."[24] Dureteste, who thought that the bakers were hoarding grain,

[16] Note from Marsin, May 30, 1653, *ibid.*, p. 91.

[17] Unidentified letter to Mazarin, no date, *ibid.*, p. 170.

[18] Vivens to Mazarin, June 12, 1653, *ibid.*, 444–46; Guron to Mazarin, June 28, 1653, *ibid.*, pp. 468–69; Vendôme to Mazarin, June 21, 1653, *ibid.*, pp. 453–55.

[19] Bertier to Mazarin, June 22, 1653, *ibid.*, pp. 455–56.

[20] Lenet to Vateville, July 1, 1653, *ibid.*, XV, 327.

[21] *A.G.*, G 1028, fol. 147.

[22] Unidentified letter to Mazarin, July 4, 1653, *Archives historiques de la Gironde*, XV, 328.

[23] Unidentified letter to Mazarin, no date, *ibid.*, VIII, 451.

[24] Unidentified letter to Mazarin, July 2, 1653, *ibid.*, pp. 473–74.

undertook a search of their storage places but found that they were indeed empty.[25]

The financial situation was equally grave. The flow of Spanish gold had ceased and Lenet's creditors would not advance him new sums. A recourse was to devalue the coinage, but this only had the effect of driving good coins out of circulation and the well-to-do out of Bordeaux. "Those with money," wrote a correspondent of Mazarin, "are buying *pistoles* at 14 *livres*; the more prosperous are departing and placing in safe keeping all the things that they cannot carry with them."[26] As a last desperate measure, the Princesses sent a portion of their plate to the mint and the rest to Durand, the munitioneer, as security for a loan of 18,000 *livres*.[27]

To add to its travails, the Ormée was now faced with another conspiracy. On the 20th of June, it arrested Jacques Filhot, the treasurer general of Montauban, who had just returned to Bordeaux from a voyage to Cadillac where he had conferred with Candalle. Filhot was taken before the *Conseil de Guerre* and charged with treason and having "wished to see the poor starve to death." His reply was that "the bourgeois had always fed the poor and that these had never before perished in the street." Asked under torture to identify "the principal bourgeois of Chapeau Rouge, La Rousselle, and elsewhere who have been in the plot," Filhot remained silent and, in his words, "saved the lives and property of a great number of brave people of all conditions whose only thought had been to serve the King and their fatherland."[28]

A last campaign against the Ormée's enemies was now begun. The *parlementaire* Dussault was arrested because he had participated in Filhot's plot. A priest who had spoken in favor of peace was exiled. Someone else who had written a subversive letter to a friend in Paris was condemned to the pillory and fined 10,000 *livres*.[29] Not content to act against individuals, the Ormée began the systematic destruction of their property. Lenet wrote to Condé: "Because the enemy has continued to burn [our houses], we have begun to do likewise to theirs. A rather nice house belonging to the *président* Pichon in the Graves has been put to the torch. The same

[25] St. Simon to Mazarin, May 23, 1653, in G.-J. Cosnac, *Souvenirs*, VII, 157.

[26] Unidentified letter to Mazarin, July 2, 1653, *Archives historiques de la Gironde*, VIII, 473–74.

[27] Lenet to Condé, June 26, 1653, *A.C.*, MS. serie P, XIII, fol. 192; Durand to Lenet, July 15, 1653, *B.N.*, MS. fonds français 6716, fol. 34.

[28] Armand Communay, *L'Ormée à Bordeaux d' après le journal inédit de Jacques Filhot* (Bordeaux, 1887), pp. 104ff.

[29] *Ibid.*, p. 142.

thing is to happen tomorrow to a house belonging to [the *avocat général*] La Vie in Plassac. If the enemy does not tire, neither shall we."[30]

There was, however, a limit to what the Ormée could do. Early in July, Bourg capitulated, thus cutting Bordeaux's water link to Libourne and the upper Dordogne. "The enemy," Lenet reported, "certainly has the necessary strength, and is ill-advised not to attack Bordeaux, where everyone, save the Ormée, is against us." Condé's representative had one last hope: "We have information that they [the Ormists] have, without our knowledge, struck an alliance with the Huguenots and the English. . . . Distasteful as this may be, the rising of the Huguenots and the connection with England may have beneficial consequences, for it will either lead to peace or permit us to continue the war."[31] Lenet had finally decided to make common cause with the radicals, but it was too late. Encouraged by the royal successes, the anti-Ormists had come to life. On July 9, the merchants who had begun to meet at the *Bourse* launched an attack on the *Place du Palais*. Lenet thought he knew how "to bring these rich bourgeois to their senses." He would permit "the most accredited among them to enter the councils where they would have the right to participate in all affairs." He then would remind them that "they too stood to suffer if the city fell into the hands of the enemy" and that, if only for that reason, "none of our friends could be abandoned, least of all Villars and Dureteste."[32] Lenet's calculations rested on the belief that the *"gros bourgeois"* would, in the end, prefer to share power with the Ormée than to be ruled by the *Parlement*. But had not events already proved otherwise?

The Ormée now attempted to repeat the stratagem of the year before; that is to rally the artisans of St. Michel and Ste. Croix, seize the cannon of the *Hôtel de Ville*, and march on the prosperous quarters. However, when the call to arms was answered by only a few hundred, all thoughts of combat quickly vanished.[33] The Ormée had lost the support of the masses and would never again pose a threat to its enemies.[34]

[30] Lenet to Condé, July 3, 1653, Henri d'Aumale, *Histoire des Princes de Condé pendant le XVIe et XVIIe siècles* (Paris, 1863–96), VI, 654.

[31] Lenet to Condé, July 3, 1653, A.C., MS. serie P, XIII, fol. 195.

[32] Lenet to Condé, July 10, 1653, A.C., MS. serie P, XIII, fol. 242.

[33] Unidentified letter to Mazarin, July 10, 1653, *Archives historiques de la Gironde*, VIII, 338; Lenet to Condé, July 10, 1653, A.C., MS. serie P, XIII, fol. 242.

[34] This development was due, no doubt, to the military situation, but fiscal exigencies may have also played a role. In February Conty imposed a salt tax which, Berthod reported, "caused a great stir with the little people [*le petit peuple*]." Berthod to Mazarin, February 3, 1653, A.E., France, vol. 891, fol. 69. And in March, the butcher Hellies Courtier was arrested "for refusing to pay the sum of 158 *livres* which represents his portion of the 5,000 *livres* [which the guild of butchers was required to pay?]" A.G., Livre de l'escroue, March 21, 1653.

Encouraged by the Ormée's latest setback, the opposition pressed its attack. Bands of youths began rampaging through the streets, attacking all suspected Ormists.[35] Conty was asked to dissolve Villars's guards and obliged, thereby prompting the chapter of St. Seurin to dispatch an emissary "to thank our Lord the Prince of Conty for the good faith he has shown in wishing to work for peace."[36] News of Conty's shift was relayed to Condé. "We have information," Lenet wrote, "that he is negotiating. . . . *Père* Romain has been in touch with a large number of *gros bourgeois* whom he hopes to enlist in the peace party. He insists that he is acting on written orders of the Prince of Conty." Lenet went on to describe the state of the city: "We are without bread. Everyone clamors for peace. Unless Bordeaux is relieved within the week, we cannot retain control."[37]

Events began to move swiftly. On July 19, an assembly of between two and three hundred which included "the entire youth of Bordeaux . . . , the *bons bourgeois*, numerous *parlementaires*, *avocats*, *procureurs* and other individuals from the Court," urged upon Conty the adoption of the following course of action:

(1) That the Ormée be abolished.
(2) That all of the captains of the militia be dismissed and that their place be taken by individuals "in whom the people of condition have confidence."
(3) That all soldiers be withdrawn from the city.
(4) That everything be done to bring about peace.[38]

Conty assured the assembly that he too favored peace. He announced that the *Conseil de Guerre* would convene to consider the assembly's demands and invited the latter to send representatives to the session.[39] The *Conseil* met the next day and approved each of the resolutions. An ordinance was thereupon drawn up outlawing the Ormée's assemblies, and the order given to dismiss all the captains of the militia. Deputies were then selected to carry the city's terms to the royalist generals. All came from the ranks of privilege and wealth: there were the *parlementaires* La Tresne and d'Espagnet, the archdeacon d'Alère, the merchants Mercier and Martinez (the

---

[35] *Journal de Filhot*, pp. 145–46.
[36] *A.G.*, G 1028, fol. 149.
[37] Lenet to Condé, July 17, 1653, in d'Aumale, *Histoire*, VI, 657.
[38] Lenet to Condé, July 24, 1653, *A.C.*, MS. serie P, XIII, fols. 283–84; *A.G.*, G 1028, fol. 150; Berthod, "Mémoires," pp. 616–17; *Journal de Filhot*, p. 154.
[39] Lenet to Condé, July 24, 1653, *A.C.*, MS. serie P, XIII, fols. 283–84.

latter a former *juge* of the *Bourse*), the lawyers Lauvergnac and Dalon, and the *jurats* Thodias and de Nort.[40]

While some deliberated, others acted. The city's gates were captured, as was the *Hôtel de Ville* whose prison was emptied of all political prisoners.[41] Bordeaux's youth were especially active. "The youth," Berthod reported to Mazarin, "marched through the city shouting '*Vive le Roi et la paix*' and forcing the Ormists to do likewise."[42] A dramatic incident followed. "A number of youths climbed the belfries in which the Ormists had placed red banners as a sign of their Spanish inclinations. These were torn down and replaced with white banners as testimony of their loyalty to France and to the King."[43]

The Ormée had been overthrown and there was nothing left to do but reach a peace settlement with the King. On July 25, the city's deputies met with Vendôme and Candalle. They presented the terms of the city: that the 2 *écus* surtax on wine be suppressed; that Bordeaux be given the right to impose its own taxes "so as to be able to pay its debts and compensate those who have suffered material losses"; that the *Parlement* be permitted to return; that there be no quartering of soldiers in the city; and that all fortresses in the environs of Bordeaux be razed.[44] The two commanders proved surprisingly accommodating, accepting most of the demands and promising that everyone would be forgiven, "including all the bourgeois and inhabitants of Bordeaux who have participated in the so-called Union of the Ormée."[45] The *jurats* now sent an appeal to Mazarin: "We implore Your Eminence . . . to confirm the articles accorded to us by His Majesty's generals and to approve the articles not yet acted upon which our deputies bring to the King."[46] But the Cardinal had already decided on a different course of action as is evident from the following instructions he sent to Vendôme and Candalle:

First, nothing must be done to tie His Majesty's hands in what regards the

---

[40] *Ibid.*; Lenet to Condé, July 28, 1653, *B.N.*, MS. fonds français 6716, fol. 51. As to the *Conseil de Guerre*, Lenet reported that it "consisted of individuals from all the bodies of the city, including the officers of the guilds, this being done in the hope of detaching the artisans from the Ormée." *Ibid.*

[41] Unidentified letter to Mazarin, July 22, 1653, *Archives historiques de la Gironde*, XV, 355.

[42] Berthod, "Mémoires," p. 616.

[43] Lenet to Condé, July 24, 1653, *A.C.*, MS. serie P, XIII, fols. 283–84.

[44] *B.N.*, MS. fonds français 18752, fols. 313–18.

[45] *B.N.*, MS. fonds français 11633, fol. 146.

[46] Jurats to Mazarin, July 30, 1653, *Archives historiques de la Gironde*, XV, 371.

erection of walls and fortifications, or the filling of moats. The same applies to the city's privileges.

Secondly, while His Majesty agrees that those who have acted against his authority should be pardoned—that is, in the event they capitulate early enough to merit this grace—nevertheless he intends to exclude from any amnesty the said Dureteste, de Villars, the first *jurat* Thodias, Luzignan, and a few others who have been equally seditious, whether they be members of the *Parlement* or simple residents of the city. . . .

Thirdly, His Majesty retains the right to transfer from the city of Bordeaux the *Parlement* and the other sovereign courts previously located therein, as well as all other subaltern bodies.[47]

The *jurats'* appeal was consequently rejected. "The articles demanded by the *Bordelais*," Mazarin commented, "are filled with insolence and cannot be the work of well-intentioned people but of factious elements . . . whose aim is to prolong the war." He ordered the royalists to observe a truce of three days and if need be to resume the attack.[48]

The resumption of warfare proved unnecessary. Told that if it permitted a token force to enter the city the siege would be lifted, but also that if the city chose to await the King's ratification of the treaty, the siege would continue, an assembly of notables meeting at the *Bourse* agreed to accept the royal peace without delay.[49] On August 2, Conty and his entourage departed—the Prince and Princesses had received permission to withdraw to their lands—and the next day, "to the great acclaim of the *gens de bien*," Vendôme and Candalle entered the city.[50] A *Te deum* was chanted at the cathedral of St. André; then the two Dukes had supper at the *Bourse* "where the bourgeois treated them magnificently."[51] Within a week, a new *Jurade* had been formed, Vendôme and Candalle each selecting three of its members.[52] The King was once more master of Bordeaux.

*

The story of the Ormée does not end with the restoration of monarchical authority in Bordeaux. The revolutionary regime had been suppressed,

---

[47] Memoirs from Mazarin to Vendôme and Candalle, July 28, 1653, *ibid.*, pp. 369–70.
[48] Mazarin to Vendôme and Candalle, August 2, 1653, *B.M.*, MS. 2241, fol. 115.
[49] Lenet to Condé, July 29, 1653, in d'Aumale, *Histoire*, VI, 658–60.
[50] *Journal de Filhot*, p. 158. Unidentified letter to Mazarin, August 4, 1653, *Archives historiques de la Gironde*, XV, 381–82.
[51] *Ibid.*, p. 383.
[52] *Ibid.*, p. 382.

but not the spirit of revolution. "The mood of sedition and rebellion has not been extinguished," Vendôme wrote to Mazarin on August 7, "on the contrary, it appears to be increasing in vigor as is attested by the placards that go up nightly and the discourses that are held almost every hour."[53] A similar message was sent by Guron, one of Mazarin's representatives in Guyenne: "This is a mutinous city with decidedly pro-English leanings and as the riff-raff [canaille] is its master, it could before long suffocate the gros bourgeois."[54] Guron had previously advocated a purge of all undesirables, but one conducted by the Bordelais and not by the royal authorities. For, as he observed, "if we undertake to remove them ourselves, there will surely be an outcry that we are not living up to the terms of the amnesty; therefore, it is necessary that the bourgeois themselves conduct the purge."[55] Mazarin was apparently impressed by the content of these letters. "I have been ordered to inform you," Le Tellier wrote to d'Estrades, the newly appointed mayor of Bordeaux, "that M. le Prince has more followers in Bordeaux now than he has ever had before and that they only await the opportune moment to rise on his behalf. . . . You are urged to take all measures necessary to avert this."[56]

The policy of repression was soon in full swing. Within a week of the capitulation, twenty-five of the principal leaders of the Ormée had been exiled.[57] By the end of September, at least one hundred had suffered this fate (or been arrested), including the former procureur syndic of Bordeaux, the father superior of the Minimes—a man called by Guron a "monstrous rebel"—and all the officers of the Parlement who had remained in Bordeaux during the revolt.[58] The number expelled from the city eventually reached three hundred, if we are to believe Berthod.[59]

While greatly pleased with the expulsions and arrests, the restored party demanded more tangible compensation for all the injuries it had suffered at the hands of the Ormée. As Salomon de Virelade, a président of the Présidial wrote to Mazarin: "Your Eminence will permit me to observe that to console the people of substance and forestall such disorders as have

[53] Vendôme to Mazarin, August 7, 1653, ibid., p. 390.
[54] Guron to Mazarin, August 18, 1653, Ibid., p. 399.
[55] Guron to Mazarin, August 4, 1653, ibid., p. 380.
[56] Le Tellier to d'Estrades, August 10, 1653. B.M., MS. 2241, fol. 130.
[57] Guron to Mazarin, August 11, 1653, Archives historiques de la Gironde, XV, 395.
[58] Guron to Mazarin, September 1, 1653, ibid., p. 421; Vendôme to Mazarin, September 22, 1653, ibid., p. 442.
[59] Berthod, "Mémoires," pp. 618–19.

recently taken place . . . it is essential that the amnesty not excuse those who have stolen property . . . from making restitution or at least rendering an account of their deeds before a court of law."[60] Virelade was not to be disappointed, for the notarial records and the registry of the prison of the *Hôtel de Ville* show that restitution was amply made. Thus Pierre Armentary, a participant in the Ithier conspiracy, regained possession of furniture that had been seized while he was in exile.[61] Pierre Augeau, *procureur* of Blaye, reclaimed 25 *louis* he had been forced to pay Laurens Rolland, "a highly esteemed member of the Ormée."[62] Marguerite d'Arnault, widow of Jean de Lanevère, *greffier des arrests et registres de la cour du Parlement de Bordeaux*, informed her respondent that she would not adhere to an earlier settlement as "being the work of the Ormée whose tyranny and violence had constrained her late husband to abandon the just and legitimate actions he had begun to take to terminate their dispute."[63] Particularly contentious were the landlords who, it will be recalled, had been forced to forfeit a quarter of their yearly rent. Jeanne de Sallignac, widow of a *parlementaire*, sought payment of the money owed her "inasmuch as the rebate of the said quarter will not be accorded to the tenants of the present city."[64] And Vallery Taranque, widow of an *avocat*, rejected the claims of her tenants with the comment: "It would be a sheer mockery to abide by the terms of a false ordinance."[65]

The outcome of the above litigations is not always known, but with the organs of justice once more in the hands of the patrician party there can be little doubt as to who received satisfaction. The following entries in the registry of the prison of the *Hôtel de Ville* provide much information on the character of the restored justice:

August 23 [1653]. Simon Laporte, house servant of M. de Salegourde, *conseiller du roy en la cour*, has been taken prisoner by order of M. de Pissebeuf [*iurat*]. August 26. Anthoine Trabarel, apprentice harness maker, has been taken prisoner by order of M. Dalesme, *jurat*, at the request of M. le *président* Pichon. August 27. Arnault d'Arnault and Guilleme Girault, valets of Mme. de Sudiurault [wife of the *conseiller*], have been taken prisoner by order of M. Lauvignac [*jurat*] and at the request of the said lady.

---

[60] Virelade to Mazarin, August 21, 1653, *Archives historiques de la Gironde*, XV, 406–7.
[61] *A.G.*, 3E 767, fol. 1045.
[62] *A.G.*, 3E 12.219, fol. 69.
[63] *A.G.*, 3E 4047, fol. 117.
[64] *A.G.*, 3E 14.850, fol. 52.
[65] *A.G.*, 3E 15.253, fol. 258.

August 30. Jean La Vialle, lackey of M. de Montaudan, *conseiller du roy*, has been taken prisoner at the request of the said Sieur de Montaudan.
September 3, Françoise Roquette, servant, has been arrested at the request of M. de Cazages, *avocat*.[66]

That so many of those arrested belonged to the households of *parlementaires* was surely not a coincidence. We have seen that when *président* Lalanne returned to Bordeaux, he discovered that his servants, "taking advantage of the prevailing disturbances," had stolen his mother's possessions.[67]

Still other examples of patrician-inspired justice are found in the decisions of the court of the *Jurade*. Jacques de Pichon, *conseiller* of the *Parlement*, had accused Jean Pantaguet and Leonard Dumas of larceny: the *Jurade* condemned the first to be executed in front of the plaintiffs house and the other to be banished from the city.[68] André Grenoulchaud, a servant of Armand de Pontac, *président* of the *Parlement*, was condemned to death for "an act of theft."[69] And Pierre le Lou and Cecille Rigade, his wife, were ordered hanged for having stolen from Louis de Martin, a former *président* of the *Présidial*.[70]

Was civil misconduct merely an excuse for punishing former Ormists? The following dispatch to Mazarin provides a clear answer: "The *Parlement* has sentenced a rebel of the Ormée who had committed a theft to life in the galleys. The sentence would not have been so harsh had the man not been an Ormist. The last crime was used as a pretext for others he had committed but which were covered by the amnesty."[71] A way had thus been found to circumvent the terms of the amnesty. But other ways existed. In a letter addressed to the King in July of 1654, the *Parlement* declared its "concern over the excessive number of civil and even criminal actions being introduced outside this court against subjects of the King who inhabit this province, which has the effect of prejudging the declaration of amnesty accorded by His Majesty."[72] Evidence more of venal apprehension than of an attachment to judicial propriety, the *Parlement*'s

---

[66] *A.G.*, Livre de l'escroue, 1653.
[67] Lalanne to Mazarin, April 26, 1654, *B.N.*, MS. fonds français 11633, fol. 246.
[68] Sentences de l'Hôtel de Ville, 1649–67, *A.G.*, 12 B7, April 18, 1654.
[69] *Ibid.*, November 6, 1653.
[70] *Ibid.*, January 14, 1654.
[71] Tallement to Mazarin, February 12, 1654, *B.N.*, MS. fonds français 11633, fol. 207.
[72] Arrest du Parlement de Bordeaux, July 10, 1654, *B.N.*, MS. fonds français 11633, fol. 297.

remonstrance confirms the fact that the prosecution of former Ormists was a deliberate policy of the royal government.

Not only were Ormists exiled, imprisoned, or sent to the galleys, but a number were put to death. The first to suffer this fate was the former leader of the Ormée, Christophe Dureteste. In hiding since Bordeaux's surrender, Dureteste was captured in January of 1654 in circumstances duly described to Mazarin:

I have thought that Your Eminence will be pleased to learn that Dureteste has been captured. . . . I found him in the Landes region, at ten leagues from Cadillac. We suspect that he was on his way to Spain, although there is nothing in his papers to indicate this. I hope that by his testimony we shall be able to uncover the entire cabal. . . . He has so far said that he spent two months in hiding in Bordeaux, and during the rest of the time was in the countryside. I have never encountered so powerful a mind in a person born so low.[73]

Mazarin lost little time in revealing his intentions. On the 25th of January he wrote to d'Estrades:

I am very pleased to learn of Dureteste's capture. . . . There can be no question but that it lies completely within the King's authority to have him executed, for not only was he exempted from the amnesty, but he has committed numerous acts of sedition since it was issued. . . . To give the judgment more *éclat*, it is His Majesty's wish that he be tried before the *Parlement*.[74]

There followed a post-script in the Cardinal's hand: "I have forgotten to tell you that if Dureteste is put to the question he should be asked about his correspondence with Vateville. Also try to get the names of his accomplices both in Bordeaux and in the province."[75] Mazarin's instructions were dutifully carried out. Dureteste was tried by the *Parlement*, found guilty of "*lèse majesté*, rebellion, sedition, and of having belonged to the Ormée," and put to death.[76] His ordeal is described by d'Estrades:

From the prison he was let through the major streets of the city to St. André before which he made the proper amends, then to the *Hôtel de Ville* where he had once presided, and finally to the square that faces the *Parlement*. There he

---

[73] St. Romain to Mazarin, January 12, 1654, *B.N.*, MS. fonds français 11633, fol. 168.

[74] Mazarin to d'Estrades, January 25,1654,*A.N.*, KK 1221, fol. 497,

[75] *Ibid.*, fol. 498.

[76] *Arrest de la Cour de Parlement de Bordeaux contre le nommé Dureteste, chef de l'Ormée* (Paris, 1654).

was broken on the wheel, beheaded, and his head placed on the point of the tower that stands at the Ormée. On his way through the city he had been guarded by my men and by one hundred reliable soldiers whom I had brought for the purpose into Bordeaux. As mayor of the city and chief of the militia, I also had under my command 400 bourgeois, 10 captains, and as many lieutenants and ensigns, and these I deployed on all the roadways leading into the square and in the square itself. The execution took place without incident, all the people expressing great satisfaction over it.[77]

D'Estrades is not convincing. If everyone was as pleased with the execution as he indicates, then what need was there for all the precautionary measures?

More executions followed. In August, a sergeant of Dureteste who was "suspected of putting up placards and who had committed a theft at two leagues from the city" was hanged.[78] A few days later, it was the turn of a man "convicted at La Réolle [by the *Parlement*] of having violated his daughter."[79] The execution was carried out, but not without difficulty as Mazarin learned: "Numerous people had begun to murmur that this man was innocent and that all of them would likewise be put to death. . . . So great was the agitation, that we were afraid of taking the prisoner out to the rack. I was finally compelled to dispatch my guards and the decree was carried out without any trouble."[80] Still another Ormist was put to death in March of 1655. This was Beaulieu, who, betrayed by one of his cohorts, had confessed having been sent to Bordeaux by Trancars and Clairac—both then in Spain—to assassinate d'Estrades and seize the government.[81] Beaulieu had been promised his life (to elicit information from him), but d'Estrades knew how to get around this:

The said Beaulieu . . . is greatly worried because of a theft and an assault he committed two years earlier and for which one of his comrades was executed six months ago, but not before he named him as the chief culprit. Therefore, as the amnesty refers only to the last conspiracy [that is that of the Ormée], our lords of the *Parlement* can always have him put to death for the other crimes he has committed and for which there are witnesses in the city. It would

[77] D'Estrades to Mazarin, February 12, 1654, *B.N.*, MS. fonds français 11633, fol. 204.
[78] D'Estrades to Mazarin, August 13, 1654, *ibid.*, fol. 339.
[79] D'Estrades to Mazarin, May 17, 1654, *ibid.*, fol. 372.
[80] *Ibid.*
[81] Gramont to Mazarin, October 29, 1654, *ibid.*, fol. 459. Gramont to Mallet, November 11, 1654, *ibid.*, fol. 468.

certainly be a great misfortune if we could not make an example of a man who has always led a bad life, and who, moreover, is lowly born.[82]

Beaulieu was eventually charged "with being an accomplice in a theft committed in the Landes region the previous year," and beheaded.[83]

Did the executions now cease? The sources do not provide a clear answer. A number of former Ormists had been arrested with Beaulieu—among them Robert, Le Breton, Rigoulet—and d'Estrades had written "we will overlook nothing to see them brought to justice,"[84] but whether they were actually put to death is not known. In June of 1655, Guyonnet, a *conseiller* who had supported the Ormée, was found guilty of *lèse majesté*, rebellion and treason. He was deprived of his office, fined 6,000 *livres*, and ordered hanged.[85] The same sentence had been passed on Trancars, Blarru, Dezert, Clairac and Villars a year earlier, at which time Virelade had written to Mazarin: "I shall be sure to carry out an enactment of the sentences at the earliest moment because these spectacles have almost as much effect on the populace as do actual executions which are always liable to evoke pity; furthermore, hangings in effigy have as much distinction as the other ones."[86] Two of those mentioned—Blarru and Villars—were eventually pardoned, but as to what befell the others, nothing is known.[87]

Such then was the fate reserved for those who had participated in the Ormée insurrection. A final word should be said about the state of the city now that the old order had been restored. According to Tallement, lieutenant general of Guyenne, all resistance ended with the execution of Dureteste. "Since Dureteste's demise," he wrote to Mazarin,

the great majority of those from whom we might have expected some trouble have returned to their duty and now only desire to live in peace. Even so factious a group as the butchers, in order to demonstrate their total loyalty to M. d'Estrades, have presented a ballet in his honor.[88]

[82] D'Estrades to Mazarin, December 27, 1654, *ibid.*, fol. 537.
[83] Pontac to Mazarin, March 15, 1655, *ibid.*, fol. 568; Registres du Parlement, 1651–58, fol. 374.
[84] Mallet to Mazarin, November 6, 1654, *B.N.*, MS. fonds français 11633, fol. 470; d'Estrades to Mazarin, November 9, 1654, *ibid.*, fol. 486.
[85] Registres du Parlement, 1651–58, fol. 415.
[86] Virelade to Mazarin, May 20, 1657, *B.N.*, MS. fonds français 11633, fol. 259.
[87] Blarru received the amnesty in 1657, at which time he was in forced residence at Bourg. G.-J. Cosnac, *Souvenirs*, VII, 8. Villars was pardoned in 1658. After the Ormée's fall he had entered Conty's household with the title of *Sieur de la Jalle, gentilhomme ordinaire de M. le Prince de Conty*. A.G., G 1039, fol. 38.
[88] Tallement to Mazarin, February 16, 1654, *B.N.*, MS. fonds français 11633, fol. 211.

The assessment of the Archbisop of Bordeaux, however, was very different:

The rupture between His Majesty and England has had the effect of encouraging the people of this city, who are by nature flighty, to entertain thoughts of renewing the recent disturbances. Countless rumors have been spread in the hope of provoking a new revolt.[89]

D'Estrades and Gramont, the governor of Bayonne, presented similar accounts. The former wrote:

I am seeking to discover the authors of rumors presently afloat in the city and countryside that I have come here to establish the salt tax [*gabelle*] . . . . Numerous assemblies of *menu peuple* have taken place in which various agitators have declared that I am going to kill all who oppose me.[90]

And Gramont:

I would like to inform you of the bad disposition of the people of Guyenne who are more inclined to rebellion now than ever before. I do not speak only of the people of Bordeaux, but of everyone in the province.[91]

Tallement's letter was written in January of 1654, the other three letters six months later. If all are to be given equal credence—not enough is known about each writer's motives to do otherwise—then one must conclude that the attitude of the lower classes had undergone a change in the interval. Such may well have taken place, for more coinage had been debased,[92] the tax on wine had been increased,[93] and prices had continued to rise—indeed, reaching such a high level that d'Estrades was compelled to order a general reduction.[94] The consequences of the wine tax was especially to be feared, as Mazarin was warned: "The *jurats* do not anticipate a revolt over the tax they intend to impose on each barrel of wine entering the city and which they will use to pay their debts. Yet what could be considered more onerous than an impost that will fall on the common people and which will serve the interests of only a few individuals?"[95]

---

[89] Archbishop of Bordeaux to Mazarin, June 29, 1654, *ibid.*, fol. 279.

[90] D'Estrades to Mazarin, July 24, 1654, *ibid.*, fol. 309.

[91] Gramont to Mazarin, July 8, 1654, *ibid.*, fol. 295.

[92] D'Estrades to Mazarin, July, 3 1655, *ibid.*, fol. 592. In February, 1655, the *Parlement* had issued a remonstrance against the "fabrication of *liards* which is resulting in the total ruin of the city and province." Registres du Parlement, 1651–58, fol. 383.

[93] Unidentified letter to Mazarin, no date, 1653, *B.N.*, MS. fonds français 11633, fol. 145.

[94] D'Estrades to Mazarin, November 13, 1654, *ibid.*, fol. 107.

[95] Unidentified letter to Mazarin, no date, 1653, *B.N.*, MS. fonds français 11633, fol. 145.

If the spirit of rebellion had indeed been stilled in the early part of 1654, it was fully alive by the end of the year. Placards were going up which urged the people "to chase the followers of Mazarin out of the city" and which asked: "Do you want to wait until you are broken on the wheel, until you are hanged, until your wives and children are in prison? Have not innocents recently been taken to the gallows?"[96] And conspirators were once more at work. At the time of his arrest, Beaulieu had on his person a letter from Clairac, addressed "to the true and loyal bourgeois of Bordeaux," which proclaimed: "The moment has come for you to prove your love for your fatherland. Rise up and carry out this action upon which the fate of all France depends!"[97] D'Estrades was not sure he could retain control of the city, as he indicated in a letter to Mazarin: "I believe that I can preserve order but am obliged to inform Your Eminence that the surest way would be to return the *Parlement* to Bordeaux, for the King will then be assured of the support of a large segment of the population which desires such a return."[98]

D'Estrades had come to see what had escaped the understanding of Mazarin: that the Crown needed the *Parlement*. The King might send his army to conquer a rebellious city; he might, with competent officials such as d'Estrades, administer its affairs; but he could not effectively rule it—that is, preserve order—without the support of the patrician element and above all of the *Parlement*. The latter would therefore have to be restored, but with sharply delineated powers. As Phellipeaux de La Vrillière, the secretary of state for Guyenne, informed the *Parlement* after its re-establishment in Bordeaux in November of 1654: "Should new revolts break out in the future, you will conduct a precise investigation and punish with severity those responsible. . . . In this way revolts in our province and in our city of Bordeaux will be discouraged. A good example must be made to preserve everyone's obedience."[99] Initially created to combat feudal power, the *Parlement* would henceforth be used to meet the challenge of the lower classes. The Ormée had taught both the Crown and the *Parlement* how much they needed each other. It was a lesson which the age of Louis XIV would remember, but which a subsequent age would forget, much to its regret.

[96] *B.N.*, fonds français 11633, fol. 483.
[97] Clairac to the loyal bourgeois of Bordeaux, October 25, 1654, *ibid.*, fol. 412.
[98] D'Estrades to Mazarin, November 24, 1654, *ibid.*, fol. 500.
[99] Registres du Parlement, 1651–58, fol. 357.

CONCLUSION

THE ORMÉE WAS BOTH A REBELLION and a revolution. Its goal was to free
Bordeaux of centralized monarchical control and to destroy the power of
the local oligarchy, above all, that of the *Parlement*. It failed in both
attempts, partly because of such adverse developments as England's
failure to provide military assistance, but also because the two goals,
neither of which could be abandoned, proved in the end mutually ex-
clusive. For to defeat the Crown the Ormée would have had to ally itself
with the *Parlement* (as the only force strong enough to turn the tide in its
favor), and to defeat the *Parlement* it would have had to ally itself with
the Crown (if only to prevent a coalition of the two). But to pursue either
course was precisely what circumstances and its own orientation would
not allow the Ormée to do: in making peace with the Crown, it would have
had to sacrifice its only ally, the Prince of Condé; in reaching an accommo-
dation with the *Parlement*, it would have had to renounce its social aims.
And so the Ormée was compelled to struggle at once against the *Parlement*
and the Crown, without hope of defeating either.

Was the Ormée a class movement? The difficulty of the question is
increased by the ambivalent nature of social stratification, a fact recognized
by Marx who observed:

The separate individuals form a class only in so far as they have to carry on a
common battle against another class; otherwise they are on hostile terms with
each other as competitors. On the other hand, the class in itself achieves an
independent existence over against the individuals, so that the latter find their
conditions of existence predestined, and hence have their position in life and

their personal development assigned to them by their class, become subsumed under it. This is the same phenomenon as the subjection of the separate individuals to the division of labour and can only be removed by the abolition of private property and of labour itself.[1]

Thus the term would seem to have static as well as dynamic properties— a class being an aggregate of persons who occupy the same position in the organization of production but also a network of relations that only emerges during moments of social strife. Excluded from class consideration if the first characterization is employed—Ormists, as we have seen, came from a variety of productive backgrounds—the Ormée is revealed as a class and indeed its revolt as a class uprising if the second is adopted. This is especially true if one follows the definition of T. H. Marshall who notes that class is "a force that unites into groups people who differ from one another, by overriding the difference between them," and that "class conflict occurs when a common interest unites adjacent social levels in opposition to more distant social levels."[2] For the Ormée membership consisted of individuals of similar standing—artisans, small merchants, petty functionaries—who shared a common hostility to the "more distant" grouping of *parlementaires*, rich merchants, and royal officials. The division may not have been perfect—a small number of *parlementaires* supported the Ormée and some artisans supported the oligarchy—but that it existed is beyond question.

Does the class nature of the Ormée struggle—and that of its enemies— suggest a pattern of hostility common to similar municipal Frondes? A definitive answer must await more detailed investigations of other urban upheavals, but what is known does suggest some parallels between Bordeaux's experience and that of other cities. In Aix-en-Provence a mob of peasants and artisans sacked the *Hôtel de Ville*, ousted the ruling *consuls*, and placed its men in the government of the city.[3] In Angers tens of thousands of "lowly bourgeois—*avocats* and *procureurs*, small merchants and artisans—and proletarians" revolted against "an oligarchy of a few

---

[1] Karl Marx, *The German Ideology*, quoted in Reinhard Bendix and Seymour Martin Lipset, "Karl Marx's Theory of Social Class," in *Class, Status and Power*, ed. Reinhard Bendix and Seymour Martin Lipset (Glencoe, 1953), pp. 30–31.

[2] T. H. Marshall, "The Nature of Class Conflict," in Bendix and Lipset, eds., *Class, Status and Power*, pp. 81, 84.

[3] René Pillorget, "Vente d'offices et journée des barricades du 20 janvier 1649 à Aix-en-Provence," *Provence Historique*, XV, (1965), 45, 50–55; Ernst H. Kossmann, *La Fronde* (Leiden, 1954), p. 121.

hundred rich bourgeois," and proceeded to establish a "popular" form of government.[4] In Carcassonne a mob invaded the *Hôtel de Ville* while the annual consular election was taking place, expelled seventeen of the twenty-four electors, and with those that remained secured the election of its own candidates.[5] In Rouen the "popular masses" first joined the *Parlement*'s war against the "wealthy bourgeois," then turned against the *Parlement* when it became evident that the latter no longer intended to continue the struggle.[6] The same occurred in Paris where the populace initially rallied to the support of the *Parlement*, then attacked the *Parlement* when it began to favor a conciliatory policy.[7]

Thus, coinciding with the political struggles being waged on the provincial and national levels—in Rouen, Aix, and Paris, the *Parlements* had, initially, fought the royal governors (or the King)—were a series of social conflicts taking place on the municipal level. The lower classes were bitterly hostile to the wealthy merchants (principally because they controlled the municipal governments and therefore the collection and disbursement of revenues); the merchants in turn opposed the officers of the *Parlements* (in part because of their elevated social positions but also because the *Parlements* had become closed corporations); finally, *parlementaires* resisted the mercantile element (because of the latter's close ties to such feudal figures as the provincial governors and because rich merchants had come to dominate the financial apparatus of the state).

Confronting the same enemies, it is not surprising that *Parlements* and lower classes should have joined forces in the early moments of the Fronde. But why had the alliance foundered? Why had the lower classes turned on the *Parlements* as they had previously turned on the "*gros bourgeois*"? Some historians have found the answer in the centrifugal pull of divergent group interests. According to Porchnev the rupture occurred when "the [office-holding] bourgeoisie became afraid of the prospects of a

---

[4] *Ibid.*, pp. 137–38; A. Débidour, *La Fronde Angevine, tableau de la vie municipale au XVIIe siècle* (Paris, 1877), pp. 85–95, 138 ff.

[5] Claude de Vic and Jean Joseph Vaisette, *Histoire générale de Languedoc* (Toulouse, 1872–1904), XIII, 337–38.

[6] Kossmann, *La Fronde*, p. 139; Paul Logie, *La Fronde en Normandie* (Amiens, 1951–52), II, 27–28.

[7] Roland Mousnier, "Quelques raisons de la Fronde. Les causes des journées revolutionaires Parisiennes de 1648," *XVIIe siècle*, nos. 2–3 (1949), 33–78; Mlle. Cubells, "Le Parlement de Paris pendant la Fronde," *XVIIe siècle*, no. 35 (1957), 193–99; Jean-Louis Bourgeon, "L'Ile de la Cité pendant la Fronde," *Paris et Ile de France, Mémoires*, XIII (1949), 127–42.

popular revolution and laid down its arms."[8] Intent on overthrowing "the feudal-absolutist order" but failing "at the critical moment," the office-holders had made their peace with the "aristocratic state and the feudal society which it protected" thereby leaving the lower classes "whose revolutionary élan remained unimpaired" no choice but to repudiate its erstwhile ally.[9] A similar argument is advanced by Kossmann: "Presented squarely with the choice of remaining absolutist and conservative or of embracing a political radicalism that would deprive royalty of all its power and a social radicalism that would inevitably entail an attack on the hostile bourgeoisie, it [the *Parlement*] withdrew from the struggle seeing that it could neither profit from it nor bring it to an end."[10] The *Parlement* preferred to make peace with the Crown rather than prolong a conflict that was inflaming the "revolutionary spirit" of the masses and the latter, feeling "abandoned and betrayed," retaliated by including the *Parlement* in its attack."[11]

While Porchnev and Kossmann point to a sudden shift of positions, Leon Bernard suggests a long-standing pattern of hostility: "The im-poverished urban worker was more inclined to regard the local parle-mentarian, municipal oligarch, or *seigneur* as an enemy than he was to lock arms even symbolically with him in common battle against royal tyranny. In his turn, the magistrate or *seigneur* tended to rally—often slowly and reluctantly—to the cause of law and order than to fire the passions of the *canaille*."[12] This view accords with that of Robert Mandrou who likewise stresses deep-seated divisions:

In the 16th and 17th centuries, the evolution [from a society of orders to one of classes] accelerates to the point of rendering obsolete earlier [corporate] ties while group ties gradually emerge as the principal element of all signifi-cant social relations. Nobles, bourgeois, peasants, small townsmen—all feel a close sense of group affinity and growing hostility toward other groups, thereby permitting one to describe them as social classes.[13]

[8] Boris Porchnev, *Les Soulèvements populaires en France de 1623 à 1648* (Paris, 1963), p. 576.

[9] *Ibid.*, p. 579.

[10] Kossmann, *La Fronde*, p. 238.

[11] *Ibid.*, pp. 111, 116.

[12] Leon Bernard, "French Society and Popular Uprisings under Louis XIV," *French Historical Studies*, III (1964), 472.

[13] Robert Mandrou, *Introduction à la France moderne, 1500–1640* (Paris, 1961), p. 138.

While the struggle between the lower classes and the *Parlements*, the gradual rapproachement of the venal and mercantile oligarchies, the eventual alliance of the officer-holders and the royal government would seem to constitute persuasive evidence of the class character of France's mid-century upheaval, a number of historians have remained unconvinced. Thus, Kossmann acknowledges the existence of "social contrasts" during the Fronde,[14] but refuses to ascribe to them a decisive character:

One greatly exaggerates the element of spontaneity when explaining the Fronde as a popular upheaval. It was evidently an aspect of the struggle— no doubt, an aspect of the greatest importance—but one that in the end could not determine the course of events, conflicts of a purely political nature being necessary for this. The social question has complicated the Fronde which, as we have noted many times, found therein a means of prolonging itself but it did not cause it, for the Fronde was above all a political struggle. Every place where this political conflict did not penetrate—in the provinces without *Parlements* or without residing governors, in regions far removed from the centers of resistance—the population remained more or less calm and did not declare itself.[15]

John Elliott reaches a similar conclusion—although on the basis of the Catalan experience:

It would be unwise to disregard the evidence for the existence of fierce social antagonisms in Early Modern Europe. . . . But it is one thing to establish the existence of social antagonisms, and another to assume that they are the principal cause of conflict. . . . A revolt may frequently have started, as in Catalonia, against the agents of the state, and then been transformed into a war on the rich. But the parallels between this and a modern class conflict cannot be automatically taken for granted, if only because the ordering of society in Early Modern Europe tended to militate against class solidarity. A society grouped into corporations, divided into orders, and linked vertically by powerful ties of kinship and clientage cannot be expected to behave in the same way as a society divided into classes.[16]

But the most emphatic rejection of the class interpretation is provided by Roland Monsnier who concludes: "I do not see a grouping of noble and bourgeois classes pitted against the lower classes nor a grouping of lower

[14] Kossmann, *La Fronde*, p. 138.
[15] *Ibid.*, p. 134.
[16] John H. Elliott, "Revolution and Continuity in Early Modern Europe," *Past and Present*, no. 42 (1969), 41–42.

classes pitted against the nobles and bourgeois."[17] The bourgeoisie may occasionally take up arms against "popular gatherings," but only because these pose a threat to law and order—not because of class antagonism.[18] Indeed the age is institutionally protected from such antagonism: "The 17th century reveals that more important than the stratification of social groups along 'horizontal' lines is the 'vertical' division integrating cultivators, solicitors, officers of the *Parlement*, priests, and lords, all bound by mutual ties of protection and service."[19] It follows that social strife can only result from "an alliance between the people and the nobles against the King" who alone stands outside the "vertical division," and not from "a monarchical-feudal alliance against the common people."[20] For the same reason, the lower classes may turn on the agents of the Crown but never on the local notables: "The revolts are not wars between the poor and the rich. The tax collectors are attacked, but rarely the *châteaux* or *hôtels*."[21]

Is one therefore to conclude—in light of the above arguments—that the Ormée owed its existence to conflicts of a largely political nature, that its principal target was the Crown with its fiscal agents rather than the ruling municipal oligarchies, and that its overriding loyalty was to such "vertical" allies as the *Parlement* and the feudal gentry? Our findings indicate otherwise. The Ormée may not have begun as a spontaneous popular uprising (can any insurrection be said to have such a beginning?), but neither are its origins to be found in extraneous rivalries—whether those of Epernon and the *Parlement* or of Condé and the Crown. These, no doubt, provided the lower classes with opportunities not found in earlier revolts, but they could not in themselves unleash the revolutionary wrath of the masses. Social tensions were needed for that, and indeed at the bottom of the Ormée's revolt was the age-old antagonism between artisans and merchants—an antagonism resulting as much from conflicting economic interests as from the fact that merchants used their control of the municipal government to shift the burden of royal taxes onto the

[17] Roland Mousnier, "Recherches sur les soulèvements populaires en France avant la Fronde," *Revue d'histoire moderne et contemporaine*, V (1958), 103.

[18] *Ibid.*, p. 105.

[19] Roland Mousnier, "Serviteurs du roi: quelques aspects de la fonction publique dans la société française du XVIIe siècle," *XVIIe siècle*, nos. 42–43 (1959), 4.

[20] Roland Mousnier, "Monarchie contre aristocratie dans la France du XVIIe siècle," *XVIIe siècle*, no. 61 (1956), 381.

[21] Roland Mousnier, *Les XVIe et XVIIe siècles* (Paris, 1954), p. 161.

lower classes. If the latter also rallied to the *Parlement* in its struggle with Epernon, it was not out of hostility to the Crown—subsequent attacks against the royal government remained primarily defensive in character— nor out of a sense of "vertical" allegiance for the *Parlement*—nothing either in the events prior to the Fronde or in those after indicates such a tie—but because Epernon had steadfastly championed mercantile rule through the *Jurade*. With the *Jurade*'s defeat, the lower classes turned on the *Parlement* which had taken advantage of the altered situation by electing its own *jurats*, gaining control of the city's funds, and taxing the unprivileged element to pay for the war. The Ormée now emerged and in a struggle that can only be called a class war proceeded to defeat the *Parlement* and seize power. Rather than speak of a political struggle with social overtones as do Kossmann and Elliott, one would be more correct to speak of a social struggle with political overtones.

The Ormée's emergence is proof not only of advanced social stratification but also of the high level of political maturity achieved by the lower classes. Urban clashes in themselves were not new—Porchnev has identified more than two hundred just between 1616 and 1647[22] and even Mousnier (who refuses to ascribe to these clashes a class character) acknowledges the existence of class divisions in the religious wars of the 16th century.[23] What was new was that for the first time the lower classes had risen against and defeated the entire ruling establishment—*Parlement* as well as royal fisc, municipal government as well as provincial overlord. The future would belong to the bourgeoisie, but the 17th century had shown that determined artisans could also make a revolution.

The Ormée's defeat was to mark the end of organized insurrections in Bordeaux until the French Revolution. The conditions which had produced the Ormée's revolt continued to exist—indeed, another anti-fiscal revolt was to break out in 1675—but there would never be a second Ormée. In part this can be explained by the actions of Louis XIV who ordered that all records pertaining to the events of 1648–52 be destroyed.[24] But the Ormée must also share responsibility for its disappearance from history, for unlike other social movements whose influence managed to survive—one can mention the Anabaptists and the Diggers—the Ormée

[22] Porchnev, *Les Soulèvements populaires*, pp. 661–64.
[23] Roland Mousnier, "Trevor Roper's 'General Crisis' Symposium," in *Crisis in Europe 1560–1660*, ed. Trevor Aston (London, 1965).
[24] Porchnev, *Les Soulèvements populaires*, pp. 506–7.

failed to produce a body of ideas useful to the future. Its attachment to the corporate system, to Bordeaux's "ancient liberties," and to traditional moral values could have little or no appeal to a rising bourgeoisie or to journeymen who had as much reason to oppose the closed society of the guilds as they did the increasingly open society of the merchants. Rather than recall the Ormée, future revolutionaries would turn to more promising voices.

APPENDIX

MEMBERS OF THE ORMÉE*

Name	Occupation	Year of Entry into Bourgeoisie	Source
Arnault, Bernard	*marchand*	—	*A.G.*, 3E 1521 fol. 26
Arnault, Martin du Pierron d'	*courtier, capitaine de la milice*	—	*A.G.*, 3E 4320 fol. 766
Aubry, Gabriel	—	—	*A.G.*, 3E 4368 fol. 784
Augier, Jacques	*marchand, capitaine de la milice, member of Cent et Trente*	1579	*A.G.*, 3E 15252 fol. 14
Augier, Paul	*prestre*	1579	*A.G.*, 3E 13495 fol. 673
Bargeaut, Pierre de	*marchand*	1645	*A.G.*, 3E 767 fol. 47
Bassibey, Jean de	*notaire*	—	*A.G.*, 3E 767
Bastide, Jacques	*procureur au Sénéchal de Guyenne*	1609	*A.G.*, 3E 10944 fol. 16v
Bault, Etienne	*maître pâtissier*	1643	*A.G.*, 3E 7675 fol. 16
Berbeilh, Pierre	*marchand*	—	*A.G.*, 3E 2448 fol. 256
Bezian, Anthoine	*maître gantier*	—	*A.G.*, 3E 15252 fol. 140
Billate, Simon	*marchand*	1640	*A.G.*, 3E 8752 fol. 182v
Bizat, Pierre	*notaire*	1584	Livre des bourgeois, 9
Blanzy, Jean	*maître gantier*	1645	*A.G.*, 3E 12353 fol. 351
Blarru, Jean	*maître orfèvre*	1645	Cosnac, *Souvenirs*, VII, 8
Boisson, Blaise		1655	*A.G.*, 3E 9160 fol. 186v
Bonmard, Simon	*avocat au Parlement*	1647	*A.G.*, 3E 12318 fol. 24v
Bonnet, ___de	*escuyer*	—	Cosnac, *Souvenirs*, VII, 8
Brimbeuf, Daniel	*marchand*	—	*A.G.*, 3E 1308 fol. 507v

*These names will be found in the text or in a letter sent to Condé on May 13, 1652, *A.C.*, MS. serie P, XII, fol. 228. The dates of *embourgeoisement* are obtained from the "Livre des bourgeois de Bordeaux" in *Archives historique de la Gironde*, XXXII, 1–149, and from the *Registres de la Jurade*, VII, 417 ff. The occupations are contained in the references found after each name, with the exception of *capitaine de la milice*, *commissaire de police*, and *trésorier de l'hospital*, which may be found in the *Registres de la Jurade* under the appropriate heading.

Name	Occupation	Year of Entry into Bourgeoisie	Source
Broqueville, Sanson	*marchand*	—	*A.G.*, 3E 7685 fol. 16
Bussereau, Samuel	—	1581	*A.G.*, 3E 10491 fol. 2
Cadroy, ———	*marchand*, member of Cent et Trente, trésorier de l'hospital	1637	*A.G.*, 3E 3723 fol. 51v
Cassaignol, Eymerie	*marchand*	1602	*A.G.*, 3E 10787 fol. 395
Castaignie, Anthoine	*procureur au Sénéchal de Guyenne*		*A.G.*, 3E 4319 fol. 213v
Castaignet, André	*marchand*, member of Cent et Trente	1631	*A.G.*, 3E 12.253 fol.258
Cavault, ———	*fermier d'impôt*	—	Cosnac, *Souvenirs*, V, 31–32
Cayrac, Pierre	*marchand, capitaine de la milice*	1626	*Revue historique de Bordeaux*, XI, 8
Clairac, Raymond	*avocat au Parlement*		Communay, *Journal de Filhot*, 61
Claverie, Pierre	*marchand, enseign de la milice*	1600	*A.G.*, 3E 7263 fol. 156v
Coderc, Jean	*marchand*	1612	*A.G.*, 3E 4819 fol. 141
Compnes, Christophe	*maître graveur*	—	*A.G.*, 3E 767 fol. 203v
Conilh, François	*praticien*	—	*A.G.*, 3E 10944 fol. 114
Cornut, Pierre	*marchand, enseign colonel de la ville*	1582	*A.G.*, 3E 3208 fol. 24
Croizet, Jacques	*procureur au Parlement*	1645	*A.G.*, 3E 6582 fol. 299
Crozillac, Guillaume	*marchand, commissaire de police*	1620	*A.G.*, 3E 5142 fol.727
Curtin, Jean	*maître pâtissier*	—	*A.G.*, 3E 1522 fol. 351
Darnault, ———	*huissier de l'Hôtel de Ville*	—	*A.G.*, 3E 10767 fol.258v *A.G.*, 3E 14,850 fol.344
Davril, Joseph	*marchand*	1640	*A.G.*, 3E 13495 fol. 93
De Habas, Jean	*marchand*	—	*A.G.*, 3E 6582 fol. 61
De Lux, Estienne	*marchand*	—	*A.G.*, 3E 4818 fol. 40
Dezert, François	*marchand*	1639	*Archives historiques de la Gironde*, XXX, 174
Dierx, Ramus	*courtier*	—	*A.G.*, 3E 13,495 fol.227
Droilhet, Paul	*marchand, enseign de la milice*	1642	*A.G.*, 3E 1308 fol. 803v

Name	Occupation	Year of Entry into Bourgeoisie	Source
Du Bourg, Jean	*praticien*	—	*A.G.*, 3E 3704 fol. 3
Du Boys, Jean	*maître écrivain*	1618	*A.G.*, 3E 12,353 fol.446
Dubuc, Jacques	*procureur au Sénéchal de Guyenne*	—	*A.G.*, 3E 5141 fol. 68
Ducoing, Julien	*maître orfèvre*	—	*A.G.*, 3E 12,353 fol.201
Duperier, Pierre	*procureur en la maison commune de Bordeaux*	1663	*A.G.*, 3E 8112 fol. 32
Du Puy, Henry	*escuyer*	—	Cosnac, *Souvenirs*, VII, 18
Dureteste, Christophe	*soliciteur de procès*	1603	*A.G.*, 3E 3208 fol. 21
Eynard, Pierre	*maître de bahutier*	1617	*Registres de la Jurade*, II, 3
Fauré, Denys	*marchand, commissaire de police*	1640	*A.G.*, 3E 15,252 fol.152
Fevielle, Antoine de	*marchand, commissaire de police, capitaine de la milice*, member of *Cent et Trente*, *trésorier de l'hospital*	1625	*A.G.*, 3E 10,491 fol. 2
Forrest, J[ean]	*maître tailleur*	1638	"Tailleurs," fonds Baurein, carton 28
Gardera, ——	*marchand graisseur*	—	*Registres de la Jurade*, III, 452
Gauselan, Jean	*marchand*	1612	Livre des bourgeois, 70
Gauvain, Pierre	*marchand, commissaire de police*	1579	*A.G.*, 3E 4368 fol. 824
Gay, ——	*prestre*	—	*B.N.*, F. Fr. 22377 fol. 103
Giraut, Pierre	*maître orfèvre*	1588	Communay, *Journal de Filhot*, 104
Griffon, Sebastien	*procureur au Parlement*	—	*A.G.*, 3E 5212 fol. 123
Guerin, Bernard	*marchand*	1605	*A.G.*, 3E 3704, fol. 33
Guillemeteau, Jullien	*notaire*	1626	*A.G.*, 3E 4319 fol. 172
Haubet, Pierre	*marchand*	1650	*A.G.*, 3E 10491 fol. 2
Hochard, Anthoyne	*maître perruquier*	—	*A.G.*, 3E 2448 fol. 1v

Name	Occupation	Year of Entry into Bourgeoisie	Source
Hosten, ——— d'	président de la Cour des Aides, capitaine de la milice	—	Chambre de Direction, Feb. 4, 1652
Hugoun, Bernard	maître boulanger	1603	A.G., 3E 10491 fol. 2
Jamart, Pierre de	courtier	1588	Registres de la Jurade, IV, 55
Jannet (or Jeanet)	ermite	1585	A.G., 4J 170
Jehan, Guillaume	receveur des gages des Présidiaux	—	A.G., 3E 3897 fol. 460
Labaille, Anthoine	maître boulanger	—	A.G., 3E 4320 fol. 949
Labat, Jacques	maître orfèvre	1663	A.G., 3E 1308 fol. 162
Labourdette, François de	procureur au Sénéchal de Guyenne	1640	Registres de la Jurade, II, 466
Lafitte, ———	marchand de jambon	—	Courrier bourdelois [XVIᵉ]
Lafon, Pierre de	notaire, trésorier de l'hospital	1649	A.G., 3E 7685
La Grave, Jean de	escuyer	—	A.G., 3E 7263 fol. 154v
Lamolie, Jean	huissier au Présidial	—	A.G., 3E 10787 fol.392v
Lanardonne, François	marchand	—	A.G., 3E 12353 fol. 341
Landé, Jean	musicien	1638	Communay, Journal de Filhot, 179
Lartigue, Pierre	praticien	—	A.G., 3E 9160 fol. 32v
Lataste, Jean de	escuyer	1663	A.G., 3E 10944 fol. 7v
Laurans, Jehan	maître gantier	1634	A.G., 3E 15252 fol.240v
Le Breton, Jean Geoffre	escuyer	1614	Communay, Journal de Filhot, 108
Leguit, ———	maître savatier	—	B.N., F. Fr. 22377 fol. 215
Leguit, ———	boulanger	—	B.N., F. Fr. 11633 fol. 470
Loignon, Jean	marchand	1651	A.G., 3E 2448 fol. 938
Mantet, ———	vice-sénéchal	—	A.G., Livre de l'escroue, May 18, 1653
Martin, Bernard	matîre charpentier de barrique	1626	A.G., 3E 10944 fol. 741

Name	Occupation	Year of Entry into Bourgeoisie	Source
Mercier, Jean de	*marchand*	1587	*A.G.*, 3E 4319 fol. 1226
Michelet, P	*maître pintier*	1687	*A.G.*, 3E 7685 fol. 14
Minvielle, Barthelemy	*officier de la monnaye*	Before 1600	*A.G.*, 3E 4319 fol. 1074
Moman, _____	*marchand*	1594	*Livre des bourgeois*, 103
Montaigne, Jacques	*huissier au Sénéchal*	—	*A.G.*, 3E 1308 fol. 148
Monleau, _____	*procureur au Parlement*	—	*Courrier bourdelois* [*XVIᵉ*]
Mouchac, Jean de	*escuyer*	—	*Archives historiques de la Gironde*, **XXX**, 174
Mouresse, Bernard	*marchand, lieutenant de la milice*	1637	*A.G.*, 3E 13495 fol. 179
Mouty, Jacques	*maître chaudronnier*	1640	*A.G.*, 3E 4368 fol. 580v
Ollivier, Jean	*marchand*	1589	*A.G.*, 3E 3208 fol.234
Pacot, Pierre	*marchand*	1617	*A.G.*, 3E 9160 fol. 232
Papineau, Jean	*marchand*	1636	*A.G.*, 3E 574 fol. 574
Peres, Pierre	*huissier au Bureau de Finance*	—	*A.G.*, 3E 6582 fol. 84v
Philipon, Pierre	*maître chirurgien*	1527	*A.G.*, 3E 3897 fol. 386v
Philipon, Pierre (*le Jeune*)	*maître chirurgien*	1527	*A.G.*, 3E 10944 fol.632v
Pinel, Louis	*procureur au Parlement*	1636	*B.N.*, F. Fr. 22377 fol. 164
Pontellier, Jean	*avocat au Parlement*	1607	Communay, *Journal de Filhot*, 158
Prades, _____	*professeur au Collège de Guyenne*	—	*B.N.*, F. Fr. 6711 fol. 57
Puylausye, Pierre	*marchand*	1639	*A.G.*, 3E 4319 fol. 56v
Puylausye, Jean (*fils*)	*marchand*	1639	*A.G.*, 3E 6878 fol. 609
Rigoulet, _____	*apothicaire*	1601	*B.N.*, F. Fr. 22377 fol. 164
Ripote, _____	*marchand*	1608	*Livre des bourgeois*, 126
Riviere, Pierre	*marchand*	1559	*A.G.*, 3E 7263 fol. 123
Robert, Pierre	*avocat au Parlement*, member of *Cent et Trente*	1567	Cosnac, *Souvenirs*, VII, 8
Rocques, _____	*procureur au Sénéchal de Guyenne*	1636	Communay, *Journal de Filhot*, 130
Rolland, Laurens	*marchand*	1636	*A.G.*, 3E 12.219 fol. 69

Name	Occupation	Year of Entry into Bourgeoisie	Source
Roy, Jean	*marchand*	1591	*A.G.*, 3E 13495 fol. 243
Saint Million, Laurens	*huissier au Parlement*	—	*A.G.*, 3E 4319 fol. 69
Samaruc, Jean	*marchand drapier*	—	*B.N.*, F. Fr. 11633, fol. 470
Sauvage, Bernard de	*escuyer*	1537	*A.G.*, 3E 4687 fol. 375
Taudin, Jacques	*maître pintier*	—	*A.G.*, 3E 4818 fol. 72
Tauzin, Guillaume	*maître potier d'estaing*	1630	Communay, *Journal de Filhot*, 122
Truchon, Pierre	*marchand*, member of *Cent et Trente*	1623	Cosnac, *Souvenirs*, VII, 8
Turquois, Blaise	*maître chaussetier*	—	*Registres de la Jurade*, III, 245
Tustal, Daniel de	*escuyer*	—	Cosnac, *Souvenirs*, VII, 8
Vallet, Anthoine	*docteur en médecine*	1584	
Veyssiere, ——	*musicien*	—	Communay, *Journal de Filhot*, 142
Vidau, Jean	*maître gantier*	1603	*A.G.*, 3E 2448 fol. 318v
Villars, Pierre	*avocat au Parlement*	1610	Cosnac, *Souvenirs*, VII, 8
Vroede, Jacob de	*marchand*	1646	*A.G.*, 3E 12353 fol. 690v

MEMBERS OF THE CENT ET TRENTE*

Name	Occupation	Year of Entry into Bourgeoisie
Augey	—	—
Andraut	*conseiller au Parlement*	1505
d'Apvril	*avocat au Parlement*	1603
Ardent	—	—
Banarvy	*marchand*	—
Barbet	*avocat au Parlement, capitaine de la milice*	—
Bechon	—	1630
Beluye	*avocat au Parlement*	1639
Bernarda	*marchand*	1545
Berguet	*chirurgien*	—
Bisabat	*avocat au Parlement*	1561
Bethouland	*avocat au Parlement*	1610
de Blanc	*escuyer*	1547
Bord	*marchand*	—
Bordes	*avocat au Parlement*	1522
Boulmer	*avocat au Parlement*	—
Branda	*avocat au Parlement*	1619
Brunet	*avocat au Parlement*	1605
Cadroy	*marchand*	1637
Calvimont	—	—
de Campaigne	*avocat au Parlement*	1548
Castaignet	*marchand*	1631
Casenave	*capitaine de la milice*	1588
Chadirac	*avocat au Parlement*	—
Chastaing	*avocat au Parlement*	1542
Chatillan	*avocat au Parlement*	1554
Chenaud	*capitaine de la milice*	1571
Chevrier	*avocat au Parlement*	1633
Chiquet	*avocat au Parlement*	1614

*This list derives from two sessions of the *Cent et Trente* (April 30, 1649 and May 14, 1649) preserved in *B.B.*, MS. fonds Itié. The date of *embourgeoisement* may be found in the "Livre des bourgeois," *Archives historiques de la Gironde*, XXXII, 1–149. Notation "prior to 1600" indicates that original letter of *embourgeoisement* was reported lost.

Name	Occupation	Year of Entry into Bourgeoisie
Clement	*avocat au Parlement*	—
Commes	—	1637
Constant	*avocat au Parlement*	1626
Dalon	*avocat au Parlement*	prior to 1600
Dalon, *le jeune*	*avocat au Parlement*	prior to 1600
Delpech	*avocat au Parlement*	1593
Devaux	—	1643
Dorat	*juge de la Bourse*	1618
Dubois	*marchand*	1616
Durand	*avocat au Parlement*	1611
Dussault	*prestre*	prior to 1600
Dussault	*conseiller au Parlement*	prior to 1600
Duval	—	1641
Fayard	*conseiller au Parlement*	prior to 1600
Fenelon	—	1613
Fevielle	*marchand*	1625
Fontenel	*avocat au Parlement*	1602
Fontenel, *le jeune*	*avocat au Parlement*	1602
Fontenel	*chanoine*	1622
Foissen	*marchand*	1622
Fortan	*avocat au Parlement*	1603
Fouquet	*marchand*	1563
de Frans	*conseiller au Parlement*	prior to 1600
Gardera	*marchand*	—
Giraud	*capitaine de la milice*	—
Grenier	*avocat au Parlement*	1617
Grenier, *le jeune*	*avocat au Parlement*	1617
Hugla	*marchand*	prior to 1600
Hugon	*avocat au Parlement*	prior to 1600
La Barriere	—	prior to 1600
La Clauzure	*capitaine de la milice*	—
Lamezas	*avocat au Parlement*	prior to 1600
Lamarque	—	1626
Larchebaut	*marchand*	1610
La Roche	*secrétaire du Roi*	—
Larzac	*avocat au Parlement*	—
Lauretan	*marchand*	1613
Lauvergnac	*avocat au Parlement*	prior to 1600
Lauvergnac, *le jeune*	*avocat au Parlement*	prior to 1600
Laville	*avocat au Parlement*	1573

Name	Occupation	Year of Entry into Bourgeoise
Legué	—	—
Lestrilles	—	prior to 1600
Liraudein	*avocat au Parlement*	1617
Mammeran	*avocat au Parlement*	—
Mantet	—	—
Mathieu	—	1605
Mercade		1537
Mercier	*consul de la Bourse*	1587
Minvielle	*consul de la Bourse*	prior to 1600
Mirat	*avocat au Parlement*	prior to 1600
Mousnier	*conseiller au Parlement*	1601
de Navarre	*capitaine de la milice*	1627
Noques	—	1605
de Paty	*marchand*	1584
Pelausse	—	1590
Peleau	*secrétaire du Roi*	1590
Pineau	*marchand*	1634
Raouil	—	1587
Robardeau	—	1606
Robert	*avocat au Parlement, capitaine de la milice*	1567
Salenave	—	
Sarsac	*avocat au Parlement*	1604
Seigneuret	*marchand*	
Soubre	*avocat au Parlement*	
Testas	—	1643
Thibaud	*conseiller au Parlement*	prior to 1550
Tillet	*avocat au Parlement*	1622
Truchon	*marchand*	1623
Venaut	—	1604
Verins	—	1584
Vitalis	—	1615
Voisin	*conseiller au Parlement*	prior to 1600

BIBLIOGRAPHY

PRIMARY SOURCES

MANUSCRIPTS

Bordeaux. Archives Départementales de la Gironde. MSS. series 1B 24, 6B 283,
12B 7, C 3794, C 3888, C 3989, C 4700, C 4726 , 3E 181, 3E 706, 3E 767,
3E 1522, 3E 2448, 3E 3208, 3E 4047, 3E 4320, 3E 4332, 3E 4369, 3E 5142,
3E 5212, 3E 6582, 3E 7228, 3E 8753, 3E 9752, 3E 10.787, 3E 10.945, 3E
12.219, 3E 12.253, 3E 12.319, 3E 12.354, 3E 14.850, 3E 15.253, 3E 24.802,
G 1028, G 1039, G 2140–42, 4J 170.
———. Archives Municipales. Fonds Drouyn, vols. XIII–XVI, XXVI. Fonds
Baurein; Extraits des registres secrets du Parlement de Bordeuax, 1648–53;
Extraits des registres de la Chambre de Direction.
———. Bibliothèque Municipale. MSS. fonds Itié.
Bayonne. Bibliothèque Municipale. MSS. fonds Communay.
Chantilly. Musée Condé. MSS. serie P. Vols. XII, XIII.
Paris. Archives du Ministère des Affaires Etrangères. Correspondence Politique.
France. Vol. 891.
———. Archives Nationales. Serie KK 1219, 1220–21.
———. Bibliothèque Mazarine. MSS. 2241.
———. Bibliothèque Nationale. MSS. fonds français 4186, 6707, 6710, 6711,
6715, 11109, 11233, 18752, 22377; fonds Dupuy, 775.

PUBLISHED SOURCE MATERIAL

Archives historiques du département de la Gironde. 58 vols. Paris-Bordeaux, 1859–
1932. Vols. II–IV, VI–VIII, XIII, XV, XIX, XXIII, XXX, XXXI,
XXXIV, XXXVI, LVIII.
Aumale, Henri d'. *Histoire des Princes de Condé pendant le XVIe et XVIIe siècles.*
Paris, 1863–96.
Barckhausen, R., ed. *Livre des privilèges.* Vol. 2. Archives Municipales de
Bordeaux, XXII. Bordeaux, 1878.
Berthod, [Père] François. "Mémoires," in *Nouvelle collection des mémoires pour
servir à l'histoire de France,* ed. J. Michaud and F. Poujoulat. Vol. X. Paris,
1838.
*Calendar of State Papers and Manuscripts Existing in the Archives and Collections of
Venice.* Ed. Allen B. Hinds. Vols. XXVIII–XXIX. London, 1927–29.
Cayrac, Pierre. "Récit de la Fronde à Bordeaux," *Revue historique de Bordeaux,*
VII (1914), 5–11, 195–209, 261–73; XI (1918) 171–81, 230–45.

Communay, Armand. *L'Ormée à Bordeaux d'après le journal inédit de Jacques Filhot.* Bordeaux, 1887.

——. "Notaires, registres paroissiaux, bourgeois de Bordeaux." Manuscript, Bibliotheque de Bayonne.

Cosnac, Daniel. *Mémoires.* Paris, 1852.

Cosnac, Gabriel-Jules de. *Souvenirs du règne de Louis XIV.* 8 vols. Paris, 1866–82.

Darnal, Jean. *Supplément des chroniques de la noble ville et cité de Bordeaux.* Bordeaux, 1666.

Fonteneil, Jacques. *Histoire des mouvemens de Bourdeaux.* Bordeaux, 1651.

Gazett [*de Renaudot*]. Paris, 1652–53.

Inventaire sommaire des registres de la Jurade, 1520–1783. Vols. I–VIII. Bordeaux, 1896–1947.

Joly, Claude. *Recueil de maximes véritables et importantes pour l'institution du roy contre la fausse et pernicieuse politique du Cardinal Mazarin.* Paris, 1663.

Lenet, Pierre. "Mémoires," in *Nouvelle collection des mémoires pour servir à l'histoire de France,* ed. J. Michaud and F. Poujoulat. 3d series vol. II. Paris, 1838.

Loret, Jean. *La muze historique, ou recueil des lettres en vers.* J. Ravenel, ed. Vol. I. Paris, 1857.

Mazarin, Jules. *Lettres du Cardinal Mazarin pendant son ministère.* Pierre-Adolphe Cheruel, ed. 9 vols. Paris, 1872–1906.

Montglat, François de. "Mémoires," in *Nouvelle collection des mémoires pour servir à l'histoire de France,* ed. J. Michaud and F. Poujoulat. 3d series, vol. V. Paris, 1838.

Robert, Samuel. *Lettres.* Saintes, 1907.

Tranchère, Hovyn de. *Les dessous de l'histoire.* 2 vols. Paris, 1886.

MAZARINADES

Apologie (l') pour l' Ormée, par un de l'assemblée de messieurs les bourgeois. N.p., n.d. Labadie, No. 11.

Arrest de la Cour de Parlement de Bordeaux, portant défense aux courretiers de prendre plus grands droits que ceux qui leurs sont attribués par l'édit vérifié audit Parlement. Bordeaux, 1648.

Arrest de la Cour de Parlement de Bordeaux, portant que tous les manans et habitants demeureront quittes et déchargez du payement des loyers d'un quartier des dites locations. Bordeaux, 1650. Labadie No. 81.

Articles de l'union de l'Ormée et de la ville de Bordeaux. Paris, n.d. Moreau, No. 408.

Courrier bourdelois apportant toutes sortes de nouvelles. Paris, 1652. Labadie, Nos. 143–59.

Courrier de la Guyenne, apportant le véritable état des affaires. Paris, 1652. Moreau, No. 822.

Evangéliste (l') de la Guyenne. Paris, 1652. Moreau, No. 1310.

Exile (l') de l'inconnu, dédié aux exilés de la ville de Bourdeaux. Paris, 1653. Moreau, No. 1330.

Extrait de tout ce qui s'est fait et passé à Bordeaux depuis le 29 juin 1652, touchant le parti de messieurs les princes et celui des Mazarins. Paris, 1652. Moreau, No. 1342.

Généreuse (la) résolution des gascons. N.p., 1652. Moreau, No. 1480.

Histoire véritable d'une colombe qui a paru miraculeusement en un lieu appelé l'Ormoye de Bordeaux. Paris, 1652. Moreau, No. 1652.

Illustres frondeurs de l'Ormaye [Les]. N.p., n.d. Labadie, No. 119.

Journal de tout ce qui s'est fait et passé en la ville de Bordeaux depuis le 24 juin jusques à présent entre les bourgeois de la ville et les Ormistes. Paris, 1652.

Journal de tout ce qui s'est passé à Bordeaux, depuis le 1er juin jusques à présent. Paris, 1652. Moreau, No. 1754.

Lettre de monseigneur le prince de Condé, gouverneur de Guyenne, à messieurs les bourgeois de l'Ormée de Bourdeaux. Bordeaux, 1651. Moreau, No. 2010.

Lettre de monseigneur le prince escrite a messieurs les maires et jurats, gouverneurs de Bordeaux avec la lettre escrite a messieurs les bourgeois. Bordeaux, 1652.

Lettre de monsieur le Prince escrite à messieurs les maires et jurats de la ville de Bordeaux. Bordeaux, 1651. Moreau, No. 2031.

Manifeste (le) des bordelois contenant le récit véritable de ce qui d'est passé dans la ville de Bordeaux les 13 et 14 du passé. Paris, 1652. Moreau, No. 2386.

Rélation des dernières nouvelles du siège de la ville de Bordeaux. Paris, 1650. Moreau, No. 3154.

Véritable (le) courrier bordelois ou nouvelles très assurées de tout qui c'est passé tant à Bourg qu'à Bordeaux. Paris, 1650. Moreau, No. 3928.

SECONDARY SOURCES

Aston, Trevor, ed. *Crisis in Europe.* London, 1965.

Bercé, Yvres-Marie. "La bourgeoisie Bordelaise et la fisc sous Louis XIII," *Revue historique de Bordeaux*, XIII, N.S. (1964). 41–46.

———. "Les soulèvements populaires du Sud-Ouest pendant la guerre de trente ans." Unpublished thesis. Ecole des Chartes, 1959.

Bernard, Léon. "French Society and Popular Uprisings under Louis XIV," *French Historical Studies*, III (1964), 454–74.

Bertrand, Louis. *La Vie de Messire Henry de Bethune 1604–1680.* 2 vols. Paris, 1902.

Boscheron des Portes, C. *Histoire du Parlement de Bordeaux 1451–1790.* 2 vols. Bordeaux, 1877.

Bourgeon, Jean-Louis. "L'Ile de la Cité pendant la Fronde," *Paris et Ile de France, Mémoires*, XIII (1949), 23–144.

Boutruche, Robert, ed. *Bordeaux 1453–1715.* Bordeaux, 1966.

Brailsford, H. N. *The Levellers and the English Revolution.* London, 1961.

Charmeil, Jean Paul. *Les trésoriers de France à l'époque de la Fronde.* Paris, 1964.

Church, William F. *Constitutional Thought in 16th Century France.* Cambridge, 1941.

Cubells, Mlle. "Le Parlement de Paris pendant la Fronde." *XVIIe Siècle.* No. 35 (1957).

Damas, Pierre. *Histoire de la juridiction consulaire de Bordeaux.* Paris, 1947.

Débidour, A. *La Fronde Angevine, tableau de la vie municipale au XVIIe siècle.* Paris, 1877.

Desgraves, Louis. *Evocation du vieux Bordeaux.* Paris, 1960.

Devienne, Dom. *Histoire de la ville de Bordeaux.* 2 vols. Bordeaux, 1771.

Doolin, Paul. *The Fronde.* Cambridge, 1935.

Elliott, John H. *The Revolt of the Catalans; a Study in the decline of Spain, 1598–1640.* Oxford, 1863.

——. "Revolution and Continuity in Early Modern Europe," *Past and Present.* No. 42 (1969), 33–56.

Goubert, Pierre. "Les offiçiers royaux des Présidiaux, Baillages et Elections dans la société française au XVIIe siècle," *XVIIe siècle.* Nos. 42–43 (1959), 54–75.

Jullian, Camille. *Histoire de Bordeaux depuis ses origines jusqu'en 1895.* Bordeaux, 1895.

Knachel, Philip A. *England and the Fronde.* Ithaca, 1967.

Kossmann, Ernst H. *La Fronde.* Leiden, 1954.

Labadie, Ernest. *Nouveau supplément à la bibliographie des Mazarinades.* Paris, 1904.

Logie, Paul. *La Fronde en Normandie.* 3 vols. Amiens, 1951–1952.

Loirette, Francois. "Un intendant de Guyenne avant la Fronde: J. de Lauson," *Bulletin philologique et historique du comité des travaux historiques et scientifiques,* 1957, 433–61.

Madelin, Louis. *La Fronde.* Paris, 1931.

Malvezin, Théophile. *Histoire du commerce de Bordeaux.* 2 vols. Bordeaux, 1892.

Mandrou, Robert. *Introduction à la France moderne 1500–1640.* Paris, 1961.

Merriman, Roger B. *Six Contemporaneous Revolutions.* Oxford, 1938.

Moreau, Célestin. *Bibliographie des Mazarinades.* 3 vols. 1850–51.

Mousnier, Roland. *Deux cahiers de la noblesse 1649–1651.* Paris, 1965.

——. *Les XVIe et XVIIe siècles.* Paris, 1954.

——. *Lettres et mémoires adressés au Chancelier Séguier.* 2 Vols. Paris, 1964.

——. "Monarchie contre aristoçratie dans la France du XVIIe siècle," *XVIIe siècle.* No. 61 (1956), 377–81.

——. "Quelques raisons de la Fronde. Les causes des journées révolutionaires Parisiennes de 1648," *XVIIe siècle.* Nos. 2–3 (1949), 33–78.

————. "Recherches sur les soulèvements populaires en France avant la Fronde," *Revue d'histoire moderne et contemporaine*, V (1958), 81–113.

————. "Serviteurs du roi: quelques aspects de la fonction publique dans la société française du XVIIe siècle," *XVIIe siècle*. Nos. 42–43 (1959), 3–7.

————. *La vénalité des offices sous Henri IV et Louis XIII*. Rouen, n.d.

O'Reilly, Patrice-John. *Histoire complète de Bordeaux*, 8 vols. Bordeaux, 1860.

Pillorget, Réné. "Vente d'offices et journée des barricades du 20 janvier 1649 à Aix-en-Provence," *Provence historique* (1965), 25–63.

Porchnev, Boris. *Les soulèvements populaires en France de 1623 à 1648*. Paris, 1963.

Quet, Simone. "La Cour des Aides de Guyenne, ses rapports avec le Parlement de Bordeaux," *Revue historique de Bordeaux*, XXXII, 97–111; 167–82; XXXIII, 17–22.

Vie, Claude de and Vaissette, Jean Joseph. *Histoire générale de Languedoc*. Toulouse, 1872–1904.

Wailly, Natalis de. *Mémoire sur les variations de la livre tournois*. Paris, 1857.

INDEX

THE JOHNS HOPKINS UNIVERSITY PRESS

This book was composed in Times Roman text and
Deepdene Bold Italic display by Baltimore Type and
Composition Corporation. It was printed by Universal
Lithographers, Inc., on Sebago Regular paper and bound
in Holliston Roxite cloth by L. H. Jenkins, Inc.